Half Horse Half Alligator

THE GROWTH OF THE
MIKE FINK LEGEND

Half Horse Half Alligator

THE GROWTH OF THE
MIKE FINK LEGEND

Edited with an Introduction and Notes by

WALTER BLAIR
and
FRANKLIN J. MEINE

University of Nebraska Press
Lincoln and London

First Bison Book printing: 1981
Most recent printing indicated by the first digit below:
1   2   3   4   5   6   7   8   9   10

Library of Congress Cataloging in Publication Data
Main entry under title:

Half horse, half alligator.

Reprint. Originally published: Chicago : University of Chicago Press, 1956.
Bibliography: p.
1. Fink, Mike, 1770–1823?—Legends—Addresses, essays, lectures.   2.
Frontier and pioneer life—Middle West—Addresses, essays, lectures.   3.
Legends—Middle West—Addresses, essays, lectures.   4. Pioneers—Middle
West—Biography—Addresses, essays, lectures.   I. Blair, Walter,
1900–   II. Meine, Franklin Julius, 1896–1968.
GR105.37.M54H34   1981   398.2'2'0977   81–3358
ISBN 0–8032–6060–1 (pbk.)   AACR2

Reprinted by arrangement with the University of Chicago
Press

Preface

IN 1933, FRANKLIN J. MEINE and I published Mike Fink: King of Mississippi Keelboatmen. "Our first hope," we then explained, "was that we might collect all original stories about our hero and print them in their most authentic forms. Persuaded that the work we contemplated could not be published, at least at this time, we hit upon the expedient of writing a narrative which made use of the most important tales about him. . . ." The present book is a realization of this first hope of ours.

Several happenings since the distant day when our account of the once famous frontiersman appeared have made this book possible. (The day, we have rueful reasons to remember, was the one when President Franklin D. Roosevelt closed all the country's banks and froze the funds of most potential buyers.) Interest in American history, literature, and folklore has grown prodigiously. Courses in these fields have multiplied in colleges and universities, and books have kept pace. Mike Fink has been discussed by scholars and writers. Even Broadway and Hollywood have discovered the hero we resurrected and have created some legends of their own about him, which we have not felt we were competent to consider with scholarly impartiality. The growing interest has encouraged us to collect the old stories, and some we have come upon since 1933, from the pages of books, almanacs, magazines, and newspapers and to publish them in their original forms.

These narratives unfold a fascinating story, the like of which no other body of documents can reveal. They show how an American, whose life was lived on three picturesque frontiers between about 1770 and 1823, became a legend; how the legend proliferated in oral tales and a number of greatly varied literary expressions; and how in the end it all but died. In more auspicious times, it is possible that the legendary lore might have inspired a noteworthy literary work, for it had real possibilities.

In the nineteenth and twentieth centuries, it inspired writings which fell short of greatness but which nevertheless have a considerable interest.

In the stories here printed, we have now and then silently corrected typographical errors and removed some of the commas and other punctuation marks which seemed to impede the reading. Otherwise, except where omissions have been indicated, the narratives have been reproduced exactly. The chief stories are ordered according to their appearance, with introductory material tracing the contributions of each to the development of the legendary Mike Fink. All but one of the varied accounts of Fink's death—that by Field (p. 142)—have been separately grouped, in chronological order, at a later point.

Franklin Meine has been active in hunting down the stories, in seeing that some of them were correctly reproduced, in working out what should be said about them, and in checking over the editorial materials. I have searched out the newly added materials, collated our texts with original texts, written all the introductory matter, and compiled the augmented Bibliography.

In 1933, we listed a number of people to whom we were indebted for help and to whom we are again indebted. To them, once more, our thanks. We also wish to express gratitude to others who have helped us with the present book: B. A. Botkin, Croton-on-Hudson, N.Y.; Thomas D. Clark, University of Kentucky; Eugene Current-Garcia, Alabama Polytechnic Institute; the late Bernard DeVoto, Cambridge, Massachusetts; Richard M. Dorson, Michigan State University; Bess Finn, Newberry Library; John T. Flanagan, University of Illinois; Barbara Kell, Missouri Historical Society; Mitford M. Mathews, University of Chicago; Frank T. Meriwether, Southwest Louisiana Institute; Dale L. Morgan, University of California; Vance Randolph, Eureka Springs, Arkansas; Julian Lee Rayford, Mobile, Alabama; Milton Rickels, John Pepperdine College; Colonel Henry W. Shoemaker, Harrisburg, Pennsylvania; Winifred Ver Nooy, University of Chicago Library.

WALTER BLAIR

[vi]

Table of Contents

ACCOUNTS OF MIKE FINK'S DEATH

BIBLIOGRAPHY

List of Illustrations

Mike Fink in History, Legend, and Story

Mike Fink in History, Legend, and Story

T HIS BOOK BRINGS TOGETHER the narratives, mostly legendary, about a frontiersman famous in the nineteenth century, Mike Fink. Though anyone who has tried to write poetically about this man has had to regret the prosaic nature of his name, the stories about him are the raw materials for a sort of buckskin and linsey-woolsey saga with appeals as American history, as legend, and (in part) as literature.

One reason is that the action, the danger, and the violence of three frontiers shaped Fink's life and the stories based upon it. In the years when his countrymen fought the British and the Indians for the Pennsylvania frontier—the gateway to the Mississippi Valley—he was born and reared there. Later, during the decades when the Mississippi and its tributaries were routes of the vast westward movement, he frolicked, fought, and worked as a river boatman. At the last, as a trapper, he followed the Missouri to its headwaters, and he was a mountain man in the Rockies when his life ended. Another reason is that his roles on the shifting frontiers and his traits (real and invented) as a man made him a symbol of his era and a hero of many legends and stories.

I. SCOUT AT FORT PITT AND IN THE INDIAN COUNTRY

Mike was born, it is generally claimed, in one of the little cabins clustered around Fort Pitt, in about 1770.[1] There is some uncertainty about both the place and his ancestry. It has been assumed that his parents were Scotch-Irish, as were many people in the settlement, but there is a strong likelihood that they belonged to the Pennsylvania German contingent.[2]

Long before Mike's birth and for a number of years after, the land between the Monongahela and Allegheny Rivers at the point where they form the Ohio River was the scene of fierce conflict. In 1753, young George Washington, en route to Fort Le Boeuf on a diplomatic mission, had written: "I spent some time in viewing the Rivers and the Land in the Fork; which I think extremely well situated for a Fort, as it has the absolute Command of both Rivers." The strategic location had made the Point an objective of both the French and the British in a bitter contest which had lasted until 1758. Thereafter, the Indians, on their own initiative or as allies of the British during the Revolution, had attacked it and the lands to the west. After the war, the Indians did not feel that they were involved in the British surrender. So sporadic Indian raids continued into the 1790's, and the danger did not end until the Battle of Fallen Timbers, forty years after Washington had first urged the building of a fort.

H. M. Brackenridge in 1824, looking back to the Pittsburgh of thirty years before, recalled that "the Ohio . . . was still the boundary of civilization; for all beyond it was called the Indian country, and associated in the mind with many a fireside tale of scalping knife, hair-breadth escapes, and all the horrors of savage warfare."[3] And Joseph Doddridge, whose memoirs give vivid pictures of life on the upper Ohio in those days, recalls that "we were few in number, and engaged in perpetual hostility with the Indians, the end of which no one could foresee."[4]

During the decades of "perpetual hostility," the folk of the settlements were gripped by terror again and again. At almost any time (except during the winter) marauding bands of Indians might swoop down upon the families in isolated cabins— or even upon those nestled close to the stockades. The redmen would burn the crops and the cabins, would ravage and kill and scalp, then would dart away with captives. Doddridge tells how it was:

I well remember, when a little boy, the family was sometimes waked up in the dead of night by an express with a report that the

Indians were at hand. The express came softly to the door or back window, and by a gentle tapping waked the family. This was easily done, as an habitual fear made us ever watchful and sensible to the slightest alarm. The whole family were instantly in motion. My father seized his gun and other implements of war. My stepmother waked up and dressed the children as well as she could, and being myself the oldest of the children, I had to take my share of the burdens to be carried to the fort. There was no possibility of getting a horse in the night to aid us . . . we caught up what articles of clothing and provision we could get hold of in the dark, for we durst not light a candle or even stir the fire. . . . Thus it often happened that the whole number of families belonging to a fort who were in the evening in their homes were all in the little fortress before the dawn. . . .[5]

It was on such a warring frontier that Mike was reared. Every male settler was at least a part-time Indian fighter, and the more adventurous, Mike among them, became scouts.

Scouts or rangers were the men who served as guides or as messengers, who defended the forts and who at times invaded the enemy territory as spies or fighters. These were militiamen, but usually they were unattached to any company or fort. They made their most useful and most dangerous forays alone. A scout would go into the forests with a small load of provisions—a bit of jerked venison, a small bag of corn meal, tow for wiping his rifle barrel, bullets, and powder—and would expect to take care of his needs and of his physical safety with his tomahawk, his knife, or his flintlock.

One story has it that Mike started as a "market hunter" who supplied the markets of Pittsburgh with fresh game. Later, according to several accounts, he became a scout. Among the most venturesome of the frontiersmen, we are told by a writer in 1829, "whilst yet a stripling, Mike acquired a reputation for boldness and cunning far beyond his companions. A thousand legends illustrate the fearlessness of his character."[6] Unless this was an overestimate, about nine hundred and ninety-nine of these legends have disappeared: this same writer tells the only well-authenticated one we have.

Skill in shooting was a prerequisite for a scout, as in fact it was for survival on the frontier. Legend has it that Mike showed unusual talent as a marksman at ten—about the time most frontier youngsters started to learn to shoot—and that at seventeen he was good enough to join the scouts. When he tried, it was said, he could win all the prizes in a match for a beef, which by an ingenious frontier calculation was divided into "six quarters." This must have meant that from childhood he had skilled himself in the selection, the care, and the use of his rifle.

The "Kentucky rifle," so historians of firearms say, was developed especially to meet the needs of frontiersmen. Developed, as it happened, in Pennsylvania, it was designed to load more quickly, to fire more accurately, to hit with more impact, to keep clean longer, and to handle better than its European ancestors.[7] The accuracy which westerners acquired with such weapons was a revelation to easterners and to the British during the Revolution. The Virginia Gazette in 1775 reported:

On Friday last there arrived at Lancaster, Pennsylvania Captain Crescap's company of riflemen consisting of 130 active and brave young fellows, many of whom were in the late expedition of Lord Dunmore against the Indians. These men have been bred in the woods to hardships and danger from their infancy. With their rifles in their hands they assume a kind of omnipotence over their enemies. Two brothers in the company took a piece of board 5 inches by 7 inches with a bit of white paper the size of a dollar nailed in the center, and while one held the board upright gripped between his knees, the other at 60 yards without any kind of rest shot 8 balls through it successfully and spared his brother's thighs. Another . . . held a barrel stave close against his body perpendicularly while one of his comrades at the same distance shot several bullets through it. The spectators were told that there were upwards of 50 persons in the company who could do the same.

Three of Crescap's men, it was reported elsewhere, "fired simultaneously at a buzzard flying overhead. The bird fell . . . and . . . examination proved that all three bullets had hit their mark."[8]

Stories of frontier marksmanship, before and after the war, are numerous and in many cases authenticated. They hold that from forty paces, shooting at the head of a nail, a good shot could hit the nail squarely; that from fifty yards on a dark night many a settler could fan a candle flame by hitting the tip, without extinguishing it. At fifty yards up to ninety yards, Daniel Boone and others of his day could "bark" squirrels—knock the animals off branches by clipping the bark from beneath their feet.[9] A knowledge of marksmanship such as this prepared contemporaries for stories about Mike's great skill with his rifle, "Bangall," and for accounts of his most renowned trick—that of shooting a tin cup perched atop a companion's head.

II. KEELBOATMAN ON WESTERN WATERWAYS

Charles Cist, Cincinnati's leading historian in the pre-Civil War period, wrote in 1845:

> The first race of boatmen were the spies and scouts whose first employment ceased when Wayne, at the battle of Fallen Timbers and the treaty of Greenville, gave repose and safety to the settlers of the West. Most of them had become unfitted for the pursuits of agriculture—a few followed the chase for subsistence when they could pursue the savage no longer as an occupation, but of the mass, part had imbibed in their intercourse with the Indians a . . . contempt as well as disrelish for regular and steady labor; and the others were . . . in distress, or in debt, or discontented. . . . A boatman's life was the very thing for such individuals. From the nature of their movements, they felt themselves scarcely responsible to the laws, as indeed they were not, except at New Orleans, where the motley crew, whether residents or strangers, have always been kept with the curb bit in the mouth and the rein drawn tightly up.[10]

Therefore when Mike ended his activity as a scout by becoming a boatman, he was one of a number who did so.

Even before the steamboat, navigation on America's great network of western waterways played an important part in the nation's development. Before the national post roads and before the railways, the Ohio, the Mississippi, and the many streams running into them were the best routes for settlers to follow and the only routes between farmers or manufacturers and consumers. Through the years up to the Revolution, movement up and down the rivers steadily increased. And the end of the war greatly accelerated river traffic.

Boatmen's horns echoed along the swarming rivers, and each

year the number of boats and passengers increased. During twelve months in 1787–88, according to one estimate, some 500 boats carrying 20,000 people, 8,000 horses, 2,400 cattle, 1,000 sheep, and 700 wagons were floated down the Ohio, and there was no falling off in the decades which followed this remarkable year. Cities and towns sprang up on the banks, and settlements dotted what had recently been wilderness. Kentucky was admitted to statehood in 1792, and by 1800 the population had come to number 220,000. And still the boats moved with the currents, bearing farmers and farmers' families, domestic animals and chickens, plows and products of new-built factories, to the rich new lands of the West. They stopped along the Ohio or the Mississippi, or they made their way into the interior on smaller streams.

The rivercraft of the movers, many hastily built at points of embarkation, were varied. One startled traveler, looking out at the swarm of boats near Pittsburgh, exclaimed, "You can scarcely imagine an abstract form in which a boat can be built that in some part of the Ohio or Mississippi you will not actually see in motion."[11] There were pirogues—great canoes, each stuffed with a family and its household goods. There were arks—huge clumsy thick-planked houseboats, which ambled along with the current, with a family housed at one end and stock at the other. There were giant rafts, galleys, canoes, and "monstrous anomalies reducible to no specific class."[12]

Especially numerous and important were flatboats and keelboats. The former (often called broadhorns because of the steering oars slanting from their two sides) were boxlike structures built of green-oak planks; they were partly covered—covered boats, like covered wagons, were great carriers of pioneers. Perhaps a million people lived on them for weeks at a time in the period 1784–1840. On these craft, twenty to forty feet long, men, women, children, kegs, cooking utensils, furniture, and cattle were most intimately jumbled together during long journeys. Or the boats carried cargoes of freight to southern ports.

But flatboats were good only for downstream journeys: they

were knocked to pieces and used for lumber on arriving at their destinations. The long slender keelboats (the larger of which were sometimes called barges) were more versatile. These were built on a keel so as to ride high in the water and were pointed at both bow and stern. They shot downstream more rapidly: the famous "Susan Amelia" "descended from the Falls of the Ohio to Natchez in 14 days and 5 hours" in 1811.[13] But their great virtue was that they could also go upstream. At its downriver destination, such a boat could increase its crew of from eight to fifteen men to a crew of from twenty to thirty-six men, load with merchandise from the South, and crawl northward against the currents. Between 40 and 120 feet in length, 7 to 20 feet in beam, a keelboat could carry from 15 to 50 tons of freight up- or downriver.[14] They therefore made possible upriver commerce on a large scale. (For an authentic drawing, see p. 51.)

These battlers of currents were necessarily manned by boat-men who were giants of might and daring. On each side of the keelboat was a cleated running board extending from prow to stern. On these boards, the boatmen, marching along and push-ing with long poles again and again and again, had to win des-perate battles against the pull of the current. A student can re-construct the picture:

. . . can see the two lines of polemen pass from the prow to the stern on the narrow running board . . . lifting and setting their poles to the cry of steersman or captain. The struggle in a swift "riffle" or rapid is momentous. If the craft swerves, all is lost. Shoul-ders bend with savage strength; poles quiver under the tension; the captain's voice is raucous, and every word is an oath; a pole breaks, and the next man, though half dazed in the mortal crisis, does for a few moments the work of two. At last they reach the head of the rapid, and the boat floats out on the placid pool above, while the "alligator-horse" who has had the mishap remarks to the scenery at large that he'd be "fly-blowed before sun-down to a certingty" if that were not the very pole with which he "pushed the broadhorn up Salt River where the snags were so thick that a fish couldn't swim without rubbing his scales off."[15]

When the channel was too deep for poling, the keelboatmen had to use other methods, equally strenuous. In "cordelling," one end of a long rope was tied to the boat's mast, the other was carried ashore, and the men tugged the boat along—not an easy chore when thick brush or cliffs edged the river or estuaries had to be crossed. Or if the shore was impossible, the crew might "warp"—carry the rope upriver on a skiff and tie an end to a snag in the river, or a tree on the bank, and then pull the boat ahead with a windlass or by hand. If the river was high, they might "bushwhack"—each grabbing a branch overhanging the stream and walking from bow to stern on the cleated running board. One can sympathize with one boatman's comment, "If it wasn't for the name of riding I'd about as soon walk!" Fifteen miles a day was the average, if one counts in the days when the wind was right for the use of the sail. The upstream trip from New Orleans to Pittsburgh took four months or more.[16]

Keelboatmen, or bargemen, were rated the best athletes in the West. They had enough wind to sing as they pushed their poles or tugged the cordelle. When the boats tied up at night, they went coon hunting, or they captured settlers' daughters and proved, as one of their songs put it, that—devils that they were—they could

> Dance all night, till broad daylight,
> And go home with the gals in the morning.[17]

The stories about Mike's love life were told by authors who knew the boatmen's reputations as heartbreakers.

But the widespread belief was that keelers preferred less gentle pastimes, such as getting roaring drunk and painting a town bright red, or demolishing barrooms in taverns,[18] or fighting man-to-man, no holds barred, against any brawler who was available. The champion of each boat wore in his hat a red feather which challenged all rival champions. Keelers and bargers felt that their particular enemies were flatboatmen and raftmen. They met crews of these inferior boats man for man, enough members of the larger crew standing aside so that the numbers would be equal. Or perhaps the champions fought a battle in which there were no genteel rules: "No natural weapons were barred. Fists flew at faces, feet kicked wherever they could find a target; knees bucked at unprotected crotches; teeth sank wherever there was flesh; fingers clutched at throats and thumbs seemed to gouge out eyes from their sockets."[19] Noses were battered, teeth splintered, and blood was plentifully shed when boatmen squared off and shot fists at one another.[20] The widespread tales of these violent battles made impressive the mere statement that Mike was the champion of the waterways and inspired stories about his violent fights and his brutal jokes.

III. TRAPPER AND MOUNTAIN MAN IN THE ROCKIES

The last episode in Mike Fink's career began in 1822 in St. Louis. From this city, since 1764, entrepreneurs had sent traders to barter with Indians along the Missouri River. Since 1794, companies, taking advantage of the discoveries of trappers and such explorers as Lewis and Clark and Pike, had been operating from there. By 1822, the fur trade had become a thriving business and an important force in the development of the West. The wide-ranging trappers, usually working on their own as Fink had in his early days as a scout, were the "pathfinders" of the Far West. They were to map the courses of empire, to shape the destiny of the redmen, to have much to do with the marking of our northern boundaries.[21] When, therefore, Fink threw in his lot with the fur traders, he stepped into another important era of our history.

A newly founded company published the following advertisement in the St. Louis Missouri Republican of March 20, 1822:

To enterprising young men. The subscriber wishes to engage one hundred young men to ascend the Missouri river to its source, there to be employed for one, two, or three years. For particulars enquire of Major Andrew Henry, near the lead mines in the county of Washington, who will ascend with, and command, the party; or of the subscriber near St. Louis. [Signed] William H. Ashley.[22]

This was the beginning of the historic Ashley-Henry operation and of an adventure for Fink which was to end with his death.

In less than a month, St. Louis and the surrounding country had produced the required men—a crew of voyageurs, boatmen, hunters, trappers, and some less-seasoned youths, who (so a rather stuffy account says) "had relinquished the most respectable employments and circles of society." Among them were two of the most famous of the mountain men—Jim Bridger, also known as "Old Gabe," later to be celebrated as a champion trapper, guide, and teller of tall tales, and Jedidiah Smith, who during a few years was to make a great reputation for himself as a trapper and trader.[23] They were to be joined by Hugh Glass, whose great fight with a grizzly bear and whose incredible journey, despite a mangled body, through scores of miles of wilderness, were to be celebrated by yarnspinners and by poets.[24] And among them was the deposed king of the keelboatmen, whose trade had languished as more and more steamboats replaced keelboats.

Mike may well have been put in command of one of the seventy-five-foot keelboats used to carry the food and equipment up a stream which was swollen with spring floods and on a rampage. Twenty to twenty-four men were required on each boat, marching along the runways with their poles or cordelling the boat through the muddy waters. The river was bristling with snags: fifty miles below the mouth of the Kansas River, one buckled through one of the keelboats, and the boat and a ten-thousand-dollar cargo lurched out of sight beneath the surface. The expedition pushed on past the tepees of the Pawnees, Otoes, and Sioux and, past the occasional lonely cabins of trappers or settlers. Northwest of the Mandan villages, a band of Assiniboine Indians made a sudden attack and stole fifty horses. Otherwise the trip was uneventful but hard.[25]

The party stopped for the season at the mouth of the Yellowstone River; Ashley and a few men went back to St. Louis to organize another party of trappers for the next spring. From the fort, small parties went out to hunt and to trap. One of these included Fink and two of his friends, Carpenter and Talbott. The men spent some of the winter on the Musselshell in the Blood Indian country.[26]

George F. Ruxton, in his classical Adventures in Mexico and

the Rocky Mountains (1847) gives an idea of the kind of men trappers had to be and of how they lived during such an expedition. "Callous to any feeling of danger," they were closer "to the primitive savage," he thought, "than perhaps any other class of civilized men": their good qualities were "those of the animal"; they were "White Indians."

During the hunt [says Ruxton] regardless of Indian vicinity, the fearless trapper wanders far and near in search of "sign." His nerves must ever be in a state of tension, and his mind ever present at his call. His eagle eye sweeps round the country, and in an instant detects any foreign appearance. A turned leaf, a blade of grass pressed down, the uneasiness of the wild animals, the flight of birds, are all paragraphs to him written in nature's legible hand and plainest language. All the wits of the subtile savage are called into play to gain an advantage over the wily woodsman; but with the natural instinct of primitive man, the white hunter has the advantages of a civilized mind, and, thus provided, seldom fails to outwit, under equal advantages, the cunning savage. . . .

At a certain time, when the hunt is over or they have loaded their pack-animals, the trappers proceed to the "rendezvous," the locality of which has been previously agreed upon; and here the traders and agents of the fur companies await them, with such assortments of goods as their hardy customers may require, including generally a fair supply of alcohol.

It was probably to such a rendezvous at the main camp that Fink and his companions returned.

Many accounts tell the rest of the story, but the details vary a great deal. A government record baldly states some facts in part of a document recording "deaths of men caused by accidents and other causes not chargeable to Indians." In a few stiff sentences we are told that in 1825, "Marshall was lost in the willow valley near Salt Lake"; in 1823, "Holly Wheeler died from wounds received from a bear"; in 1824, "Thomas, a half breed, was killed by Williams, on the waters of Bear River." "In 1822 [probably in 1823] Mike Fink shot Carpenter—Talbot soon after shot Fink, and not long after was drowned at the Tetons."[27]

A somewhat more detailed version, the first, as a matter of

fact, to be printed, appeared in the Missouri Republican of
July 16, 1823:

> By a letter received in town from one of Gen. Ashley's expedi-
> tion we are informed that a man by the name of Mike Fink well
> known in this quarter as a great marksman with the rifle . . . was
> engaged in his favorite amusement of shooting a tin cup from off
> the head of another man, when aiming too low or from some other
> cause shot his companion in the forehead and killed him. Another
> man of the expedition (whose name we have not heard) remon-
> strated against Fink's conduct, to which he, Fink, replied, that he
> would kill him likewise, upon which the other drew a pistol and
> shot Fink dead upon the spot.

Many writers were to expand and modify the story set down so
briefly here: their varied accounts were to afford interesting data
for the folklorist and the historian.

There was a gruesome sequel to the melodrama at Fort Henry
on the Yellowstone which has been noticed by historian Dale L.
Morgan:[28] Later in 1823, a party of Blackfoot Indians wandered
into the fort, which had been abandoned. We have a report
about them: "They found nothing except the bodies of two men
[Fink and Carpenter] that had been buried therein. According
to their usual barbarity, they commenced to open the graves in
order to strip the bodies of whatever clothes might be wrapped
around them, but finding they were in a putrid state, they left
them without further molestation."[29] Thirty-five years later, an
Indian interpreter, who bore the intriguing name of Zephyr
Rencontre, was able to point out Fink's grave to A. H. Redfield,
Indian Agent for the Upper Missouri.[30]

We have, then, good evidence that Mike Fink's body lay
a-mouldering in the grave. His soul—or, one hopes, a reasonable
facsimile—went marching on in the many narratives about him.

IV. ORAL TRADITION AND PRINTED STORIES

In 1825, sixteen-year-old Abe Lincoln was living near the
mouth of Anderson Creek on the Ohio River. He was a farm
hand and the operator of a ferryboat which crossed the river.
Carl Sandburg tells how he talked with customers of many sorts,

and "Occasionally came a customer who looked as if he might be one of the 'half-horse, half-alligator men' haunting the Ohio water course in those years. There was river talk about Mike Fink . . . the toughest of the crowd . . . a famous marksman and fighter."[31]

Sandburg does not give his evidence, and he may have been guessing. But there is a strong likelihood that Lincoln did hear stories about Mike in 1825 or during one of his flatboat trips to New Orleans in 1828 and 1831. For oral stories appear to have been going the rounds in those years. Morgan Neville of Pittsburgh in 1828 said that even during Fink's lifetime "a thousand legends" (including one told by Fink himself) showed his bravery as a scout; and on the rivers, "from Pittsburg to St. Louis and New Orleans his fame was established." Neville also testified that the tale of the boatman's death was told to him by a steamboat pilot. In 1829, a fur trader wrote from St. Louis, "Many shooting feats of Mike's are related here by persons who profess to have witnessed them." An almanac, published in Nashville in 1837, quotes one Captain Jo Chunk's claim: "There arn't a man from Pittsburgh to New Orleans but what's heard of Mike Fink."[32] In New Orleans in 1842[33] and in Cincinnati in 1845 and 1847,[34] writers spoke of widespread oral lore. In 1847, Joseph M. Field, a widely traveled actor turned newspaper editor, ticked off five places where he had heard stories: "Fifteen years ago, the writer listened to some stories of Mike told by the late Morgan Neville, Esq., of Cincinnati. . . . In Louisville, subsequently, many 'yarns' respecting the early river hero were repeated to the writer; and since that time in New Orleans, Natchez, and, finally, in St. Louis, anecdotes and stories. . . ."[35]

It may have been in the same decade that young Sam Clemens, in the riverside town of Hannibal, heard the yarn which he knew about Fink—possibly from an old-time boatman, who introduced him to typical keelboatmen's lingo.[36] It was in the 1840's that Lieutenant J. W. Abert, on an expedition into New Mexico, at a camp near Valverde, heard some stories: "This afternoon," he wrote, "we had a festive scene at the camp of a trader from Missouri, who still had some fine claret and some good old brandy. We had many tales of wild adventures of prairie life, and hair-breadth escapes. We heard of Mike Fink, who, with two other desperadoes, for a time lived in the Rocky Mountains."[37] And in 1858, A. H. Redfield was shown on the Yellow River "the grave of the celebrated" Mike Fink.[38]

The wide geographic spread and the lengthy time span of these testimonials suggest oral diffusion. There are some other signs: Anecdotes about the king of the boatmen which are merely referred to in early stories are later recounted more fully by writers at some distance in both location and time.[39] Again, some stories, when retold, offer variations which would have been impossible if details had been fixed in printed versions. In particular, the accounts of Fink's death—as set down in widely separate places, at times distant from one another—differ considerably.[40] Finally, some writers about Fink appear to know only local phases of his wide-ranging history, some mentioning only his fame as a hunter or marksman, some his celebrity as a boatman, some only his notoriety as a mountain man.[41] If the authors had read much about him, it seems probable that they would have picked up—and would have mentioned—other phases of his biography.

However, there is no doubting that printed stories as well as oral traditions contributed to Fink's fame. In some instances, authors, one is sure, based their statements about oral traditions upon published claims rather than upon personal experiences. In other instances, authors may well have invented stories on their own or may have adapted to Fink printed or oral tales originally told about others. Mody Boatright believes, in fact, that writers were chiefly responsible for Fink's fame.

Folk tales [he says] tend to cluster around certain heroes. Thus Peter Cartwright, most famous of the frontier circuit-riders, complains that "almost all these various incidents that had gained currency throughout the country concerning Methodist preachers had been located on me. . . ."

But the accretion of folk tales around a few names is mainly the work of writers, not the folk. Crockett becomes famous as a hunter and backwoods politician, and this makes him a suitable peg upon which almanac makers hang a host of anecdotes originally attributed to others. Mike Fink attains notoriety as a fighting keelboatman. Humorists supplying copy for newspapers, almanacs, and thrillers assigned him any traditional adventures they consider to be in character.[42]

Journalists did indeed assign adventures to Fink which seemed appropriate to him. Probably the story Cassedy told in 1852 about Mike and the sheep was stolen from another boatman, as were probably the two stories, "The Disgraced Scalp-Lock" (1842) and "Lige Shattuck's Reminiscence" (1848).[43] Some stories that were told about the king of the boatmen were not even particularly appropriate, for instance, "Deacon Smith's Bull" (1851).[44] However, since there is pretty good evidence that there was an accretion of tales around Fink in oral lore, even before many writers got at him, and since oral diffusion apparently continued long after, we suggest that both oral and written stories helped the process, the two types probably interacting. What we appear to have here, in other words, is a type of semioral, semiliterary lore. This combination seems to have been characteristic of the United States and different from the folklore of Europe in some ways but like it in others.[45]

However the narratives in print originated, there was a considerable body of them, and the story of their appearance shows how Mike Fink's fame waxed and waned.

The mediums in which they were published were, to put it mildly, varied. Take the nineteenth-century appearances of the first noteworthy treatment—Morgan Neville's "The Last of the Boatman." This was first printed in 1828, in what was then sometimes called (appropriately enough) a "female gift book." Thence it moved in 1829, 1832, and 1834 to successive editions of Samuel Cummings, The Western Pilot, Containing Charts of the Ohio River and of the Mississippi . . . Accompanied with Directions for Navigating the Same, a handbook for the use of pioneers and boatmen. In 1832, Mary Russell Mitford, a British lady, placed it in her collection of sketches from the United States—Lights and Shadows of American Life, published in

London, and a British magazine reproduced it from the book. Thirteen years later, it was picked up by Hiram Kaine and printed in the Cincinnati Miscellany or Antiquities of the West (antiquities did not need to be very antique in 1845). In 1847, it was appended to a pamphlet describing an extraordinary painting being displayed throughout the nation and abroad— Description of Banvard's Panorama of the Mississippi, Painted on Three Miles of Canvas, Exhibiting a View of a Country 1,200 Miles in Length, Extending from the Mouth of the Missouri River to the City of New Orleans, Being by Far the Largest Picture Ever Executed by Man, with the Story of Mike Fink, the Last of the Boatmen, a Tale of River Life, published in Boston. (Longfellow and Queen Victoria, among others, viewed the picture; but if they read the story, they inconsiderately neglected to comment upon it.) And in 1859, a man impressively named A. De Puy Van Buren found a place for it in a travel book, Jottings of a Year's Sojourn in the South.

The next tale had travels almost as varied. The Rev. Timothy Flint (probably) copied it from a letter sent to him, as he said, by "an intelligent and respectable" fur trader in St. Louis, and published it in his magazine, the Western Monthly Review (Cincinnati, July, 1829). The same year it was reprinted in two St. Louis newspapers. We find it next in a western historical miscellany, Henry Howe's The Great West (Cincinnati, 1847); then in Ben Cassedy's The History of Louisville . . . (Louisville, 1852); then in a German travel book, Moritz Busch, Wanderungen zwischen Hudson und Mississippi . . . (Stuttgart und Tübingen, 1854); and then in a hack publication, Frank Triplett, Conquering the Wilderness . . . (New York and St. Louis, 1883).[46]

Meanwhile, other stories had been printed and in some instances reprinted in a variety of other publications. Illustrated with quaint but lively woodcuts, they appeared in the popular Crockett Almanacs of 1837, 1839, 1851, 1852, and 1853—the first published in Nashville, the later ones in several eastern cities. They appeared in a sportsmen's magazine, comic maga-

zines, a literary journal, a boatmen's magazine, and the eminent-
ly respectable Harper's Magazine. They were published in newspapers scattered throughout the country. Editors included them
in anthologies for British readers published in London—Transatlantic Tales, Sketches and Legends (1842) and Traits of
American Humour, by Native Authors (1852). A journalist
named Thomas W. Knox included one tale in a very miscellaneous compilation—The Underground World: A Mirror of Life
below the Surface, with Vivid Descriptions of the Hidden
Works of Nature and Art, Comprising Incidents and Adventures beyond the Light of Day . . . etc., etc. (Hartford, 1873).
Mike, one presumes, came under one of the "etcs." Mike's adventures were also included in histories, in a steamboat directory,
in collections of tales and legends, in a paper-backed novel, and
in three autobiographies of preachers.

The list is of course incomplete, but it does seem safe to say
that during the nineteenth century readers of many sorts and in
many parts of the country over a rather lengthy period were introduced, one way or another, to Mike Fink. The dates of publication of the stories we have found show, it seems likely, how
his reputation fared. The period most prolific of "original"
stories was between 1842 and 1860, when twenty-three were first
published—compared with four between 1828 and 1841 and four
between 1861 and 1883. Original stories plus reprints and rewrit-
ten stories grouped as follows:

1828–40	10
1841–50	24
1851–60	23
1861–70	1
1871–80	4
1881–90	7
1891–1900	3

The great decades were the 1840's and the 1850's. In the 1840's,
there were two periods of one year each and one period of two
years when no stories appeared; in the 1850's, there were two
periods of one year each when none appeared. Between 1828
and 1900, the longest spans without original stories or reprints

ran from 1861 through 1865 and from 1867 through 1872, periods of five and six years respectively. Fink's fame, then, grew up to the 1860's; then, abruptly, began to fade. By 1900, he was no longer a vital tradition, although a few original stories about him (some of dubious authenticity) were to appear in the twentieth century. When—in the 1920's and 1930's—his name again began to occur frequently in print, he had become a figure of history rather than of living legend.

V. FOLKLORISH ASPECTS

In both oral and printed narratives, Mike Fink cavorted precariously on a line between history and legend or between folklore and more sophisticated fiction.

Some material classifies pretty safely as history. There is, for instance, the oral testimony of one Claudius Cadot of Scioto County, Ohio (born in 1793), set down on the basis of an interview by James Keyes in his Pioneers of Scioto County: Being a Short Biographical Sketch of Some of the First Settlers of Scioto County, Ohio (Portsmouth, 1880), pp. 3–4:

When the war [of 1812] was ended Claudius went on the river to follow keel boating for the purpose of raising money to buy a piece of land. Keel boating on the river was the only place where a man could go to earn money at all; and the wages paid was very low even there. The first boat he applied to was commanded by the celebrated Mike Fink. The boat belonged to John Finch who was one of a company that run keel boats from Pittsburgh to all the various points in the west. Fink eyed young Claudius very closely, and asked him if he could push. Claudius replied that he could try. So Fink, liking the appearance of the young man, agreed to give him 50 cents a day, that being the wages for a common hand on the Ohio at that time. Claudius soon learned the art of keel boating and stayed with Fink a long time. As he went on to the river to make money, he did not spend it as fast as he got it, which was the usual practice among boatmen at that time. He very soon acquired a considerable pile, all in silver. He got Mike to put it in his trunk for safe keeping. Mike observed to him as he had the biggest pile he ought to carry the key.

It was the usual practice among boatmen at that time when they landed at a town to go up into town and get on a spree. Mike Fink was as fond of spreeing and rowdying as any of his hands, and it was always necessary for some one to stay with the boat. Claudius, not choosing to spend his money in that way always remained with the boat, which suited him better than spending his money in drinking and carousing, and was very satisfactory to the captain and the rest of the crew.

Mike Fink was a very noted character in his day. He could scarcely be called a good man, although he had some good traits in his composition. He was one of the most wild and reckless rowdying men of his class. Yet he had respect for a man of different habits, and when a man like Claudius Cadot, whose sole aim was to do his duty and save his money [worked for him], Fink placed greater confidence in him and gave him greater privileges than the rest of his crew. When he paid him at the end of the year he gave him sixty two and a half cents a day, when the bargain was for only fifty cents a day.

Mr. Cadot followed keel boating four years, during which time he saved money enough to purchase a quarter section of land and settle down to the life of a farmer.

This bears evidence of authenticity partly because of its context, partly because its picture of Mike as an intelligent businessman is somewhat at odds with the popular conception of Fink which was contemporaneous with it. Yet it is possible that even this apparently straightforward reminiscence is touched by the lore about the boatman, since it makes a great deal of Mike's constant roistering—one of the most persistent motifs in tales about him.

A similar reminiscence of eighty-two-year-old Captain John Fink appears to be a compound of history and legend. Also based upon an interview—this one in 1887—it was published in the Ohio Centennial Edition of Henry Howe's Historical Collections of Ohio (Columbus, 1888), I, 321–22:

Capt. John Fink in his youthful days arose bright and early. He was smart, and so he got to Bellaire long before the town; indeed, officiated at its birth. He was born in Pennsylvania in 1805. Mike Fink, the last and most famous of the now extinct race of Ohio and Mississippi river boatmen, was a relative, and he knew Mike—knew him as a boy knows a man. "When I was a lad," he told me, "about ten years of age, our family lived four miles above Wheeling, on the river. Mike laid up his boat near us, though he generally had two boats. This was his last trip, and he went away to the farther West; the country here was getting too civilized, and he was disgusted. This was about 1815.

In the management of his business Mike was a rigid disciplinarian; woe to the man who shirked. He always had his woman along with him, and would allow no other man to converse with her. She was sometimes a subject for his wonderful skill in marksmanship with the rifle. He would compel her to hold on the top of her head a tin cup filled with whiskey, when he would put a bullet through it. Another of his feats was to make her hold it between her knees, as in a vice, and then shoot."

Here some new facts have the appearance of being part of the informant's recollection—that Mike "generally had two boats" and that he at one time moored his boat near Wheeling. The claim that Mike went "to the farther West" in 1815 seems dubious unless (as is possible) it means that Mike thereafter operated only on rivers west of Wheeling. Also, Mike's sternness as a disciplinarian is in contrast with the usual picture of him.[47] But the rest of the interview is based upon widespread stories about Mike and his women, except for one detail which, according to Victorian standards, had been considered too horrible to record[48]—that he tested his girl friend's faithfulness by shooting a cup held between her knees.[49]

A purported interview with an old-time boatman, Captain Jo Chunk, published in 1837, classifies as legend. It appeared in a publication not noteworthy for historical accuracy, a Crockett Almanac. Chunk was quoted as saying, "There arn't a boatman on the river to this day but what he strives to imitate him [Fink]. . . . Mike was looked upon as a kind of king among the boatmen, and he sailed the prettiest craft there was to be found about these 'ere parts." The information may be correct, but it is also quite in line with tradition. Chunk's further claim that Mike was "the first boatman who dared to navigate a broad horn down the falls of the Ohio" almost certainly is fiction or legend rather than history.[50]

These reminiscences, true and legendary, not only represent the tendency of fantasy to mingle with fact, they also, it happens, give us almost all the information available concerning Fink's skill or activity as a boatman.[51] Mike's fame rests upon other talents. As one historian, quoting Mike's traditional challenge, remarks, Mike has "left the record, not that he could load a keelboat in a certain length of time, or lift a barrel of whiskey with one arm, or that no tumultuous current had ever compelled him to back water, but that he could 'out-run, out-hop, out-jump, throw down, drag out, and lick any man in the county.' "[52] One reason may be that the stories as a rule were recorded by writing fellows who knew little about boating. A more important reason probably is that the most memorable stories dealt with something more significant—Mike as an archetype and as a heroic figure.

Since the development of the backwoodsman and of his kin spirit, the boatman, as a type, has been traced and documented elsewhere,[53] we shall merely sketch it here. The story starts in the early days of the nineteenth century when the Kentuckian or the backwoodsman, as the generic frontiersman was called, became as well known a type as, say, the stingy Scotsman in many anecdotes of today. He was, in general belief, a man who was lawless, ignorant, rough mannered, strong, a heavy drinker, and a ferocious fighter. Story after story so pictured him. Later, when former Indian scouts, ex-Revolutionary soldiers and fugitives from the law or the plow found that boating offered the roughest adventures and the best tests of a man's toughness, boatmen won fame as a breed of super-Kentuckians. "With the freer ways of the waters," as Constance Rourke suggests, "the boatman perhaps emerged more quickly as master of his scene than the backwoodsman."

When, eventually, western settlers became worried about their reputation, there was, on occasion, a tendency to suggest that the Kentuckians had been maligned because they had been confused by outsiders with the more savage men of the rivers. In 1830, for instance, Mathew Carey wrote:

. . . the character of the citizens of Kentucky . . . is on the whole estimable. . . . I am well aware that it by no means corresponds with the prejudices of the generality of the citizens of the other states. . . . One circumstance which tends to perpetuate the prejudice is the conduct of the Kentucky boatmen on the Ohio and Mississippi, some of whom appear to pride themselves on the roughness and rudeness of their manners—"half horse, half alligator, &c."[54]

And James H. Perkins, writing on "The Pioneers of Kentucky" in 1846, said:

The first settlers of Kentucky have had no little injustice done them, in consequence of the existence at a later period of a class of "river men," who became, in the view of many, the representatives of the whole race of pioneers. But nothing could be more unlike the boasting, swearing, fighting, drinking, gouging Mike Finks than Boone, Logan, Harrod, and their comrades, the founders of the commonwealth.[55]

The indication is that there was a succession of type portrayals: first the Kentuckian or backwoodsman emerged; then an attempt was made to transfer his fame, such as it was, to the boatmen. When Mike Fink rose to pre-eminence among the boatmen, he became the personification of their qualities. As Leland D. Baldwin has remarked:

Mike Fink was the archetype of the western boatmen. [As we read about him] from the depths of our easy chairs we . . . follow him in his relaxations of raiding camp meetings, battling with berserk rage against other mighty "gougers," shooting the tin cup from his comrades' heads, and chasing the spangled skirts of New Orleans. Boastful, blasphemous, and brutal, save for rhetorical purposes he acknowledged no code nor deity not of his own making— that is, none beyond the spirits that dwelt within the whisky jug. With this familiar oracle ever waiting at his elbow to be consulted Mike toiled and rollicked and gouged his way through the world. . . .[56]

Baldwin's summary of the stories is excellent. The accounts we have of Mike's victories in single combat, to be sure, are more generalized than we would like. Time and again, we are told that the red feather in his hat—and his boasts—proclaimed him king bully-boy of the rivers. We are told that when he was stimulated by whiskey—and we are instructed that he could drink a gallon a day without staggering—he was able to "clear three ball rooms" and to lick two New Orleans gens d'armes sent to arrest him. But the most extensive stories are those which tell of his defeats. One account of a fight, said to have been published between 1824 and 1826, we have been unable to find: it may be an exception.[57] A few stories, recorded only recently, tell of victories. For the rest—in stories at least—he was humbled by Peter Cartwright, Jack Pierce, the sheriff of Westport, and probably others. (It may be worth noticing that all these tales came late in the development of the legend.) When he and his crew were involved, they came out better, notably in the narratives of Field and Bennett. But in at least one late unprinted story, he and his crew suffered ignominious defeat.[58]

Other stories about Fink during his period as a boatman for the most part tell of his brutal or lawless practical jokes and his marksmanship, often in combination. Early and late, we hear of his unchivalrous treatment of his wenches. We hear often of his shooting off a Negro's heel for the fun of it, and one story tells how he shot off an Indian's scalp-lock. We learn of his playfully stealing some of the cargo with which he had been entrusted and of his making a mockery of law courts on several occasions. So he emerges from a whole series of anecdotes and tales as a boatman's boatman—a champion of the unrestrained and unrestrainable roughnecks.

The nature of the stories, and the attitudes which they reveal, cast an interesting light upon the Americans who cherished them. As Daniel C. Hoffman remarks:

> In a folk group the areas of shared interest and common sympathy encompass almost the whole of the people's lives. Hence, from their socially accepted stories we can infer a great deal about the ways in which members of a group look at their relationships to each other, to nature, to the supernatural, and to others outside the group. In short, we can generalize from the folk tale about the society which it represents.[59]

In Fink we have, in Constance Rourke's words, "one of those minor deities whom men create in their own image to magnify themselves." In the tales about this savage and lawless brawler, his creators were either tolerant or actually adulatory: "Many of the tales exhibited the broad, blind cruelty of the backwoods; yet many of them insisted that Fink was good."[60] A British critic comments: "He endeared himself as a lawbreaker to men who were hindered by the law in exploiting the lucrative possibilities of the frontier; and he was the more admired for being as distinguished as a drinker as he was as a gunman."[61] And Bernard DeVoto furnishes an excellent summary:

> The boatmen were the sublimate of frontier hardness. And America, incurably artistic, demanded a culture hero. Mike Fink . . . became the symbol. The legend of Mike Fink is the boatman apotheosized. He was the marksman who could not miss, the bully-boy who could not be felled, unmatchable in drink, invincible to wenches. He was a Salt River roarer. . . . To the admiration of the frontier, he shot the protruberant heel from a nigger's foot or the scalplock from an Indian's head. He fought a thousand combats, whose resonance increases through the years till they are hardly separable from Paul Bunyan's. He was superior to the ethics of timid souls and no court restrained him, though, for a favor, he might ride to one in a keelboat pulled by oxen. . . . His purer escapades rippled across the nation. . . . The water fronts of three thousand miles cherished the less printable stories of a frontier Casanova. Casanova, together with Paul Bunyan, merges into Thor, and Mike is a demigod of the rivers even before he dies—the boatman immortally violent, heroic, unconquerable.[62]

The final sentence in the paragraph by DeVoto introduces another way in which the stories were shaped, since it compares Mike with several mythical heroes. As early as 1828, Morgan Neville (partly for literary reasons) had compared the river champion with another assortment of such figures—Hercules, Roland, "the favourite Knight of the Lion Heart," and Rob Roy. Thereafter his name was frequently linked with that of Hercules. J. M. Field in 1844 compared him with Jason and "a river god." In 1933, a British admirer saw him doubling "the character parts of two national heroes—the strong man, Kwasind, and the great boaster, Iagoo . . . like Iagoo he was a great story-teller."[63] Beyond the resemblance to particular heroes, however, there is a resemblance to the typical hero. Although the tales about Fink were never fused into a saga or an epic,[64] one may say of them what Richard M. Dorson has said of the stories of Davy Crockett, that in many ways they "possess the leading motives and conform to the growth structure of all Old World heroic story."[65]

Fink, like Old World heroes, is (to quote Dorson) "a mighty hero whose fame in myth has a tenuous basis in fact." He does not have a "remarkable birth" but he has "precocious strength," which enables him to handle a rifle, to take part in the defense of the Fort Pitt stockade, and to become a ranger at an early age. He utters "vows and boastings" in story after story, and these parallel in many ways the vauntings of ancient heroes.[66] One of his boasts, in an 1838 almanac story, runs: "I've got the handsomest wife, and the fastest horse, and the sharpest shooting iron in all Kentuck." This follows the formula of "pride of the hero in his weapons, his horse, his dog, his woman"—and the personal name Mike has for his gun, "Bang-all," or "Old Bets," also is in the tradition. "From precocious infancy," says Dorson, ". . . the heroic life cycle is apt to follow an established pattern embroidered with fierce hand-to-hand encounters and conquests, ardent wooings, travels in far lands, and superhuman exploits"— and again the parallel is clear.

Finally: "A fundamental requirement of heroic legend is some means of terminating the career of the unconquerable hero in a way that crowns rather than mars his record. Accordingly death, characterized always by a strong sense of fatalism, comes through supernatural decree or artifice, through treachery or overwhelming odds; omens, visions, warnings, and portents inform the champion that his time is up," says Dorson. Fink died an extraordinary assortment of deaths. When he left the rivers to go to the Far West, it was something like a defeat and a departure for Valhalla. Then came a death which, according to the earliest accounts of it, was sordid enough. But as time passed, folk fancy and the fancy of fiction writers changed the story time after time, bringing it closer to the patterns of the heroic story. Field in 1844 had Mike treacherously killed because he pleaded for understanding from a man who was afraid of him. In 1847, Bennett had an old crone, who was a fortuneteller, predict the dire event. In 1847, also, Field, in another account, had a superstitious character, Jabe Knuckles, issue a series of cryptic warnings, while a chain of strange coincidences and vengeful pursuits

[27]

led to three interrelated deaths, of which Mike's was one; "as if," he said, "fate had but one end reserved for all those who through life had been woven in his checkered history." And many others modified the account in a variety of ways.[67]

Of course there were divergences from the pattern which were unmistakably American. The Old World heroic story was about royalty: these stories were about a king, but a king of keelboatmen. The society of the American stories had as its equivalent for the central hall or gathering place the deck or the cabin of a keelboat or the brothels of New Orleans. And many of the elements were comically represented: the boasts and the vows were consciously comic, and so were the accounts of many of the superhuman deeds. Even in its Heroic Age, America was too sophisticated, or perhaps too lacking in the sense of religion, to take all the heroic ingredients without a pinch of salt or a dash of pepper. Yet the tales, relieved though they were by laughter and satire, conformed to many of the traditions of ancient mythology.

VI. LITERARY ASPECTS

In the field of "respectable" American fiction during the years of Mike Fink's waxing fame, the giants were Washington Irving, Nathaniel Hawthorne, James Fenimore Cooper, and Herman Melville. These may seem to be pretty remote from the relatively "unrespectable" writers who wrote about the legendary boatman, yet they had some relationships. Irving showed how legends such as "Rip Van Winkle" (1819), "The Legend of Sleepy Hollow" (1820), and "The Devil and Tom Walker" (1824) could be adapted to the American scene; and in "A Tour of the Prairies" (1835), Astoria (1836), and Adventures of Captain Bonneville (1837), he used life in the Far West as his subject matter. Hawthorne, too, between 1830 and 1851, discovered the attractions and the possibilities of native legends. Cooper in his Leatherstocking novels (1823–41) and other writings wrote vastly popular narratives, with a legendary quality, about frontiersmen and Indians. Melville in his picaresque travel romances

and his sea stories recorded the comic adventures and wander-
ings of common sailors; here and elsewhere he frequently referred to the West;[68] and in Moby-Dick (1851) he wrote what
several discerning critics have seen to be a superbly transfigured
tall tale.

And during the first half of the nineteenth century these great
writers as well as lesser ones were much concerned with theoriz-
ings about fiction which shaped the forms of the writings about
Fink. They were worried, for instance, about finding ways to
give their writings a national coloration and (astonishing though
it now seems) about the possibility of finding characters who
were distinctly American.[69] In time, they managed to see that,
although Americans did not divide into classes like those of the
Old World, they did divide into sectional and occupational
classes which were somewhat analogous. "We do most seriously
deny," wrote the critic W. H. Gardiner belligerently in 1822,
"that there is any . . . fatal uniformity among us. . . . We boldly insist that in no country on the face of the globe can there be
found a greater variety of specific character than is at this moment developed in these United States." He asks rhetorical
questions, providing instances: "Is the Connecticut pedlar, who
travels over mountain and moor . . . the same animal with the
long shaggy boatman 'clear from Kentuck' who wafts him on
his way over the Mississippi or the Ohio? . . . Is there no bold
peculiarity in the white savage who roams over the remote hunting tracts of the West?"[70] Gardiner was not unique in seeing
boatmen as a class to be pictured imaginatively. Ralph Waldo
Emerson in "The Poet" (1844) spoke of "our boats" as part of
the "incomparable materials" available for American poetry.
And in 1860, Walt Whitman in "Our Old Feuillage," talking
of the "free range and diversity" within the unified nation, gave
this picture among others of similar classes:

On rivers boatmen safely moor'd at nightfall in their boats under
shelters of high banks,
Some of the younger men dance to the sound of the banjo or fiddle,
others sit on the gunwale smoking and talking. . . .

Longfellow in "Evangeline" (1847) made his heroine's lover a rather ethereal boatman and trapper in the Far West.

But most critics and authors tended to feel that members of such groups were unsatisfactory as main characters in novels or poems. Gardiner said of the "varieties of specific character" he had discovered that they were proper for a minor fictional form, "the popular and domestic tale." "But where," he asked, "are your materials for the higher order of fictitious composition? What have you of the heroic and the magnificent?" The trouble, he implied, was that there were no buildings in America with antique associations, and, although the forests were magnificent, "they are connected with no legendary tales of hoary antiquity." Thus like many writers of his day, including Cooper and Hawthorne,[71] he was worried about America's brief past.

These attitudes meant two things about the writings on Fink —that they were likely to be brief and unpretentious rather than long and heroic, and that they would do what could be done to give him at least a touch of antiquity. Essays, tales, and anecdotes—rather than novels or epic poems—were used for most of the incidents in Mike's life. When he got into a longer fiction, such as Bennett's novel of 1848, though his name was in the title, he almost had to be, in accordance with the fashion, a minor character, disappearing from the book for chapters at a time, while a milksop hero and a peaches-and-cream heroine took over the stage. Or if he became the hero of a longer narrative—Field's serial of 1847, for instance—the novelette was destined to remain in its obscure place in a St. Louis newspaper, never to be published as a book. The popular tale was the place for such a lowly character.

Even in writing such tales, however, authors had a try at pushing Mike back into the past. Beginning five years after his death, three stories and a play all took for their title or subtitle "The Last of the Boatmen," and it was customary for authors to use the phrase in writing about him. Actually he was nothing of the sort. As late as the year 1840, there were four hundred and fifteen arrivals of keelboats (presumably manned by boat-

men) at Pittsburgh; and in 1847, some fifty-five keelboats were
still plying the Mississippi. Keelboats were operated in numbers
as late as 1885.[72] Why, then, this dubbing of Fink as "the last of
the boatmen" by men who knew better? The reason probably is
that the writers were trying to connect this fairly recent figure
with a fairly remote age. "Last" was a favorite word during the
era—as in The Lay of the Last Minstrel (1806), "The Last Rose
of Summer" (1808), The Last of the Lairds (1826), The Last
of the Mohicans (1826), "The Last Leaf" (1831), The Last of
the Foresters (1856), and, in the form of a juvenile story, The
Last of the Huggermuggers (1856). Edward Bulwer-Lytton, who
knew a good thing when he found it, used the word in The Last
Days of Pompeii in 1834 and thereafter in the titles of three of
his novels.[73] Writers about Mike were doing what they could
with the magic word to give the embarrassingly new fellow a
little antiquing. The same desire doubtless led writers to compare him on numerous occasions with such ancient heroes as
Hercules, Jason, Apollo, Roland, and others. One author had
the gall to put words into Mike's mouth that were an elegy for
the past—"Where's the fun, the frolicking, the fighting? Gone!
gone! The rifle won't make a man a living now—he must turn
nigger and work. If forests continue to be used up, I may yet be
smothered in a settlement."[74] But most stuck at giving Fink
words so incongruous with his reputation.

The narratives which gave him that reputation were shaped
by two influences in addition to the theories about portraying
such a character in fiction—the nature of their origin and the
nature of the genre to which they belonged. The folklore from
which many stories derived, as Ruth Benedict has pointed out,
is often characterized by the use of authentic details: "Among
any people . . . the pictures of their own daily life is incorporated in their tales with accuracy and detail. . . . People's folk
tales are in this sense their autobiography and the clearest mirror
of their life."[75] Furthermore, many of the stories were humorous. Particularly in a romantic period, humor tends to be anti-
romantic, emphasizing the incongruity between its characters

and its style and the pretentious characters and the ornate style of romantic writings. And in tall tales, mundane or even vulgar characters and diction are wonderfully incongruous with the soaringly imaginative scenes and happenings. As Bernard DeVoto has said: "The Fink stories belong to the category of legend—or fable, if you like, or folklore. And yet . . . they are the vehicle of realism. Wearing the form of . . . humor, realism first enters American fiction; it is with the frontier humor that the realistic depiction of character first becomes a literary force. There had been before it no opposition to the swooning Angelinas, the bearded barons with pasts in piracy or bastardy, of our romance."[76] DeVoto somewhat overstates the case, but the claim that these stories and others like them were important in initiating the development of realism in fiction is a valid one.

The realism in the stories meant that these narratives gave emphasis to an important aspect of the westward movement elsewhere neglected. V. L. Parrington noticed this in relation to the lore about Crockett and Fink (of whom he disapproved):

The crossing of the Appalachian barrier . . . was an undertaking that had fired the imagination. Romantic in spirit and scope, it was meanly picaresque in a thousand unlovely details. Plain men engaged in it, provident and improvident, hard-working and shiftless; heroes had a share in it, but blackguards and outlaws and broken men—the lees and settlings thrown off from the older communities —had a share as well. The world that provided a stage for the courage of Daniel Boone and the fighting qualities of George Rogers Clark bred also the Davy Crocketts and Mike Finks and Col. William [sic] Sugges, who discovered their opportunities for the development of less admirable qualities; and it engulfed in its depths a host of nameless adventurers who drifted into the wilderness settlements, drank and quarreled and begot children, . . . spread a drab poverty along the frontier.[77]

Parrington is possibly too severe with men such as Fink, and his implication that they scattered poverty as they went westward is subject to some doubt. Some of the rascals doubtless prospered tremendously. And they were important in the movement. When it came to fighting Indians, steering downstream, or battling upstream, and when it came to blazing trails into the wilderness, the roughnecks were as useful as the pious brethren, perhaps even more useful. As a British critic suggests: ". . . it is not irrational to admire those of whom Mike was typical, for their defects were defects of qualities which were to make the frontier habitable for law-abiding but less enterprising citizens. They were reckless, and because they were reckless they were useful."[78]

One other literary aspect of the stories is worth a few words—the handling of dialogue. The theory of the time recognized that the use of dialect was one of the important devices for the depiction of low characters. Reviewing ten recent novels, Jared Sparks in 1825 found a new vogue of which he approved: "The actors . . . have not only a human but also a national, and often a provincial character . . . exemplified in modes of speech."[79] A few years later a southern critic was telling authors that novelists' "success . . . as delineators of real life . . . is in proportion to the fidelity with which they copy the diction of whatever rank they introduce—of the vulgar, no less than the exalted."[80]

In the varied narratives about Fink, this injunction was quite faithfully followed. Mike had to follow frontier ritual and shout boasts, and writer after writer gave this chamipon of boasters the most imaginative boast he could concoct.[81] He was reputed to be a witty tall talker, and throughout the stories there runs a fine stream of figurative speech mingled with earthiness—the typical amalgam of this kind of utterance. In an almanac of 1839, for instance, after telling how wonderful he is, he shouts, "and if any man dare doubt it, I'll be in his hair quicker than hell can scorch a feather." Following the idyllic elegy he is given to mouth in Thorpe's story of 1842, he gets back into character by saying, "If the Choctaws or Cherokee or the Massassip don't give us a brush as we pass along, I shall grow as poor as a strawed wolf in a pitfall." In Robb's story of 1847, he suggests, "Jest pint out a muskeeter at a hundred yards and I'll nip off his right hinder eend claw at the second jint afore he kin hum, Oh, don't!" He emerges from the tangled web of coincidences and improbabilities of Field's story in 1847 to say, ". . . that cussed old cow . . . had the orfullest holler hind its shoulders you ever did see, and the old folks being petiklar careful about the crittur, they jest insisted that I should foller it around in wet weather and bale its back out. . . ." In Bennett's melodramatic novel of 1848, he addresses his crew: "Boys, this here's a night. . . . How the wind rolls and trembles about like a dying craw-fish, and sprinkles the water in your faces, my hearties; and all for your own good, too. . . . Why, ef it warn't for sech times like this what in natur would become on ye, my angels? . . . fur ye never git water nearer to ye nor the river. . . ." Even the pious biographer of the Rev. Peter Cartwright in his anecdote of 1850 gives Mike an appropriate speech: "By golly, you're some beans in a bar-fight. I'd rather set to with an old he in dog-days."

Passages such as these led Constance Rourke to say of Fink, "His language was one of his glories, matching his power to push a pole. The ear attuned to delicate melodies may hear only the roar. Yet a loosely strung poetry belongs to these apostrophes, and its elements are worth mastering."[82] "As a talker," agrees Mark Van Doren, "he is sublime."[83]

Here the American language began to bring about a revolution in American writing by finding its way into subliterature. Before the end of the century, Mark Twain, reared in a town by the Mississippi, was going to put it into literature to stay. Snatches of talk such as this make the reading of a fair share of these narratives about Mike Fink rewarding even today. Furthermore, these combinations of history and legend, of humor and of fiction—good, mediocre, and downright bad—teach the reader a great deal about our American past.

NOTES

1. Pittsburgh is given as his birthplace as early as 1829 (see p. 57). Several contemporaries dated his birth in the last quarter of the eighteenth century. Morgan Neville, who quite possibly knew him, indicated that it was earlier; Hiram Kaine in 1845 gave it as 1780. But Mike's activity as an Indian scout, even if he began and ended it at an early age, seems to indicate 1770 or, at the latest, 1775.

2. Colonel Henry W. Shoemaker says that he was told by John Rathfon of Millersburg, allegedly an old friend of the Fink family, that Mike, the son of a German miller, was born "in the Lykens Valley but early in his life went to Pittsburg," where he was reared by an aunt and uncle, Mr. and Mrs. Adam Taub (Letter of December 1, 1955, and story of December 1, 1950 [see p. 242]. Fink is the German word for "finch" and is a common German name. A will dated September 1, 1821, and recorded October 4, 1824, in Pittsburgh casts a great deal of doubt upon Rathfon's recollection. This is the will of one Mary Fink, who leaves certain property "to her sons"—"Jacob, Michael, Daniel, Andrew, and Abraham Fink" (Ella Chafant [ed.], *A Goodly Heritage: Earliest Wills on an American Frontier* [Pittsburgh, 1955], pp. 146–47).

3. *Recollections of Persons and Places in the West* (2d ed.; Philadelphia, 1868), p. 59.

4. *Notes on the Settlement and Indian Wars* (Wellsburg, 1824).

5. *Ibid.* For details about the warfare with the Indians on the Pennsylvania frontier see also Leland D. Baldwin, *Pittsburgh: The Story of a City* (1937); and Randolph C. Downes, *Council Fires on the Upper Ohio* (1940), both published by the University of Pittsburgh Press; Samuel P. Hildreth, *Pioneer History* . . . (Cincinnati, 1848); C. Hale Sipe, *The Indian Wars of Pennsylvania* (2d ed.; Harrisburg, 1931).

6. See p. 53.

7. Harold T. Williamson, *Winchester, the Gun That Won the West* (Washington, 1952), pp. 3–4; Charles Winthrop Sawyer, *Our Rifles* (Boston, 1946), pp. 9–17.

8. Charles Winthrop Sawyer, *Firearms in American History* (Boston, 1910), pp. 78–79.

9. T. B. Thorpe, "Remembrances of the Mississippi," *Harper's Magazine*, XII (December, 1855), 30.

10. "The Last of the Girtys," *Western Literary Journal and Monthly Review*, I (February, 1845), 234.

11. Timothy Flint, *Recollections of the Last Ten Years* . . . (Boston, 1826), p. 14.

12. Seymour Dunbar, *A History of Travel in America* (Indianapolis, 1915), I, 288–92; and A. B. Hulbert, *Waterways of Western Expansion* (Cleveland, 1903), give accounts of early Ohio boating from which the details in this and the following paragraph have been drawn.

13. Thomas Sharf, *History of St. Louis and County* (Philadelphia, 1883), II, 1088.

14. Leland D. Baldwin, *The Keelboat Age on Western Waters* (Pittsburgh, 1941), pp. 44–45. Baldwin distinguishes between the keelboat and the barge. We have grouped the two together.

15. A. B. Hulbert, *The Paths of Inland Commerce* (New Haven,

1920), p. 71. For a good contemporary description see S. Wilke-son's article in *The American Pioneer*, II (June, 1843), 271–73, or Neville's sketch on pp. 50–51 of this book. See also cut, p. 51.

16. Baldwin, *The Keelboat Age on Western Waters*, pp. 64–66.

17. W. P. Strickland, *The Pioneers of the West* (New York, 1856), p. 197.

18. *Ibid.*, p. 198; and Wilkeson, *op. cit.*, p. 272.

19. Herbert and Edward Quick, *Mississippi Steamboatin'* . . . (New York, 1926), p. 27.

20. A. B. Hulbert, in *The Ohio River, a Course of Empire* (New York, 1906), pp. 209–10, gives an authentic account of a rough-and-tumble fight during which two battlers suffered, between them, two gouged eyes, a nose clipped off close to the face, a lower lip torn over the chin, and two heads sadly bereft of hair. The traveler who described the struggle said that he had been told that he could tell "a good from a vicious" frontier tavern by noticing whether or not the keeper had lost his ears.

21. Trappers guided the Mormons to their future home, the United States army to battlefields in New Mexico, the migrants to California and Oregon. See Hiram M. Chittenden, *History of the American Fur Trade of the Far West* (New York, 1902), I, x–xii.

22. Quoted in Chittenden, *op. cit.*, p. 262.

23. Bridger figured in several dime novels by Ned Buntline and, later, in Emerson Hough's *The Covered Wagon*; see Grenville M. Dodge, *Biographical Sketch of James Bridger* (New York, 1905); see also Dale L. Morgan, *Jedidiah Smith and the Opening of the West* (Indianapolis, 1953).

24. The story has reached print many times. John G. Neihardt's epic, *The Song of Hugh Glass*, was published in 1915.

25. For accounts of the journey, see Dale L. Morgan, *op. cit.*; John G. Neihardt, *The Splendid Wayfaring* (New York, 1920); J. Cecil Alter, *James Bridger: Trapper, Frontiersman, Scout and Guide* (Salt Lake City, 1925).

26. This was the testimony of a trapper, *Western Review*, July, 1829. See the story reproduced on pp. 56–61.

27. Smith, Jackson, and Sublette, Record Book, Vol. XXXII, containing copies of letters from Indian agents and others to the Superintendent of Indian Affairs at St. Louis, September 10, 1830, to April 1, 1832.

28. Morgan, *op. cit.*, p. 49.

29. Extract from *Edmonton Factory Journal* (written by Duncan Finlayson) published in "The International Significance of the Jones and Immell Massacre and of the Aricara Outbreak in 1823," ed. A. P. Nasatir, *Pacific Northwest Quarterly*, XXX (January, 1939), 85–86.

30. ". . . on the sixth of July, the boats for the conveyance of the

Crow annuities being finished and loaded, we started on our Yellowstone trip. We ran down in the afternoon six miles and encamped for the night at the mouth of the Yellowstone. Here my own interpreter, Zephyr Rencontre, pointed out the grave of the celebrated Mike Finch [sic] (Report of A. H. Redfield, September 1, 1858, to A. M. Robinson, 35th Cong., 2d Sess., Sen. Exec. Doc. I [Serial 974], 440).

31. *Abraham Lincoln: The Prairie Years* (New York, 1926), I, 78–79.

32. Pp. 52, 60, 64.

33. T. B. Thorpe in the *Spirit of the Times*, July 16, wrote: "Among the flatboatmen [sic], there were none that gained the notoriety of Mike Fink: his name is still remembered along the whole of the Ohio as a man who excelled in everything. . . ."

34. Hiram Kaine wrote in the *Cincinnati Miscellany or Antiquities of the West*, October, 1845: "Mike Fink was . . . the most celebrated of all the 'River men.' To this day there is scarce a city between Pittsburgh and New Orleans that has not some tradition in which he bears a conspicuous part . . . it would take a whole volume to detail half of the strange legends of which Mike was the hero. . . ." Emerson Bennett, in the preface to his novel in 1847, tells of having heard "spicy anecdotes" about Fink which, unfortunately, he does not repeat.

35. *St. Louis Reveille*, June 8, 1844. Field's description of Neville makes rather doubtful the claim that he had talked with him fifteen years before.

36. A passage in *Mark Twain's Letters to Will Bowen*, ed. Theodore Hornberger (Austin, 1941), p. 18, recalls the instruction received from General Gaines, for a time Hannibal's leading drunkard. Clemens mentioned Fink, twice. In his Notebook No. 16 (February 11 to September 20, 1882) he wrote, "Mike Fink shooting the tin cup off Carpenter's head." His working notes for *Huckleberry Finn* included this one: "Let some old liar of a keelboat man on a raft tell about the earthquake of 1811 . . . & about Carpenter & Mike Fink" (Bernard DeVoto, *Mark Twain at Work* [Cambridge, 1942], p. 65). It is impossible to say whether these passages recorded a remembrance from childhood or a story Twain heard or read when revisiting the Mississippi and reading about the river preparatory to writing the latter part of *Life on the Mississippi*.

37. "Report of Lieut. J. W. Abert on His Examination of New Mexico in the Years 1846–47," U.S. 30th Cong., 1st Sess., Exec. Doc., No. 41 (Washington, 1848), IV, 503. See p. 271.

38. See n. 30, p. 36.

39. The story about Mike's test of his woman's fidelity is mentioned in 1829 but no details are given. A version is given in 1839 and the story is told in full in 1888. Again, the story of Mike's

death is only sketched at first; later many contradictory details are added.

40. See pp. 260–77.

41. For "Scroggins" and some anonymous almanac writers, he was a hunter and a fine shot—nothing more. For a number of authors, he was simply a boatman. Lieutenant Abert knew him only as a desperado who lived in the Rocky Mountains. Whether A. H. Redfield knew anything about him before he talked with an Indian interpreter is doubtful, since he called him "the celebrated Mike *Finch*" (authors' italics).

42. *Folk Laughter on the American Frontier* (New York, 1949), pp. 93–94.

43. See pp. 67, 143, 226. Cassedy says his story had been told about another boatman. The 1842 story may well have been suggested by two widely current stories about Mike, one about his shooting a cup off a companion's head, the other about his shooting off a Negro's heel. The 1848 story was appropriate for any hearty drinker who told tall tales.

44. Pp. 220–25.

45. See Richard M. Dorson, "Print and American Folk Tales," *California Folklore Quarterly*, IV (July, 1945), 207–15, for a discussion of such tales and the problems involved in their study.

46. For details about the publication of stories during the nineteenth century and beyond see the Bibliography, pp. 281–90.

47. Here and in Cadot's account there is the possibility that an old man is, humanly enough, showing wisdom superior to that of people who have actually known the boatman by attacking stories which he has heard or read.

48. In 1829, an anonymous author, probably the Rev. Timothy Flint, had mentioned a rifle shot test but had felt impelled to omit the anecdote (see p. 58), and in 1839, a *Crockett Almanac* had presented a censored version (p. 56).

49. One may wonder whether the story in all its horrors ever appeared in print. Is it possible that Mike was so beyond the pales of decency that on occasion he had his woman hold the cup between her thighs while he shot at it?

50. See pp. 64, 262. It should also be noted that Chunk erroneously placed Mike's death "at Smithland, behind the Cumberland bar."

51. One very recent story (p. 244) tells about Mike's winning a seven-mile keelboat race. This is the only reference to keelboat races which we have encountered prior to 1955, when Walt Disney produced a movie in which Mike raced Davy Crockett. Disney stated that his story was based upon a legend, but we have not had the pleasure of seeing his source.

52. A. B. Hulbert, *The Paths of Inland Commerce* (New Haven,

1921), p. 64. A similar comment is made by Dale L. Morgan, *op. cit.*, p. 47.

53. See Constance Rourke, *American Humor: A Study of the National Character* (New York, 1931), pp. 33–55; Walter Blair (ed.), *Native American Humor (1800–1900)* (New York, 1937), pp. 27–37; Mody C. Boatright, *Folk Laughter on the American Frontier* (New York, 1949), pp. 1–33.

54. *Miscellaneous Essays* (Philadelphia, 1830), p. 396.

55. *North American Review*, LXII (January, 1846), 87.

56. *Western Pennsylvania Historical Review*, XVI (May, 1933), 146.

57. A letter from Professor Gilbert H. Barnes of Ohio Wesleyan, August 11, 1930, mentioned his seeing the account in a Pittsburgh newspaper.

58. William E. Connelly, Secretary of the Kansas State Historical Society, said in a letter of May 10, 1930: "In some of my manuscript writings I have an account of a fight between three Big Sandy backwoodsmen who had taken some produce to Louisville in canoes, for sale. Mike Fink and his crew came along and attacked these . . . pioneers who lived in what is now Johnson county, Kentucky. They were powerful men and they completely defeated Mike Fink and all his keelboatmen. One . . . was Henderson Milum, who was six feet, six, and supposed to be the strongest man in the Big Sandy Valley in his day. I knew his discendents [sic] very well. Another was a man named Hanna who had killed a bear on the Big Sandy River without weapons. . . . Another . . . was Peter Mankins, who lived many years on the . . . River but finally moved to Washington county, Arkansas, where he died at the age of 111 years. . . . This fight was on a wharf boat." A keelboat crew usually totaled at least six men.

59. *Paul Bunyan: Last of the Frontier Demigods* (Philadelphia, 1952), p. 19.

60. Rourke, *op. cit.*, p. 54.

61. *Times Literary Supplement* (London), November 16, 1933, p. 794.

62. *Mark Twain's America* (Boston, 1932), p. 60.

63. *Times Literary Supplement* (London), November 16, 1933, p. 794.

64. Neihardt's *Song of Three Friends* (1919) is based upon only three of the stories.

65. *Southern Folklore Quarterly*, VI (June, 1942), 95–102. Dorson cites as authorities consulted on heroic literature H. M. and N. K. Chadwick, *The Growth of Literature* (3 vols.; Cambridge, 1932–40); W. P. Ker, *The Heroic Age* (Cambridge, 1912); W. P. Ker, *Epic and Romance* (London, 1922), chap. i; and N. K. Sidhanta, *The Heoric Age of India* (London, 1929). A book pub-

lished since Dorson's article was written and which extends these studies is C. M. Bowra, *Heroic Poetry* (London, 1952), pp. 91–131. Constance Rourke (*op. cit.*, p. 55) was, we believe, the first student to point out that "Mike Fink embodied the traditional history of the hero. . . ." She did not, however, elaborate upon this claim. In 1844, J. M. Field had seen the "gathering of the mythic haze . . . which . . . invests distinguished mortality with the sublimer attributes of the hero and the demi-god" (see pp. 93–142 and 260–77).

66. See Dorothy Dondore, "Big Talk! The Flyting, the Gabe, and the Frontier Boast," *American Speech*, VI (October, 1930), 45–55.

67. Field's long narrative is on pp. 93–142. For other versions of the story see p. 263.

68. In chap. lxxxii of *Moby Dick* he reverses the procedure of writers about Mike Fink who compare the keeler with Hercules when he characterizes Hercules as "that antique Crockett and Kit Carson." Elsewhere in the book he talks of the legendary White Steed of the Prairies.

69. For a brief consideration of the problem and its initial solution see Blair, *op. cit.*, pp. 17–37.

70. *North American Review*, XV, 251–52. Compare Ruxton's characterization of western trappers, p. 13.

71. See Arvid Shulenberger, *Cooper's Theory of Fiction* (Lawrence, Kansas, 1955), pp. 11–37; Nathaniel Hawthorne, "Prefaces" to *Blithedale Romance* (1852) and *The Marble Faun* (1860).

72. Baldwin, *The Keelboat Age on Western Waters*, p. 194.

73. *Rienzi, the Last of the Tribunes* (1835), *The Last of the Barons* (1843), and *Harold, the Last of the Saxon Kings* (1848).

74. T. B. Thorpe, "The Disgraced Scalp-Lock" (1842). For a discussion of the elegiac motif in frontier literature see Henry Nash Smith, *Virgin Land: The American West as Symbol and Myth* (Cambridge, 1950), pp. 51–89.

75. "Folklore," *Encyclopaedia of the Social Sciences*, VI (New York, 1931), 291.

76. "Bully Boy," *Saturday Review of Literature*, April 8, 1933, p. 523.

77. *The Romantic Revolution in America* (New York, 1927), p. 138.

78. *Times Literary Supplement* (London), November 16, 1933, p. 794.

79. "Recent American Novels," *North American Review*, XXI (July, 1825), 82–83.

80. *Southern Literary Messenger*, III (November, 1837), 692.

81. Our favorite is the one given to him by T. B. Thorpe on p. 78.

82. *New York Herald Tribune*, April 2, 1933, p. 4.

83. *The Nation*, CXXXVI (May 3, 1933), 507.

The Growth of an American Legend

The Last of the Boatmen (1828)

MORGAN NEVILLE

THE MEDIUM OF PUBLICATION and the authorship of the first-known literary work about Mike Fink were, in some ways, rather surprising. For the story about the rambunctious keelboatman turned up in late 1828, of all places, in a "ladies' book," and the author was a gentleman.

Ladies' books—gift books or annual miscellanies—were the quintessence of nineteenth-century gentility. Between 1825 and 1865, such volumes were issued by the thousands around Christmas time to serve as suitable presents for the nicest "females." They cost demonstrative swains, as a rule, between $2.50 and $20.00 apiece, in a day when dollars were dollars; and they had the look of being worth such huge prices. They were bound in silk, velvet, or embossed leather, and they were lavishly illustrated and handsomely printed. They bore titles such as The Opal, The Lily, The Casket of Love, and The Offering to Beauty. The contents were appropriate. In the 1840's Huck Finn found a typical specimen, Friendship's Offering, on the table of an aristocratic family in the deep South. A look at it led him to decide that it was "full of beautiful stuff and poetry." So were they all, and both ingredients were likely to be ineffably refined and perfumed to the most ladylike taste.

The Western Souvenir, a Christmas and New Year's Gift for 1829 was in some ways typical, a 324-page duodecimo, bound in satin, "embellished" with engravings and dashed with sentimentality and highfalutin romance. But it differed from eastern compilations, since it appeared in Cincinnati, and its editor, James Hall, boasted, "It is written and published in the Western country . . . and is chiefly confined to subjects connected with

the history and character of the country which gives it birth."
The illustrations showed Ohio Valley scenes and people, and
the poems and tales (many by Hall) dealt with the new country. The most famous item was "The Last of the Boatmen,"
signed "N."

"N." was Morgan Neville (1783–1840). Grandson of two
Revolutionary War generals, son of a colonel, Neville belonged
to a wealthy Pittsburgh family. He studied Latin and Greek in
the Pittsburgh Academy, then had a varied career as bank
cashier, business secretary, lawyer, and newspaper editor. But
scion of an established family though he was, he had a taste for
fun and adventure. We have glimpses of him dancing the horn-
pipe for fellow students, performing in amateur theatricals, joining a company who tried to assist Aaron Burr's mysterious military expedition, acting as a second in a duel, serving as sheriff of
Allegheny County, and leading a militia regiment. Few lives during Neville's youth in Pittsburgh or his later years in Cincinnati
were likely to be sheltered; and his was less sheltered than most.
Neville's acquaintances and background furnished materials for
this, his most famous sketch. His claim that Fink was "an old
acquaintance, familiarly known to me from my boyhood" is
completely credible, since Mike evidently had been an Indian
scout in Pittsburgh when Neville was a boy there. Neville may
well have seen the feat of Mike's marksmanship which he de-
scribes. And couched though it is in fairly ornate language,
sprinkled though it is with classical allusions, his sketch gives
evidence of being based upon oral stories. He may, as he claims,
have heard the "legend" of the deer and the Indian from Mike's
own lips. He may also—as he alleges at the end of the sketch
(see p. 260)—have heard the tale of Mike's death from an old
keelboatman turned pilot. His pictures of himself spinning yarns
about the boatman on the moonlit deck of a steamboat and
listening to an old pilot's narrative in a pilot house provide valuable testimony concerning his hero's fame "from Pittsburgh to
St. Louis, and New Orleans" as early as 1828—five years after
Fink's death.

I embarked a few years since at Pittsburg for Cincinnati, on board of a steam boat—more with a view of realising the possibility of a speedy return against the current than in obedience to the call of either business or pleasure. It was a voyage of speculation. I was born on the banks of the Ohio, and the only vessels associated with my early recollections were the canoes of the Indians which brought to Fort Pitt their annual cargoes of skins and bear's oil. The Flat boat of Kentucky, destined only to float with the current, next appeared; and after many years of interval, the Keel boat of the Ohio and the Barge of the Mississippi were introduced for the convenience of the infant commerce of the West.

At the period at which I have dated my trip to Cincinnati, the steam boat had made but few voyages back to Pittsburg. We were generally skeptics as to its practicability. The mind was not prepared for the change that was about to take place in the West. It is now consummated; and we yet look back with astonishment at the result.

The rudest inhabitant of our forests—the man whose mind is least of all imbued with a relish for the picturesque—who would gaze with vacant stare at the finest painting—listen with apathy to the softest melody, and turn with indifference from a mere display of ingenious mechanism, is struck with the sublime power and self-moving majesty of a steam boat—lingers on the shore where it passes—and follows its rapid and almost magic course with silent admiration. The steam engine in five years has enabled us to anticipate a state of things which, in the ordinary course of events, it would have required a century to have produced. The art of printing scarcely surpassed it in its beneficial consequences.

In the old world, the places of the greatest interest to the philosophic traveller are ruins and monuments that speak of faded splendour and departed glory. The broken columns of Tadmor—the shapeless ruins of Babylon, are rich in matter for almost endless speculation. Far different is the case in the western regions of America. The stranger views here, with wonder, the rapidity with which cities spring up in forests; and with which barbarism retreats before the approach of art and civilization. The reflection possessing the most intense interest is not what has been the character of the country but what shall be her future destiny.

As we coasted along this cheerful scene, one reflection crossed my mind to diminish the pleasure it excited. This was caused by the sight of the ruins of the once splendid mansion of Blennerhassett. I had spent some happy hours here when it was the favourite residence of taste and hospitality. I had seen it when a lovely and accomplished woman presided—shedding a charm around, which made it as inviting, though not so dangerous, as the island of Calypso—when its liberal and polished owner made it the resort of every stranger, who had any pretensions to literature or science. I had beheld it again under more inauspicious circumstances—when its proprietor, in a moment of visionary speculation, had abandoned this earthly paradise to follow an adventurer—himself the dupe of others. A military banditti held possession, acting "by authority." The embellishments of art and taste disappeared beneath the touch of a band of vandals: and the beautiful domain which presented the imposing appearance of a palace, and which had cost a fortune in the erection, was changed in one night into a scene of devastation! The chimneys of the house remained for some years—the insulated monument of the folly of their owner, and pointed out to the stranger the place where once stood the temple of hospitality. Drift wood covered the pleasure grounds; and the massive cut stone that formed the columns of the gateway were scattered more widely than the fragments of the Egyptian Memnon.

When we left Pittsburgh, the season was not far advanced in vegetation. But as we proceeded, the change was more rapid than the difference of latitude justified. I had frequently observed this in former voyages; but it never was so striking as on the present occasion. The old mode of travelling in the sluggish flat boat seemed to give time for the change of season; but now a few hours carried us into a different climate. We met spring with all her laughing train of flowers and verdure rapidly advancing from the south. The buck-eye, cotton-wood, and maple had already assumed in this region the rich livery of summer. The thousand varieties of the floral kingdom spread a gay carpet over the luxuriant bottoms on each side of the river. The thick woods resounded with the notes of the feathered tribe—each striving to outdo his neighbour in noise, if not in melody. We had not yet reached the region of paroquets; but the clear toned whistle of the cardinal was heard in every bush; and the cat-bird was endeavouring, with its usual zeal, to rival the powers of the more gifted mocking-bird.

A few hours brought us to one of those stopping points known by the name of "wooding places." It was situated immediately above Letart's Falls. The boat, obedient to the wheel of the pilot, made a graceful sweep towards the island above the chute, and rounding to, approached the wood pile. As the boat drew near the shore, the escape steam reverberated through the forest and hills like the chafed bellowing of the caged tiger. The root of a tree concealed beneath the water prevented the boat from getting sufficiently near the bank, and it became necessary to use the paddles to take a different position.

"Back out! Mannee! and try it again!" exclaimed a voice from the shore. "Throw your pole wide—and brace off!—or you'll run against a snag!"

This was a kind of language long familiar to us on the Ohio. It was a sample of the slang of the keel-boatmen.

The speaker was immediately cheered by a dozen of voices from the deck; and I recognised in him the person of an old acquaintance, familiarly known to me from my boyhood. He was leaning carelessly against a large beech; and as his left arm negligently pressed a rifle to his side, presented a figure that Salvator would have chosen from a million as a model for his wild and gloomy pencil. His stature was upwards of six feet, his proportions perfectly symmetrical, and exhibiting the evidence of Herculean powers. To a stranger, he would have seemed a complete mulatto. Long exposure to the sun and weather on the lower Ohio and Mississippi had changed his skin; and, but for the fine European cast of his countenance, he might have passed for the principal warrior of some powerful tribe. Although at least fifty years of age, his hair was as black as the wing of the raven. Next to his skin he wore a red flannel shirt, covered by a blue capot, ornamented with white fringe. On his feet were moccasins, and a broad leathern belt, from which hung suspended in a sheath a large knife, encircled his waist.

As soon as the steam boat became stationary, the cabin passengers jumped on shore. On ascending the bank, the figure I have just described advanced to offer me his hand.

"How are you, Mike?" said I.

"How goes it?" replied the boatman—grasping my hand with a squeeze that I can compare to nothing but that of a blacksmith's vice.

"I am glad to see you, Mannee!" continued he in his abrupt manner. "I am going to shoot at the tin cup for a quart—off hand—and you must be judge."

I understood Mike at once, and on any other occasion should have remonstrated and prevented the daring trial of skill. But I was accompanied by a couple of English tourists who had scarcely ever been beyond the sound of Bow Bells and who were travelling post over the United States to make up a book of observations on our manners and customs. There were, also, among the passengers, a few bloods from Philadelphia and Baltimore, who could conceive of nothing equal to Chesnut or Howard streets; and who expressed great disappointment at not being able to find terrapins and oysters at every village— marvellously lauding the comforts of Rubicum's. My tramontane pride was aroused; and I resolved to give them an opportunity of seeing a Western Lion—for such Mike undoubtedly was—in all his glory. The philanthropist may start and accuse me of want of humanity. I deny the charge, and refer for apology to one of the best understood principles of human nature.

Mike, followed by several of his crew, led the way to a beech grove some little distance from the landing. I invited my fellow passengers to witness the scene. On arriving at the spot, a stout, bull-headed boatman, dressed in a hunting shirt—but bare-footed—in whom I recognised a younger brother of Mike, drew a line with his toe; and stepping off thirty yards—turned round fronting his brother—took a tin cup which hung from his belt, and placed it on his head. Although I had seen the feat per-formed before, I acknowledge I felt uneasy whilst this silent preparation was going on. But I had not much time for reflec-tion; for this second Albert exclaimed—

"Blaze away, Mike! and let's have the quart."

My "compagnons de voyage," as soon as they recovered from the first effect of their astonishment, exhibited a disposition to interfere. But Mike, throwing back his left leg, levelled his rifle at the head of his brother. In this horizontal position the weapon remained for some seconds as immoveable as if the arm which held it was affected by no pulsation.

"Elevate your piece a little lower, Mike! or you will pay the corn," cried the imperturbable brother.

I know not if the advice was obeyed or not; but the sharp crack of the rifle immediately followed, and the cup flew off thirty or forty yards—rendered unfit for future service. There was a cry of admiration from the strangers, who pressed forward to see if the fool-hardy boatman was really safe. He remained as immoveable as if he had been a figure hewn out of stone. He had not even winked when the ball struck the cup within two inches of his skull.

"Mike has won!" I exclaimed; and my decision was the signal which, according to their rules, permitted him of the target to move from his position. No more sensation was exhibited among the boatmen than if a common wager had been won. The bet being decided, they hurried back to their boat, giving me and my friends an invitation to partake of "the treat." We declined, and took leave of the thoughtless creatures. In a few minutes afterwards, we observed their "Keel" wheeling into the current, the gigantic form of Mike bestriding the large steering oar, and the others arranging themselves in their places in front of the cabin that extended nearly the whole length of the boat, covering merchandize of immense value. As they left the shore, they gave the Indian yell; and broke out into a sort of unconnected chorus—commencing with—

> "Hard upon the beech oar!—
> She moves too slow!—
> All the way to Shawneetown,
> Long while ago."

In a few moments the boat "took the chute" of Letart's Falls, and disappeared behind the point with the rapidity of an Arabian courser.

Our travellers returned to the boat, lost in speculation on the scene, and the beings they had just beheld; and, no doubt, the circumstance has been related a thousand times with all the necessary amplifications of finished tourists.

Mike Fink may be viewed as the correct representative of a class of men now extinct; but who once possessed as marked a character, as that of the Gipsies of England or the Lazaroni of Naples. The period of their existence was not more than a third of a century. The character was created by the introduction of trade on the Western waters; and ceased with the successful establishment of the steam boat.

There is something inexplicable in the fact that there could be men found, for ordinary wages, who would abandon the systematic but not laborious pursuits of agriculture to follow a life, of all others except that of the soldier distinguished by the greatest exposure and privation. The occupation of a boatman was more calculated to destroy the constitution and to shorten the life than any other business. In ascending the river, it was a continued series of toil, rendered more irksome by the snail like rate at which they moved. The boat was propelled by poles against which the shoulder was placed; and the whole strength and skill of the individual were applied in this manner. As the boatmen moved along the running board with their heads near-ly touching the plank on which they walked, the effect pro-duced on the mind of an observer was similar to that on be-holding the ox rocking before an overloaded cart. Their bodies, naked to their waist for the purpose of moving with greater ease, and of enjoying the breeze of the river, were exposed to the burning suns of summer, and to the rains of autumn. After a hard day's push, they would take their "fillee," or ration of whiskey, and having swallowed a miserable supper of meat half

burnt, and of bread half baked, stretch themselves without covering on the deck, and slumber till the steersman's call in-vited them to the morning "fillee." Notwithstanding this, the boatman's life had charms as irresistible as those presented by the splendid illusions of the stage. Sons abandoned the com-fortable farms of their fathers, and apprentices fled from the service of their masters. There was a captivation in the idea of "going down the river"; and the youthful boatman who had "pushed a keel" from New Orleans felt all the pride of a young merchant after his first voyage to an English sea port. From an exclusive association together, they had formed a kind of slang peculiar to themselves; and from the constant exercise of wit with "the squatters" on shore and crews of other boats, they acquired a quickness and smartness of vulgar retort that was quite amusing. The frequent battles they were engaged in with the boatmen of different parts of the river, and with the less civilized inhabitants of the lower Ohio, and Mississippi, invested them with that ferocious reputation which has made them spoken of throughout Europe.

On board of the boats thus navigated, our merchants entrusted valuable cargoes without insurance, and with no other guarantee than the receipt of the steersman, who possessed no property but his boat; and the confidence so reposed was seldom abused.

Among these men, Mike Fink stood an acknowledged leader for many years. Endowed by nature with those qualities of intellect that give the possessor influence, he would have been a conspicuous member of any society in which his lot might have been cast. An acute observer of human nature has said, "Opportunity alone makes the hero. Change but their situations, and Caesar would have been but the best wrestler on the green." With a figure cast in a mould that added much of the symmetry of an Apollo to the limbs of a Hercules, he possessed gigantic strength; and accustomed from an early period of life to brave the dangers of a frontier life, his character was noted for the most daring intrepidity. At the court of Charlemagne he might have been a Roland; with the Crusaders he would have been the favourite of the Knight of the Lion-heart; and in our revolution, he would have ranked with the Morgans and Putnams of the day. He was the hero of a hundred fights, and the leader in a thousand daring adventures. From Pittsburg to St. Louis and New Orleans, his fame was established. Every farmer on the shore kept on good terms with Mike—otherwise there was no safety for his property. Wherever he was an enemy, like his great prototype, Rob Roy, he levied the contribution of Black Mail for the use of his boat. Often at night, when his tired companions slept, he would take an excursion of five or six miles, and return before morning rich in spoil. On the Ohio, he was known among his companions by the appellation of the

"Snapping Turtle"; and on the Mississippi, he was called "The Snag."

At the early age of seventeen, Mike's character was displayed, by enlisting himself in a corps of Scouts—a body of irregular rangers, which was employed on the North-western frontiers of Pennsylvania, to watch the Indians, and to give notice of any threatened inroad.

At that time, Pittsburgh was on the extreme verge of white population, and the spies, who were constantly employed, generally extended their explorations forty or fifty miles to the west of this post. They went out, singly, lived as did the Indian, and in every respect became perfectly assimilated in habits, taste, and feeling with the red men of the desert. A kind of border warfare was kept up, and the scout thought it as praiseworthy to bring in the scalp of a Shawnee as the skin of a panther. He would remain in the woods for weeks together, using parched corn for bread and depending on his rifle for his meat—and slept at night in perfect comfort, rolled in his blanket.

In this corps, whilst yet a stripling, Mike acquired a reputation for boldness and cunning far beyond his companions. A thousand legends illustrate the fearlessness of his character. There was one which he told himself with much pride, and which made an indelible impression on my boyish memory. He had been out on the hills of Mahoning, when, to use his own words, "he saw signs of Indians being about." He had discovered the recent print of the moccasin on the grass; and found drops of the fresh blood of a deer on the green bush. He became cautious, skulked for some time in the deepest thickets of hazle and briar; and, for several days did not discharge his rifle. He subsisted patiently on parched corn and jerk, which he had dried on his first coming into the woods. He gave no alarm to the settlements, because he discovered with perfect certainty that the enemy consisted of a small hunting party who were receding from the Alleghany.

As he was creeping along one morning, with the stealthy tread of a cat, his eye fell upon a beautiful buck, browsing on the edge of a barren spot, three hundred yards distant. The temptation was too strong for the woodsman, and he resolved to have a shot at every hazard. Re-priming his gun and picking his flint, he made his approaches in the usual noiseless manner. At the moment he reached the spot from which he meant to take his aim, he observed a large savage, intent upon the same object, advancing from a direction a little different from his own. Mike shrunk behind a tree with the quickness of thought, and keeping his eye fixed on the hunter, waited the result with patience. In a few moments the Indian halted within fifty paces and levelled his piece at the deer. In the meanwhile, Mike presented his rifle at the body of the savage; and at the moment the smoke issued from the gun of the latter, the bullet of Fink passed through the red man's breast. He uttered a yell, and fell dead at the same instant with the deer. Mike re-loaded his rifle and remained in his covert for some minutes, to ascertain whether there were more enemies at hand. He then stepped up to the prostrate savage, and having satisfied himself that life was extinguished, turned his attention to the buck, and took from the carcase those pieces suited to the process of jerking.

In the meantime, the country was filling up with a white population; and in a few years the red men, with the exception of a few fractions of tribes, gradually receded to the Lakes and beyond the Mississippi. The corps of Scouts was abolished, after having acquired habits which unfitted them for the pursuits of civilized society. Some incorporated themselves with the Indians; and others, from a strong attachment to their erratic mode of life, joined the boatmen, then just becoming a distinct class. Among these was our hero, Mike Fink, whose talents were soon developed; and for many years he was as celebrated on the rivers of the West, as he had been in the woods.

I gave to my fellow travellers the substance of the foregoing narrative as we sat on deck by moonlight and cut swiftly through the magnificent sheet of water between Letart and the Great Kanhawa. It was one of those beautiful nights which permitted every thing to be seen with sufficient distinctness to avoid danger;—yet created a certain degree of illusion that gave reins to the imagination. The outline of the river hills lost all its harshness; and the occasional bark of the house dog from the shore, and the distant scream of the solitary loon, gave increased effect to the scene. It was altogether so delightful that the hours till morning flew swiftly by, whilst our travellers dwelt with rapture on the surrounding scenery, which shifted every moment like the capricious changes of the kaleidescope—and listening to tales of border warfare, as they were brought to mind by passing the places where they happened. The celebrated Hunter's Leap,[1] and the bloody battle of Kanhawa, were not forgotten.

The afternoon of the next day brought us to the beautiful city of Cincinnati, which, in the course of thirty years, has risen from a village of soldiers' huts to a town, giving promise of future splendour equal to any on the sea-board.[2]

1. A man by the name of Huling was hunting on the hill above Point Pleasant, when he was discovered by a party of Indians. They pursued him to a precipice of more than sixty feet, over which he sprang and escaped. On returning next morning with some neighbours, it was discovered that he jumped over the top of a sugar tree which grew from the bottom of the hill [Neville's note].

2. Neville's story ends with an account of Mike Fink's death, which will be found on p. 260.

Mike Fink: The Last of the Boatmen (1829)

TIMOTHY FLINT (1780–1840), born and reared in Massachusetts and educated at Harvard, traveled westward in 1815 by coach, flatboat, and keelboat to be a missionary. For years as a preacher he went from one part of the Mississippi Valley to another. His experiences furnished materials for one of the best travel books of the period and for a number of romantic tales and novels. Between 1827 and 1830, he edited The Western Monthly Review, published in Cincinnati, "to foster," so he said, "polite literature in the west." "Mike Fink: The Last of the Boatmen" appeared in the issue of July, 1829.

Since Rev. Flint wrote three-fourths of the contents of the magazine, it is more than likely that he put this article into shape. He was probably, however, more of an editor than an author, since the details about Mike came to him pretty indirectly by his own testimony—from "a valued correspondent at St. Louis," who in turn got them "from an intelligent and respected fur-trader."

The piety of the editor led him to protest that he was showing Fink merely as a specimen of "the monstrous anomalies of the human character under particular circumstances." It also, unfortunately, caused him to "omit some strange curses and circumstances of profanity," which we would be glad to have, and to keep from his readers facts about Mike's rifle shot test of his mistress's fidelity. (After this tantalizing hint and others, the details were finally to appear in 1888.) Fortunately, though, he says he thought it desirable to follow his correspondent's example and give the fur trader's account "nearly in his own words." One wishes that the "nearly" had been unnecessary, since the *language is still rather too literary for modern taste. But the fur trader, after all, was "respectable"; and the style is close enough to that of talk to convince us that it is fairly authentic.*

The anecdotes also look like authentic oral lore transferred to paper. And the fur trader got some of his facts pretty accurate, even though some had not appeared before in print. The story of Mike's shooting the Negro's heel had been briefly mentioned in the 1823 news story of his death. However, the raconteur may, as he says, have read court records of his trial for the offense: the old story said nothing about a trial. And the story of Mike's death (p. 260) mentioned for the first time (so far as we know) the real names of the other two men involved in it. The other anecdotes contain specific details which show knowledge of the river and the frontier and are of a sort likely to have been in circulation. The fur trader and his friend and Flint thus made an important contribution to the growing lore about the boatman. If only Flint had been a bit less pious!

Every reader of the Western Souvenir, so undeservedly brushed, like a summer butterfly, from among its more fortunate sister butterflies, into the pool of oblivion, will remember the vivid and admirable portrait of Mike Fink, the last of the boatmen. People are so accustomed, in reading such tales, to think them all the mere fairy web fabric of fiction that, probably, not one in a hundred of the readers of that story imagined for a moment that it gave, as far as it went, a most exact and faithful likeness of an actual personage of flesh and blood, once well known on our waters, and now no more. We are obliged to omit some strange curses, and circumstances of profanity and atrocity, though they seemed necessary to a full development of character, which it cannot be supposed for a moment we exhibit with any other view than to show the monstrous anomalies of the human character under particular circumstances, as Dr. Mitchell would show a horned frog or a prairie dog in relation to the lower animals. The most eccentric and original trait in his whole character was the manner in which he subjected his chere amie, when he doubted her fidelity, to a rifle shot test similar to those hereafter described. We are compelled to omit the anecdote altogether. The following addenda to the sketch given in the Western Souvenir are furnished us by a valued correspondent at St. Louis. He has them, as he informs us, from an intelligent and respectable fur-trader who has frequently extended his peregrinations beyond the Rocky Mountains and who was to start, the day after our correspondent wrote, for Santa-Fe, in New-Mexico. Our correspondent assures us that he gives the account of this gentleman, touching the extraordinary Mike Fink, nearly in his own words. We only add that we have followed his example, in the subjoined, in relation to the narrative of our correspondent.

Mike Fink was born in Pittsburgh, Pa. where his brothers, &c. still reside. He had but little knowledge of letters, especially of their sounds and powers, as his orthography was very bad, and he usually spelled his name Miche Phinck, whilst his father spelled his with an F. When he was young, the witchery which is in the tone of a wooden trumpet called a river horn, formerly used by keel and flat boat navigators on the western water, entranced the soul of Mike, while yet a boy; and he longed to become a boatman. This soon became his ruling passion; and he served as a boatman on the Ohio and Mississippi rivers and their tributary streams, which occupation he pursued until this sort of men were thrown out of employment by the general use of steam boats. When Mike first set foot on a keel boat, he could mimick all the tones of a trumpet, and he longed to go to New Orleans, where he heard the people spoke French and wore their Sunday clothes every day. He served out his pupilage with credit. When the Ohio was too low for navigation, Mike spent most of his time in the neighborhood of Pittsburgh, killing squirrels with his rifle, and shooting at a target for beef at the frequent Saturday shooting matches and company musters of the militia. He soon became famous as "the best shot in the country," and was called bang-all, and on that account was frequently excluded from participating in matches for beef; for which exclusion he claimed, and obtained the fifth quarter of the beef, as it is called (the hide and tallow) for his forbearance. His usual practice was to sell his fifth quarter to the tavern or dram shop keeper for whiskey with which he "treated" everybody present, partaking largely himself. He became fond of strong drink, but was never overpowered by its influence. He could drink a gallon of it in twenty-four hours without the effect being perceivable. His language was a perfect sample of the half-horse and half-alligator dialect of the then race of boatmen. He was also a wit; and on that account he gained the admiration and excited the fears of all the fraternity of boatmen; for he usually enforced his wit with a sound drubbing, if any one dared to dissent by neglecting or refusing to laugh at his jokes; for as he used to say, he told his jokes on purpose to be laughed at in a good humored way, and that no man should "make light" of them. The consequence was Mike always had a chosen band of laughing philosophers about him. An eye bunged up and a dilapidated nose, or ear, was sure to win Mike's sympathy and favor, for Mike made proclamation—"I am a salt river roarer; and I love the wimming, and how I'm chock-full of fight," &c. So he was in truth, for he had a chere amie in every port which he visited, and always had a circle of worshippers around him who would fight their deaths (as they called it) for him. Amongst these were two men, Carpenter and Talbot, Mike's fast friends, and particular confidants. Each was a match for the other, in prowess, in fight, or skill in shooting, for Mike had diligently trained them to all these virtues and mysteries. Carpenter and Talbot figure hereafter. Mike's weight was about one hundred and eighty pounds; height about five feet nine inches; broad round face, pleasant features, brown skin, tanned by sun and rain; blue, but very expressive eyes, inclining to grey; broad white teeth, and square brawny form, well proportioned, and every muscle of the arms, thighs and legs, were fully developed, indicating the greatest strength and activity. His person, taken altogether, was a model for a Hercules, except as to size. He first visited St. Louis as a keel boat man in the year 1814 or 1815, and occasionally afterwards, till 1822, when he joined Henry and Ashley's company of Missouri trappers. Many shooting feats of Mike's are related here by persons who profess to have witnessed them. I will relate some of them, and you can make such use of them, as you please. In ascending the Mississippi above the mouth of the Ohio, he saw a sow with eight or nine pigs on the river bank; he declared in boatman phrase he wanted a pig, and took up his rifle to shoot one; but was requested not to do so. Mike, however, laid his rifle to his face and shot at each pig successively, as the boat glided up the river under easy sail, about forty or fifty yards from shore, and cut off their tails close to their rumps, without doing them any other harm. In 1821, a short time before he ascended the Missouri with Henry and Ashley's company, being on his boat at the landing in this port, he saw a negro lad standing on the river bank, heedlessly gaping in great wonderment at the show about him. This boy had a strange sort of foot and heel peculiar to some races of the Africans. His heel protruded several inches in the rear of the leg, so as to leave nearly as much of the foot behind as before it. This unshapely foot offended Mike's eye, and outraged his ideas of symmetry so much, that he determined to correct it. He took aim with his rifle, some thirty paces distant, at the boy's unfortunate heel, and actually shot it away. The boy fell, crying murder, and badly wounded. Mike was indicted in the circuit court of this county for the offence, and was found guilty by a jury. I have myself seen the record of the court. It appeared in evidence that Mike's justification of the offence was "that the fellow's long heel prevented him from wearing a genteel boot." His particular friend, Carpenter, was, also, a great shot; and he and Mike used to fill a tin cup with whiskey, and place it on their heads by turns, and shoot at it with a rifle at the distance of seventy yards. It was always bored through, without injury to the one on whose head it was placed. This was often performed; and they liked the feat the better because it showed their confidence in each other.[1]

. . . .

There are several other strange characters who have spent most part of their lives beyond the verge of civilized society, among the savages. You have recorded the chronicles of Bte. Roy. But the story of Bte. Kiewa, a Frenchman, would surpass it. The history of Mike Shuck, a misanthropic trapper of the Missouri, would be still more strange. He holds communion with no man except to barter his furs and peltries for powder, lead, traps, &c. and then disappears for years, no body knows where. His story has been written after a sort, some years since, by Major Whitmore, of the United States Army.

The sufferings and almost incredible adventures and miraculous escapes of Glass, a Scotchman, would astonish and please all that have a taste for adventures. If my friend, to whom I am indebted for the story of Mike Fink, in part, were not about to depart so soon, I would procure the leading facts in relation to these several persons, as he is familiar with their true history and has frequently seen all of them.

1. At this point occurs an account of Mike Fink's death, which has been placed on pp. 260–62.

Crockett Almanack Stories (1837, 1839)

IN 1834 AND 1835, AS IN 1954 AND 1955, DAVY CROCKETT was the
westerner best known and most talked about by his countrymen. In 1834, the New York Transcript reported that "negroes,
dogs, horses, steamboats, omnibuses and locomotive engines"
were being named after the famous frontiersman. Books about
him were selling briskly, newspapers were dotted with anecdotes
headed "Crockett's Latest," and a political tour he was making
brought huge crowds out to hear his speeches. In 1836, after his
death in the Alamo, he became even more famous than he had
been when alive, and he remained so for many years.

In 1834, in Nashville, Tennessee, a little paper-backed book-
let was published—Davy Crockett's Almanack. This was the
first of many such booklets put out not only in Nashville but—
after 1836 and up to 1856—in New York, Philadelphia, Boston,
Baltimore, Albany, and Louisville as well. These contained, in
addition to the usual data about the weather, biographies of
sundry frontier heroes and characters, accounts of Indian fights,
essays about western flora and fauna, and tall tales about legendary characters. They were illustrated with woodcuts, most of
them crude and fantastic, but some well wrought.

It was almost a certainty that a character such as Fink would
be celebrated in these publications. "Mike Fink, the Ohio Boatman" was printed in an almanac in 1837 along with what was
probably the first published portrait (a quaint, stiff woodcut) of
that hero. This bore the title, Davy Crockett's Almanack, of
Wild Sports in the West, Life in the Backwoods, Sketches of
Texas, and Rows on the Mississippi. Its publishers identified
themselves, one suspects quite deceitfully, as "the heirs of Davy
Crockett." The sketch, like many others in the Nashville al-

manacs, *is on the realistic rather than the fantastic side. It adds to testimony about the oral fame of the boatman, gives the interesting (but questionable) information that Mike was "the first boatman who dared navigate a broadhorn down the falls of the Ohio," and coolly shifts the scene of his death several hundred miles. Captain Jo Chunk's monologue, compared with the talk of the pilot at the end of Neville's story (p. 260), shows how writers were progressing in the rendition of colloquial speech.*

"Col. Crockett Beat at a Shooting Match" appeared in 1839 in another Nashville issue, The Crockett Almanac, Containing Adventures, Exploits, Sprees, & Scrapes in the West, & Life and Manners in the Backwoods. . . . Published by Ben Harding. . . . Crockett Scared by an Owl. Go Ahead! This story, supposedly told in Davy's own words, is more typical than the first and more in keeping with the style and the materials of the general run of almanac stories. The language, for the time, is wildly vernacular. The story follows one of the most popular patterns for frontier yarns—the exchange of boasts followed by a contest. To this pattern it adapts the story about the pigtails first told in 1829. It may also have adapted or developed an oral anecdote merely referred to in 1829 ("the manner in which he subjected his chere amie, when he doubted her fidelity, to a rifle shot test"). The drinks proposed in the final sentence, "eye-openers," "phlegm-cutters," and "anti-fogmatics," occur often in tales about the drinking prowess of westerners and southerners. The American English Dictionary quotes passages which show that in Massachusetts in 1789 and in Nauvoo in 1845 "antifogmatics" protected drinkers from the unwholesome morning damps.

MIKE FINK, THE OHIO BOATMAN (1837)

Of all the species of mankind existing under heaven, the western boatmen deserve a distinct and separate cognomen.

They are a sort of amphibious animal—kind-hearted as a Connecticut grandmother, but as rough as a Rocky Mountain bear. In high water they make the boat carry them, and in low water they are content to carry the boat—or in other words, they are ever ready to jump in and ease her over the sand-bar, then jump on board and patiently wait for the next. Spending the greater portion of their time on the water, they scarce know how to behave on shore, and feel only at home upon the deck of their craft, where they exercise entire sovereignty.

They have not degenerated since the days of *Mike Fink*, who was looked upon as the most fool-hardy and daring of his race. I have heard Captain Jo Chunk tell the story of some of his daring exploits. "There ar'nt a man," said Captain Jo, "from Pittsburgh to New Orleans but what's heard of *Mike Fink*; and there aint a boatman on the river, to this day, but what strives to imitate him. Before them 'ere steamers come on the river, *Mike* was looked up to as a kind of king among the boatmen, and he sailed a little the prettiest craft that there was to be found about these 'ere parts. Along through the warm summer afternoons, when there wa'nt nothing much to do, it used to be the fashion among the boatmen to let one hold up a tin cup in the stern of the boat, while another would knock out the bottom with a rifle ball from the bow; and the one that missed had to pay a quart for the good of the crew. Howsomever," continued Capt. Jo, "this wa'nt sport enough for Mike, and he used to bet that he could knock the tin cup off a man's head; and there was one fellow fool-hardy enough to let him do it; this was Mike's brother, who was just such another great strapping fellow as himself, but hadn't as much wit in his head as Mike had in his little finger. He was always willing to let Mike shoot the cup off his head, provided that he'd share the quart with him; and Mike would rather give him the whole of it than miss the chance of displaying his skill."[1]

1. At this point the captain gives an account of Mike's death, which has been placed on pp. 262–63.

COL. CROCKETT BEAT AT A SHOOTING MATCH
(1839)

I expect, stranger, you think old Davy Crockett war never beat at the long rifle; but he war tho. I expect there's no man so strong, but what he will find some one stronger. If you havent heerd tell of one Mike Fink, I'll tell you something about him, for he war a helliferocious fellow, and made an almighty fine shot. Mike was a boatman on the Mississip, but he had a little cabbin on the head of the Cumberland, and a horrid handsome wife, that loved him the wickedest that ever you see. Mike only worked enough to find his wife in rags, and himself in powder, and lead, and whiskey, and the rest of the time he spent in nocking over bar and turkeys, and bouncing deer, and sometimes drawing a lead on an injun. So one night I fell in with him in the woods, where him and his wife shook down a blanket for me in his wigwam. In the morning sez Mike to me, "I've got the handsomest wife, and the fastest horse, and the sharpest shooting iron in all Kentuck, and if any man dare doubt it, I'll be in his hair quicker than hell could scorch a feather." This put my dander up, and sez I, "I've nothing to say again your wife, Mike, for it cant be denied she's a shocking handsome woman, and Mrs. Crockett's in Tennessee, and I've got no horses. Mike, I dont exactly like to tell you you lie about what you say about your rifle, but I'm d——d if you speak the truth, and I'll prove it. Do you see that are cat sitting on the top rail of your potato patch, about a hundred and fifty yards off? If she ever hears agin, I'll be shot if it shant be without ears." So I blazed away, and I'll bet you a horse, the ball cut off both the old tom cat's ears close to his head, and shaved the hair off clean across the skull, as slick as if I'd done it with a razor, and the critter never stirred, nor knew he'd lost his ears till he tried to scratch 'em. "Talk about your rifle after that, Mike!" sez I. "Do you see that are sow away off furder than the eend of the world," sez Mike, "with a litter of pigs round her," and he lets fly. The old sow give a grunt, but never stirred in her tracks, and Mike falls to loading and firing for dear life, till he hadn't left one of them are pigs enough tail to make a tooth-pick on. "Now," sez he, "Col. Crockett, I'll be pretticularly obleedged to you if you'll put them are pig's tails on again," sez he. "That's onpossible, Mike," sez I, "but you've left one of 'em about an inch to steer by, and if it had a-ben my work, I wouldn't have done it so wasteful. I'll mend your host," and so I lets fly, and cuts off the apology he'd left the poor cretur for decency. I wish I may drink the whole of Old Mississip, without a drop of the rale stuff in it, if you wouldn't have thort the tail had been drove in with a hammer. That made Mike kinder sorter wrothy, and he sends a ball after his wife as she was going to the spring after a gourd full of water, and nocked half her coom out of her head, without stirring a hair, and calls out to her to stop for me to take a blizzard at what was left on it. The angeliferous critter stood still as a scarecrow in a cornfield, for she'd got used to Mike's tricks by long practiss. "No, no, Mike," sez I, "Davy Crockett's hand would be sure to shake, if his iron war pointed within a hundred mile of a shemale, and I give up beat, Mike, and as we've had our eye-openers a-ready, we'll now take a flem-cutter, by way of an anti-fogmatic, and then we'll disperse."

The Disgraced Scalp-Lock, or Incidents on the Western Waters (1842)

T. B. THORPE

JUST AS EVENTUALLY a story about Fink was destined to turn up in a Crockett Almanac or two, one was bound to appear in the Spirit of the Times (New York, 1831–61). This magazine was, in the 1840's, the outstanding medium for publishing most of the best anecdotes and yarns produced by certain authors. These were southern and southwestern gentry of the "sporting crowd" of the day interested in the varied (though not unrelated) topics set forth in the journal's subtitle, "A Chronicle of the Turf, Agriculture, Field Sports, Literature, and the Stage."

As the editor, William Trotter Porter, boasted in 1846, "In addition to correspondents who described with equal felicity and power the stirring incidents of the turf and the chase, [the Spirit of the Times] enlisted another and still more numerous class who furnished the most valuable and interesting reminiscences of the Far West—sketches of thrilling scenes and adventures in the then comparatively unknown region and the extraordinary characters occasionally met with. . . ."

Porter himself on July 9, 1842, wrote an account of Fink's death which he had, doubtless, from one of his many widely scattered friends (see p. 263). And in the Spirit for July 16, 1842, he published "The Disgraced Scalp-Lock" by Thomas Bangs Thorpe. This story was to be frequently republished in both the nineteenth and twentieth centuries.

Thorpe (1815–78) was a New Englander, whose ill health caused him to move to Baton Rouge's mild climate in 1836. In

[67]

Louisiana and other parts of what was then the frontier, Thorpe, who was an artist of some skill, pictured various western scenes. He edited several newspapers and wrote numerous very popular sketches and stories, one of them the most famous tall tale from the section before the Civil War, "The Big Bear of Arkansas," published in the Spirit in 1841.

"The Disgraced Scalp-Lock" testifies with believable authority to Fink's popularity among southwestern yarnspinners. It is good (as are other sketches by this writer) in its depiction of the class to which its leading character belongs and in its description of western scenery. Also—like "The Big Bear"—it renders some of its hero's monologues very well, even including (as few other sketches do) some of Mike's picturesque profanity. For all this, it strikes one as more synthetic than authentic: It endows Mike with a romantic love of nature and a nostalgia which are hardly in character with his known or even his legendary character. Its happenings, furthermore, are closer to those of melodrama than to those of actuality. Written though it was for one of the most masculine publications of the period, Thorpe's tale does its best to sentimentalize the rowdy boatman.

In an account of the death of Fink published in 1855, Thorpe similarly was to prettify the grim incident (see p. 272).

Occasionally may be seen on the Ohio and Mississippi rivers singularly hearty looking men that puzzle a stranger as to their history and age. Their forms always exhibit a powerful development of muscle and bone; their cheeks are prominent, and you would pronounce them men enjoying perfect health, in middle life, were it not for their heads, which, if not bald, will be sparsely covered with grey hair. Another peculiarity about these people is that they have a singular knowledge of all the places on the river, every bar and bend is spoken of with precision and familiarity—every town is recollected before it was half as large as the present, or no town at all. Innumerable places are marked out, where once was an Indian fight or a rendezvous of robbers.

The manner, the language, and the dress of these individuals are all characteristic of sterling common sense; the manner modest, yet full of self reliance, the language strong and forcible, from superiority of mind rather than from education, the dress studied for comfort rather than fashion; on the whole, you insensibly become attached to them, and court their society. The good humor, the frankness, the practical sense, the reminiscences, the powerful frame, all indicate a character at the present day extinct and anomalous; and such indeed is the case, for your acquaintance will be one of the few remaining people now spoken of as the "last of the flat-boatmen."

Thirty years ago the navigation of the Western waters was confined to this class of men; the obstacles presented to the pursuit in those swift running and wayward waters had to be overcome by physical force alone; the navigator's arm grew strong as he guided his rude craft past the "snag" and "sawyer," or kept off the no less dreaded bar. Besides all this, the deep forests that covered the river banks concealed the wily Indian who gloated over the shedding of blood. The qualities of the frontier warrior associated themselves with the boatman, while he would, when at home, drop both these characters in the cultivator of the soil.

It is no wonder, then, that they were brave, hardy, and openhanded men; their whole lives were a round of manly excitement, they were hyperbolical in thought and in deed, when most natural, compared with any other class of men. Their bravery and chivalrous deeds were performed without a herald to proclaim them to the world—they were the mere incidents of a border life, considered too common to outlive the time of a passing wonder. Obscurity has obliterated nearly the actions and the men—a few of the latter still exist, as if to justify their wonderful exploits, which now live almost exclusively as traditions.

Among the flat-boatmen, there were none that gained the notoriety of *Mike Fink*: his name is still remembered along the whole of the Ohio as a man who excelled his fellows in every thing—particularly in his rifle-shot, which was acknowledged to be unsurpassed. Probably no man ever lived who could compete with Mike Fink in the latter accomplishment. Strong as Hercules, free from all nervous excitement, possessed of perfect health, and familiar with his weapon from childhood, he raised the rifle to his eye, and having once taken sight, it was as firmly fixed as if buried in a rock. It was Mike's pride, and he rejoiced on all occasions where he could bring it into use, whether it was turned against the beast of prey or the more savage Indian, and in his day these last named were the common foe with which Mike and his associates had to contend.

On the occasion that we would particularly introduce Mike to the reader, he had bound himself for a while to the pursuits of trade, until a voyage from the head-waters of the Ohio and down the Mississippi could be completed; heretofore he had kept himself exclusively to the Ohio, but a liberal reward, and some curiosity, prompted him to extend his business character beyond his ordinary habits and inclinations. In accomplishment of this object, he was lolling carelessly over the big "sweep" that guided the "flat" on which he officiated; the current of the river bore the boat swiftly along, and made his labor light; his eye glanced around him, and he broke forth in extacies at what he saw and felt. If there is a river in the world that merits the name of beautiful, it is the Ohio, when its channel is

"Without o'erflowing, full."

The scenery is everywhere soft—there are no jutting rocks, no steep banks, no high hills; but the clear and swift current laves beautiful and undulating shores that descend gradually to the water's edge. The foliage is rich and luxuriant, and its outlines in the water are no less distinct than when it is relieved against the sky. Interspersed along its route are islands, as beautiful as ever figured in poetry as the land of fairies; enchanted spots indeed, that seem to sit so lightly on the water that you almost expect them as you approach to vanish into dreams. So late as when Mike Fink disturbed the solitudes of the Ohio with his rifle, the canoe of the Indian was hidden in the little recesses along the shore; they moved about in their frail barks like spirits, and clung, in spite of the constant encroachments of civilization, to the place which tradition had designated as the happy places of a favored people.

Wild and uncultivated as Mike appeared, he loved nature and had a soul that sometimes felt, while admiring it, an exalted enthusiasm. The Ohio was his favorite stream; from where it runs no stronger than a gentle rivulet, to where it mixes with the muddy Mississippi, Mike was as familiar as a child could be with the meanderings of a flower garden. He could not help noticing with sorrow the desecrating hand of improvement as he passed along, and half soliloquizing, and half addressing his companions, he broke forth: "I knew these parts afore a squatter's axe had blazed a tree; 'twasn't then pulling a ——— sweep to get a living, but pulling the trigger done the business. Those were times, to see; a man might call himself lucky." "What's the use of improvements? When did cutting down trees make deer more plenty? Who ever cotched a bar by building a log cabin, or twenty on 'em? Who ever found wild buffalo, or a brave Indian in a city? Where's the fun, the frolicking, the fighting? Gone! Gone! The rifle won't make a man a living now—he must turn nigger and work. If forests continue to be used up, I may yet be smothered in a settlement. Boys, this 'ere life won't do— I'll stick to the broad horn 'cordin' to contract, but once done with it, I'm off for a frolic. If the Choctaws or Cherokee or the Massassip don't give us a brush as we pass along, I shall grow as poor as a strawed wolf in a pitfall. I must, to live peaceably, point my rifle at something more dangerous than varmint. Six months, and no Indian fight, would spile me worse than a dead horse on a prairie."

Mike ceased speaking. The then beautiful village of Louisville appeared in sight; the labor of landing the boat occupied his attention—the bustle and confusion that in those days followed such an incident ensued, and Mike was his own master by law until his masters ceased trafficking, and again required his services.

At the time we write of, there were a great many renegade

Indians who lived about the settlements, and which is still the case in the extreme south-west. These Indians are generally the most degraded of the tribe, outcasts, who, for crime or dissipation, are no longer allowed to associate with their people; they live by hunting or stealing, and spend their precarious gains in intoxication.

Among the throng that crowded on the flat-boat on its arrival were a number of these unfortunate beings; they were influenced by no other motive than that of loitering round, in idle speculation at what was going on. Mike was attracted towards them at sight, and as he too was in the situation that is deemed most favorable to mischief, it struck him that it was a good opportunity to have a little sport at the Indians' expense.

Without ceremony, he gave a terrific war-whoop, and then mixing the language of the aborigines and his own together, he went on savage fashion, and bragged of his triumphs and victories on the war path, with all the seeming earnestness of a real "brave." Nor were taunting words spared to exasperate the poor creatures, who, perfectly helpless, listened to the tales of their own greatness, and their own shame, until wound up to the highest pitch of exasperation. Mike's companions joined in, thoughtless boys caught the spirit of the affair, and the Indians were goaded until they in turn made battle with their tongues. Then commenced a system of running against them, pulling off their blankets, together with a thousand other indignities; finally they made a precipitate retreat ashore, amidst the hooting and jeering of an unfeeling crowd, who considered them, poor devils, destitute of feeling and humanity.

Among this crowd of outcasts was a Cherokee, who bore the name of Proud Joe; what his real cognomen was no one knew, for he was taciturn, haughty, and in spite of his poverty, and his manner of life, won the name we have mentioned. His face was expressive of talent, but it was furrowed by the most terrible habits of drunkenness; that he was a superior Indian was admitted, and it was also understood that he was banished from his mountainous home, his tribe then numerous and powerful, for some great crime. He was always looked up to by his companions, and managed, however intoxicated he might be, to sustain a singularly proud bearing, which did not even depart from him while prostrated on the ground.

Joe was filthy in his person and habits; in these respects he was behind his fellows; but one ornament of his person was attended to with a care which would have done honor to him if surrounded by his people, and in his native woods. Joe still wore with Indian dignity his scalp-lock; he ornamented it with taste and cherished it, as report said, that some Indian messenger of vengeance might tear it from his head, as expiatory of his numerous crimes. Mike noticed this peculiarity, and reaching out his hand, plucked from it a hawk's feather, which was attached to the scalp-lock.

The Indian glared horribly on Mike as he consummated the insult, snatched the feather from his hand, then shaking his clenched fist in the air, as if calling on heaven for revenge, retreated with his friends. Mike saw that he had roused the savage's soul, and he marvelled wonderfully that so much resentment should be exhibited, and as an earnest to Proud Joe that the wrong he had done him should not rest unrevenged, he swore he would cut the scalp-lock off close to his head the first convenient opportunity he got, and then he thought no more of the matter.

The morning following the arrival of the boat at Louisville was occupied in making preparations to pursue the voyage down the river. Nearly every thing was completed, and Mike had taken his favorite place at the sweep, when looking up the riverbank he beheld at some distance Joe and his companions, and from their gesticulations, they were making him the subject of conversation.

Mike thought instantly of several ways in which he could show them all together a fair fight, and then whip them with ease; he also reflected with what extreme satisfaction he would enter into the spirit of the arrangement and other matters to him equally pleasing, when all the Indians disappeared save Joe himself, who stood at times viewing him in moody silence and then staring round at passing objects.

From the peculiarity of Joe's position to Mike, who was below him, his head and upper part of his body relieved boldly against the sky, and in one of his movements he brought his profile face to view. The prominent scalp-lock and its adornments seemed to be more striking than ever, and it again roused the pugnacity of Mike Fink; in an instant he raised his rifle, always loaded and at command, brought it to his eye, and before he could be prevented, drew sight upon Proud Joe and fired. The rifle ball whistled loud and shrill, and Joe, springing his whole length into the air, fell upon the ground.

The cold-blooded murder was noticed by fifty persons at least, and there arose from the crowd an universal cry of horror and indignation at the bloody deed. Mike himself seemed to be much astonished, and in an instant reloaded his rifle, and as a number of white persons rushed towards the boat, Mike threw aside his coat, and taking his powder horn between his teeth, leaped, rifle in hand, into the Ohio, and commenced swimming for the opposite shore.

Some bold spirits present determined Mike should not so easily escape, and jumping into the only skiff at command, pulled swiftly after him. Mike watched their movements until they came within a hundred yards of him, then turning in the water, he supported himself by his feet alone, and raised his deadly rifle to his eye; its nuzzle, if it spoke hostilely, was as certain to send a messenger of death through one or more of his pursuers as if it were the lightning, and they knew it; dropping their oars, and turning pale, they bid Mike not to fire. Mike waved his hand towards the little village of Louisville, and again pursued his way to the opposite shore.

The time consumed by the firing of Mike's rifle, the pursuit, and the abandonment of it, required less time than we have taken to give the details, and in that time to the astonishment of the gaping crowd around Joe, they saw him rising with a bewildered air; a moment more and he recovered his senses, and stood up—*at his feet lay his scalp-lock!* The ball had cut it clear from his head; the cord around the root of it, in which were placed feathers and other ornaments, held it together; the concussion had merely stunned its owner; farther he had escaped all bodily harm! A cry of exultation rose at this last evidence of the skill of Mike Fink; the exhibition of a shot that established his claim, indisputably, to the eminence he ever afterwards held; the unrivalled marksman of all the flat-boatmen of the Western waters.

Proud Joe had received many insults; he looked upon himself as a degraded, worthless being, and the ignominy heaped upon him, he never, except by reply, resented; but this last insult, was like seizing the lion by the mane, or a Roman senator by the beard—it roused the slumbering demon within, and made him again thirst to resent his wrongs, with an intensity of emotion that can only be felt by an Indian. His eye glared upon the jeering crowd around; like a fiend, his chest swelled and heaved, until it seemed that he must suffocate. No one noticed this emotion, all were intent upon the exploit that had so singularly deprived Joe of his war-lock; and smothering his wrath he retreated to his associates, with a consuming fire at his vitals; he was a different man from an hour before, and with that desperate resolution on which a man stakes his all, he swore by the Great Spirit of his forefathers that he would be revenged.

An hour after the disappearance of Joe, both he and Mike Fink were forgotten. The flat-boat, which the latter had deserted, was got under way, and dashing through the rapids in the river opposite Louisville, wended on its course. As is customary when night sets in, the boat was securely fastened in some little bend or bay in the shore, where it remained until early morn. Long before the sun had fairly risen, the boat was pushed again into the stream, and it passed through a valley presenting the greatest possible beauty and freshness of landscape, the mind can conceive.

It was Spring, and a thousand tints of green developed themselves in the half formed foliage and bursting buds. The beautiful mallard skimmed across the water, ignorant of the danger of the white man's approach; the splendid spoonbill decked the shallow places near the shore, while myriads of singing birds filled the air with their unwritten songs.

In the far reaches down the river, there occasionally might be seen a bear, stepping along the ground as if dainty of its feet, and snuffing the intruder on his wild home, he would retreat into the woods.

To enliven all this, and give the picture the look of humanity, there might also be seen, struggling with the floating mists, a column of blue smoke, that came from a fire built on a projecting point of land, around which the current swept rapidly, and carried everything that floated on the river. The eye of a boatman saw the advantage of the situation which the place rendered to those on shore, to annoy and attack, and as wandering Indians, in those days, did not hesitate to rob, there was much speculation as to what reception the boat would receive from the builders of the fire.

The rifles were all loaded, to be prepared for the worst, and the loss of Mike Fink lamented, as a prospect of a fight presented itself where he could use his terrible rifle. The boat in the meantime, swept round the point, but instead of an enemy, there lay in a profound sleep Mike Fink, with his feet toasting at the fire, his pillow was a huge bear that had been shot on the day previous, while at his sides, and scattered in profusion around him, were several deer and wild turkeys.

Mike had not been idle; after picking out a place most eligible to notice the passing boat, he had spent his time in hunting, and he was surrounded by trophies of his prowess. The scene that he presented was worthy of the time and the man, and would have thrown Landseer into a delirium of joy, could he have witnessed it. The boat, owing to the swiftness of the current, passed Mike's resting place, although it was pulled strongly to the shore. As Mike's companions came opposite to him, they raised such a shout, half in exultation of meeting him, and half to alarm him with the idea that Joe's friends were upon him.

Mike at the sound sprang to his feet, rifle in hand, and as he looked around, he raised it to his eyes, and by the time he discovered the boat, he was ready to fire.

"Down with your shooting iron, you wild critter," shouted one of the boatmen.

Mike dropped the piece, and gave a loud haloo, that echoed among the solitudes like a piece of artillery. The meeting between Mike and his fellows was characteristic. They joked, and jibed him with their rough wit, and he parried it off, with a most creditable ingenuity. Mike soon learned the extent of his rifle shot—he seemed perfectly indifferent to the fact that Proud Joe was not dead. The only sentiment he uttered was regret that he did not fire at the vagabond's head, and if he hadn't hit it, why he made the first bad shot in twenty years. The dead game was carried on board of the boat, the adventure was forgotten, and everything resumed the monotony of floating in a flat-boat down the Ohio.

A month or more elapsed, and Mike had progressed several hundred miles down the Mississippi; his journey had been remarkably free from incident; morning, noon, and night presented the same banks, the same muddy water, and he sighed to see some broken land, some high hills, and he railed, and swore that he should have been such a fool as to desert his favorite Ohio for a river that produced nothing but alligators, and was never at best half-finished.

Occasionally, the plentifulness of game put him in spirits, but it did not last long, he wanted more lasting excitement, and declared himself as perfectly miserable, and helpless, as a wild cat without teeth or claws.

In the vicinity of Natchez rise a few, abrupt hills, which tower above the surrounding lowlands of the Mississippi like monuments; they are not high, but from their loneliness and rarity, they create sensations of pleasure and awe. Under the shadow of one of these bluffs, Mike and his associates made the customary preparations to pass the night. Mike's enthusiasm knew no bounds at the sight of land again; he said it was as pleasant as "cold water to a fresh wound"; and, as his spirits rose, he went on making the region round about, according to his notions, an agreeable residence.

"The Choctaws live in these diggins," said Mike, "and a cursed time they must have of it. Now, if I lived in these parts, I'd declare war on 'em, just to have something to keep me from growing dull; without some such business, I'd be as musty as an old swamp moccasin. I could build a cabin on that ar hill yonder, that could from its location, with my rifle repulse a whole tribe, if they came after me."

"What a beautiful time I'd have of it. I never was particular about what's called a fair fight, I just ask a half a chance, and the odds against me; and if I then don't keep clear of snags and sawyers, let me spring a leak, and go to the bottom. Its natur that the big fish should eat the little ones. I've seen trout swallow a perch, and a cat would come along and swallow the trout, and perhaps on the Massissip, the alligators use up the cat, so on until the end of the row."

"Well, I walk tall into varmint and Indian, it's a way I've got, and it comes as natural as grinning to a hyena. I'm a regular tornado, tough as a hickory withe, long winded as a nor'-wester. I can strike a blow like a falling free, and every lick makes a gap in the crowd that lets in an acre of sunshine. Whew, boys," shouted Mike, twirling his rifle like a walking-stick around his head, at the ideas suggested in his mind. "Whew, boys! if the Choctaw devils in them ar woods, thar, would give us a brush, just as I feel now, I'd call them gentlemen. I must fight something, or I'll catch the dry rot—burnt brandy won't save me."

Such were some of the expressions which Mike gave utterance to, and in which his companions heartily joined; but they never presumed to be quite equal to Mike, for his bodily prowess, as well as his rifle were acknowledged to be unsurpassed. These displays of animal spirits generally ended in boxing and wrestling matches, in which falls were received and blows struck without being noticed, that would have destroyed common men. Occasionally angry words and blows were exchanged; but like the summer storm, the cloud that emitted the lightning purified the air, and when the commotion ceased, the combatants immediately made friends, and became more attached to each other than before the cause that interrupted the good feelings occured. Such were the conversation and amusements of the evening, when the boat was moored under one of the bluffs we have alluded to.

As night wore on, one by one of the hardy boatmen fell asleep, some in its [the boat's] confined interior, and others protected by a light covering in the open air. The moon rose in beautiful majesty, her silver light behind the high lands gave them a powerful and theatrical effect, as it ascended, and as its silver rays grew perpendicular, they finally kissed gently the summit of the hills, and poured down their full light upon the boat with almost noonday brilliancy. The silence with which the beautiful changes of darkness and light were produced made it mysterious. It seemed as if some creative power was at work, bringing form and life out of darkness.

In the midst of the witchery of this quiet scene, there sounded forth the terrible rifle, and the more terrible war-whoop of the Indian. One of the flat boat men asleep on the deck, gave a stifled groan, turned upon his face, and with a quivering motion ceased to live. Not so with his companions—they in an instant, as men accustomed to danger and sudden attacks, sprang ready armed to their feet; but before they could discover their foes, seven sleek and horribly painted savages leaped from the hill into the boat. The firing of the rifle was useless, and each man singled out a foe and met him with the drawn knife. The struggle was quick and fearful, and deadly blows were given, screams and imprecations rent the air. Yet the voice of Mike Fink could be heard in encouraging shouts above the clamor.

"Give it to them, boys," he cried, "cut their hearts out, choke the dogs, here's hell afire, and the river rising!" then clenching with the most powerful of the assailants, he rolled with him upon the deck of the boat. Powerful as Mike was, the Indian seemed nearly a match for him; the two twisted and writhed like serpents, now one seeming to have the advantage and then the other.

In all this confusion there might occasionally be seen glancing in the moonlight the blade of a knife, but at whom the thrusts were made, or who wielded it, could not be discovered.

The general fight lasted less time than we have taken to describe it. The white men gained the advantage, two of the Indians lay dead upon the boat, and the living, escaping from their antagonists, leaped ashore, and before the rifle could be brought to bear, they were out of its reach.

While Mike was yet struggling with his antagonist, one of his companions cut the boat loose from the shore, and with powerful exertion, managed to get its bows so far into the current that it swung round and floated, but before this was accomplished, and before any one interfered with Mike, he was on his feet, covered with blood, and blowing like a porpoise; by the time he could get his breath, he commenced talking.

" 'Ain't been so busy in a long time," said he, turning over his victim with his foot, "that fellow fou't beautiful; if he's a specimen of the Choctaws that live in these parts, they are screamers, the infernal sarpents, the d———d possums."

Talking in this way, he with others took a general survey of the killed and wounded. Mike himself was a good deal cut up with the Indian's knife, but he called his wounds mere blackberry scratches; one of Mike's associates was severely hurt but the rest escaped comparatively harmless. The sacrifice was made at the first fire, for beside the dead Indians, there lay one of the boat's crew, cold and dead, his body perforated with four different balls; that he was the chief object of attack seemed evident, yet no one of his associates knew of his having a single fight with Indians.

The soul of Mike was affected, and taking the hand of his deceased friend between his own, he raised his bloody knife towards the bright moon, and swore that he would desolate "the nation" that claimed the Indians who had made war upon them that night, and turning to his stiffened victim, that, dead as it was, retained the expression of implacable hatred and defiance, he gave it a smile of grim satisfaction, and then joined in the general conversation which the occurences of the night would naturally suggest.

The master of the "broad horn" was a business man, and had often been down the Mississippi; this was the first attack he had received, or knew to have been made, from the shores inhabited by the Choctaws, except by the white man, and he, among other things, suggested the keeping of the dead Indians, until daylight, that they might have an opportunity to examine their dress and features, and see with certainty who were to blame for the occurences of the night. The dead boatman was removed with care to a respectful distance, and the living, except the person at the sweep of the boat, were soon buried in profound slumber.

Not until after the rude breakfast was partaken of, and the funeral rites of the dead boatman were solemnly performed, did Mike and his companions disturb the corpses of the red men. When both these things had been leisurely and gently got through with, there was a different spirit among the men. Mike was astir, and went about his business with alacrity; he stripped the bloody blanket from the corpse of the Indian he had killed, as if it enveloped something disgusting, and required no respect; he examined carefully the moccasin on the Indian's feet, pronouncing them at one time Chickasas, at another time Shawnese; he stared at the livid face, but could not recognise the style of paint that covered it.

That the Indians were not strictly national in their adornments was certain, for they were examined by practised eyes that could have told the nation of the dead, if such had been the case, as readily as a sailor could distinguish a ship by its flag. Mike was evidently puzzled, and as he was about giving up his task as hopeless, the dead body he was examining, from some cause turned on its side, Mike's eyes distended, as some of his companions observed, "like a choked cat," and became riveted. He drew himself up in a half serious, and half comic expression, and pointing at the back of the dead Indian's head, there was exhibited a dead warrior in his paint, destitute of his scalp-lock, the small stump which was only left, being stiffened with red paint; those who could read Indian symbols learned a volume of deadly resolve in what they saw. The body of Proud Joe was stiff and cold before them.

The last and best shot of Mike Fink cost a brave man his life; the corpse so lately interred was evidently taken in the moonlight by Proud Joe and his party, as that of Mike's, and they had resigned their lives, one and all, that he might with certainty be sacrificed. Nearly a thousand miles of swamps had been threaded, large and swift running rivers had been crossed, hostile tribes passed through by Joe and his friends, that they might revenge the fearful insult, of destroying, *without the life*, the sacred scalp-lock.

Letter to the "Western General Advertiser" from "K" (1845)

K WAS AN UNIDENTIFIABLE CORRESPONDENT of the Western General Advertiser, published in Cincinnati, his home town. In the issue of that paper for January 22, 1845, the editor Charles Cist (1793–1868), Cincinnati's leading historian, had reprinted one of his own articles. Speaking of the lawlessness of the boatmen, Cist had cited an example. "The graphic pen of Morgan Neville," said he, "has given celebrity to Mike Fink . . . to whose exploits as a marksman Mr. Neville has done justice; but to whose character otherwise he has done more than justice, in classing him with the boatmen to whose care merchandise in great value was committed with a confidence which the owners never had cause to repent. This was true of those who had charge of the boat; but did not apply to Fink, who was nothing more than a hand on board, and whose private character was worthless and vile. Mike was in fact an illustration of the class . . . who did not dare show their faces in their early neighborhoods or homes. . . ."

K's answer, dated February 11, 1845, retailed an anecdote, recently told him by "one of the oldest and most respected commanders of steamboats in the Nashville trade, to prove that Fink "did have charge of merchandise." The circumstantial identification of the informant, the specific minutiae of the account, and the unspectacular nature of the story itself all point to its authenticity. Furthermore, it coincides with the testimony to be given later, independently, by Claudius Cadot (p. 20) and Captain John Fink (p. 21). K's second story is offered in support of Cist's claim that Mike was "vile." It is about Mike's punishment of his wife Peg who, at least under that name, makes a unique appearance here. *Its specification of the date and the setting is persuasive, and the action is in character for Mike. The editors admit a slight uneasiness about the story as biography, however, because (although they can cite no parallels) it sounds much like a traditional narrative which may have been told about others.*

In strong contrast with Thorpe's sentimentalized picture of 1842, this pair of anecdotes, about two and a half years later, is remarkably realistic. K's greater closeness to the scene of Mike's activity and to authentic oral lore probably is an important reason for the contrast.

———

MR. CIST: In your paper of January 22d, there is an article from your pen entitled "The Last of the Girtys," in which you say Morgan Neville has done more than justice to Mike, by classing him with that portion of the keel boat men of his day who were intrusted with the property of others. There is no doubt but that Mike has had charge of many keel boats, with valuable cargoes; and a friend of mine, one of the oldest and most respected of the commanders of steamboats in the Nashville trade, related to me within the last four days that, in 1819, he was employed to leave Pittsburgh, and go down the Ohio in hunt of Mike and his cargo, which had been detained by some unaccountable delay. At some distance above Wheeling he found the loiterer lying to, in company with another keel, apparently in no hurry to finish the trip. Mike did not greet our envoy in very pleasant style, but kept the fair weather side out, knowing that my friend was able to *hoe his own row.* Mike was determined not to leave good quarters that night, and all went to bed wherever they could. In the night my friend was awakened by some noise or other, and before falling asleep again, he heard Mike say in a low voice, "Well, boys, who's going to *still* to-night?" This question drew his attention, as it was something he did not understand. Watching for some time, he saw Mike take a tin bucket, that had apparently been fixed for the purpose, with a small pipe inserted in its bottom, about the size of a common gimblet. This was taken to a cask of wine or brandy, and a hole made in either cask, the pipe put in, and then a couple of quarts of water turned into the bucket. Then the "*still*" began to operate, as they drew from the head of the cask until the water in the bucket disappeared.

Thus they obtained the liquor, and the cause of their long detention [was] ascertained. The very casks of wine that Mike drew from, were returned to the merchant in Pittsburgh, more than a year afterwards, having soured.

Thus you see Mike *did* have charge of merchandize, and to considerable extent.

But I did not intend to defend Mike from the charge you have made against him, for in truth, he was all that was "worthless and vile." I intended to tell you an anecdote that occurred about the year 1820, just below the mouth of the Muskingum, in which Mike was prominent. There had been several keel boats landed there for the night, it being near the middle of November. After making all fast, Mike was observed, just under the bank, scraping into a heap the dried beach leaves which had been blown there during the day, having just fallen from the effects of the early autumn frosts. To all questions as to what he was doing he returned no answer, but continued at his work, until he had piled them up as high as his head. He then separated them, making a sort of oblong ring, in which he laid down, as if to ascertain whether it was a good bed or not. Getting up he sauntered on board, hunted up his rifle, made great preparations about his priming, and then called in a very impressive manner upon his wife to follow him. Both proceeded up to the pile of leaves, poor "Peg" in a terrible flutter, as she had discovered that Mike was in no very amiable humor.

"Get in there and lie down," was the command to Peg, topped off with one of Mike's very choicest oaths.

"Now *Mr.* Fink," (she always mistered him when his blood was up,) "what have I done, I dont know, I'm sure—"

"Get in there and lie down, or I'll shoot you," with another oath, and drawing his rifle up to his shoulder. Poor Peg obeyed, and crawled into the leaf pile, and Mike covered her up with the combustibles. He then took a flour barrel, and split the staves into fine pieces, and lighted them at the fire on board the boat, all the time watching the leaf pile, and swearing he would shoot Peg if she moved. So soon as his splinters began to blaze, he took them into his hand and deliberately set fire in four different places to the leaves that surrounded his wife. In an instant, the whole mass was on fire, aided by a fresh wind which was blowing at the time, while Mike was quietly standing by enjoying the fun. Peg, through fear of Mike, stood it as long as she could; but it soon became too hot, and she made a run for the river, her hair and clothing all on fire. In a few seconds she reached the water, and plunged in, rejoiced to know she had escaped both fire and rifle so well. "There," said Mike, "that'll larn you to be winkin at them fellers on the other boat."

There were many occasions of this kind, where Mike and Peg were the actors, all going to show that Mike was one of the very lowest of mankind, and entirely destitute of any of the manly qualities which often were to be found among the bargemen of his day.

Trimming a Darky's Heel (1847)

JOHN S. ROBB [SOLITAIRE]

THE ST. LOUIS REVEILLE, founded in 1844, shortly became famous as a newspaper in which good western stories were published. John S. Robb, apparently a journeyman printer who had worked his way from the East to St. Louis, contributed some of the newspaper's best tall tales, signing them with the pseudonym "Solitaire." One of these, "Trimming a Darky's Heel," appeared in the Reveille at an undetermined date and later, like many stories from that paper, was reprinted in Porter's Spirit of the Times—on February 13, 1847, probably not long after its first appearance.

The story is an enlargement upon a feat of Mike's which had been mentioned in a news story of 1823 and again in an 1829 article about the boatman. Whether Robb got it orally or not is hard to say, but there is evidence that he got some material orally, since he tells of Mike's shooting a cup between a companion's knees. Heretofore the stories had placed the cup on the friend's head, although a story of his shooting a cup held between a woman's knees was probably being transmitted orally (see p. 22).

Partly because modern readers find it hard to be as blithe as the author about the serious wounding of Mike's victim, partly because the repartee between Mike and the justice hardly seems sparkling, it is not likely to be considered one of Robb's best efforts. But it does add to the growing body of lore about Fink's carefree attitude toward courts of law.

In the early days of St. Louis, before the roar of commerce or manufactures had drowned the free laugh and merry song of the jolly keel boatmen, those primitive navigators of the "Father of Waters" tied up their crafts beneath the bluff, which then, eighty feet in height, rose perpendicular from the water's edge in front of the city. On the top of the bluff then, as now, a number of doggeries held forth their temptations to the hardy navigator, and they were often the scene of the wildest kind of revelry.

At that time *Mike Fink*, the chief among keel boatmen, was trading to St. Louis, and he frequently awoke the inhabitants by his wild freaks and dare-devil sprees. Mike was celebrated for the skill with which he used the *rifle*—then the constant companion of western men. It was his boast that he could "jest shoot whar he'd a mind to with his *Betsy*," as he familiarly termed his "shooting iron," and his companions, for the pleasure of noting his skill, or exhibiting it to some stranger, would often put him to the severest kind of tests.

One day, while lying upon the deck of his boat below the St. Louis bluff, with two or three companions, the conversation turned upon Mike's last shot; and one of the party ventured the opinion that his skill was departing. This aroused the boatmen into a controversy, and from their conversation might be learned the manner of the shot which was the subject of dispute. It was thus: One of the party, at a distance of one hundred yards, had placed a tin cup between his knees, and Mike had, at that distance, bored the centre of the cup.

"I'll swar I don't hold that cup agin for you, Mike," remarked the doubter, "for thur is the delicatest kind of a trimble comin' in your hand, and, some of these yur days, you'll miss the cup clar."

"Miss thunder!" shouted Mike; "why, you consarned corndodger mill, it war you that had the trimbles, and when I gin old Bets the wakin' tetch, you *squatted* as ef her bark war agoin' to bite you!"

"Oh, well," was the reply, "thar's mor'n one way of gettin' out of a skunk hole, and ef you kin pass the trimbles off on me, why, you kin *pass*, that's all; but I aint goin' to trust you with a sight at my paddles agin at an hundred paces, that's sartin."

"Why, you scary varmint," answers Mike, bouncing to his feet and reaching for "*Betsy*," which stood by the cabin door of the boat, "jest pint out a muskeeter at a hundred yards, and I'll nip off his right hinder eend claw at the second jint afore he kin hum, *Oh, don't!*"

"Hit a muskeeter, ha, ha!" was the tantalizing response of the other; "why, you couldn't hit the hinder part of that nigger's heel up thar on the bluff, 'thout damagin' the bone, and that ain't no shot to crow about."

The negro referred to was seated at the very edge of the bluff, astride of a flour barrel, and one foot hung over the edge. The distance was over one hundred yards, but Mike instantly raised his rifle, with the remark: "I'll jest trim that feller's heel so he kin wear a decent boot!" and off went "Betsy."

The negro jumped from his seat, and uttered a yell of pain, as if, indeed, his whole heel had been trimmed off, and Mike stood a moment with his rifle, listening to the negro's voice, as if endeavoring to define from the sound whether he was really seriously hurt. At last the boatman who had been doubting Mike's present skill remarked:

"You kin *leave*, now, Mike, fur that darky's master will be arter you with a sharp stick"; and then he further added as a taunt—"I knowed Betsy was feelin' for that nigger's bones jest by the way you held her!"

Mike now became a little wrathy, and appeared inclined to use *his* bones upon the tormentor, but some of the others advised him to hold on—that he would have a chance to exercise them upon the constable. In a short time an officer appeared with a warrant, but as soon as Mike looked at him he gave up the thought of either flight or resistance, and quietly remarked to his companions that the officer was a clever fellow, and "a small *hoss* in a fight."

"The only way you kin work him is to fool him," says Mike, "and he's a weazel in that bisness hisself!"

The warrant was produced by the officer and read to the offender, who signified his assent to the demand for his body, and told the representative of the law to lead the way. He did so, and when about to step off the boat he cast his eye back, supposing that Mike was following him, yet a little suspicious. The movement was a prudent one, for he discovered the tail of Mike's hunting shirt at the very moment the owner was retreating into the small cabin at the rear of the boat, which was immediately locked on the inside! All the boatmen, as if by previous concert, began to leave their craft, each bearing away upon his shoulder any loose implement lying about, with which an entrance into the cabin could be forced. The officer paused a moment, and then went to the cabin door, which he commenced persuading the offender to open, and save him the trouble of forcing it. He received no answer, but heard a horrible rustling within. At length getting out of patience, he remarked aloud:

"Well, if you won't open the door I can burn you out!" and he commenced striking fire with a pocket tinder box. The door immediately flew open, and there stood a boatman in Mike's dress: but it *wasn't Mike!*

"You aint arter me, are you, hoss?" inquired the boatman. The officer, without reply, stepped inside of the small cabin and looked around. There appeared to be no place to hide a figure as large as Mike, and there was a fellow dressed just like him. The thought immediately came uppermost in the officer's mind that the offender had changed coats outside while his back was turned, to go off the boat, and one of the parties that had walked off was Mike in disguise! He was about to step out when a moccasin-covered heel, sticking out of a hole in a large mattress, attracted his attention, and when he touched it the heel vanished. He put his hand in to feel, and Mike burst out in a hoarse laugh!

"Quit your ticklin'!" shouted he. "Consarn your cunnin' pictur', I'll *gin in* 'thout a struggle."

The other boatman now joined in the laugh, as he helped the

officer to pull Mike out of his hiding place. He had changed his garments *inside* the cabin instead of outside. A crowd of the boatmen also gathered around, and they all adjourned to the bluff, where, after taking drinks, they started in a body for the magistrate's office, who, by the way, was one of the early French settlers.

"Ah, ha!" he exclaimed, as the party entered the door; "here is ze men of ze boat, raisin' ze *diable* once more time. I shall not know what to do wiz *him*, by gar. Vat is de mattair now?"

"Why, Squire," broke in Mike, "I've jest come up with the Colonel to collect a small bill offen you!"

"You shall collect ze bill from *me?*" inquired the Justice. "What for you do the city good to de amount of von bill? Ah, ha! You kick up your *heel* and raise de batter and de salt of de whole town wiz your noise so much as we nevair get some sleep in de night!"

All eagerly gathered around to hear what Mike would reply, for his having a bill against the justice was news to the crowd.

"You jest hit the pint, Squire," said Mike, "when you said that thar word *heel!* I want you to pay me fur trimmin' the heel of one of your town niggers! I've jest altered his breed, and arter this his posterity kin warr the neatest kind of a boot!"

The boatmen burst into a yell of laughter, and the magistrate into a corresponding state of wrath. He sputtered French and English with such rapidity that it was impossible to understand either.

"Leave ze court, you ras*kells* of ze boat!" shouted the Squire above the noise. "*Allez vous-en, vous* rogues, I shall nevair ave nosing to do wiz you. You ave treat ze court wiz *grand contempt.*"

The boatmen, all but Mike, had retired to the outside of the door, where they were still laughing, when Mike again, with a sober and solemn phiz, remarked to the Squire:

"Well, old dad, ef you allays raise *h-ll* in this ere way fur a little laffin' that's done in your court, I'll be cussed ef I gin you any more of my cases!"

Another roar from the boatmen hailed this remark.

"Constable, clear ze court in *une* instant, right avay! *Les sacre diables* of ze river, no know nosing about how to treat wiz de law. I shall ave nosing to do wiz de whole what you call pile of ze rogues!"

"I aint agoin' to stand any more sich law as this," remarked Mike. "Consarn my pictur' ef I don't leave the town!"

"Go to ze *devil!*" shouted the magistrate.

"I won't," says Mike; "mabbe he's anuther French Jestis!"

Amid a torrent of words and laughter Mike retreated to his boat, where he paid the officer for his trouble, and sent a handful of silver to the darky to extract the pain from his shortened heel.

Mike Fink: "The Last of the Boatmen" (1847)

JOSEPH M. FIELD

JOSEPH M. FIELD (1810–56), who twice wrote about Fink in the St. Louis Reveille, was active in two fields, the theater and journalism. As actor, playwright, and theater manager, and as journalist and editor, he traveled widely, and it is credible that during his travels he heard yarns about the boatman, as he claimed, in Cincinnati, Louisville, New Orleans, Natchez, and St. Louis. He mentioned two storytellers—Morgan Neville and Colonel Charles Keemle. Since he described the former as having been "a noble old gentleman" at the age of forty-nine, there may be doubt about Field's claim that he had talked with him. Keemle, however, was a very close associate as coeditor of the Reveille. Moreover, Keemle had been on the Yellowstone River, at the site of Fink's death in the spring of 1823. Part of the evidence is an interesting letter of recommendation which he wrote for a Blackfoot Indian named Iron Shirt—and there is other evidence (see Nasatir's article, Pacific Northwest Quarterly, XXX [Jan., 1939], 83, 101). In 1844, furthermore, Keemle had given Field previously unpublished information about the place of Mike's death. Field may have had an additional literary source—a drama, probably never produced and now lost, The Last of the Boatmen, by an associate of his in the New Orleans theater a few years before—James Rees.

The account Field wrote in 1844 of "The Death of Mike Fink" was a pretty straightforward one (see p. 263). The following is a serial published in 1847. It introduces Mike as a ballad composer, rather believably, since it seems unlikely that either

*Field or his friend Keemle would have been capable of compos-
ing a ballad as unsophisticated as "Neal Hornback." Other oral
traditions seem, as Field says, to have supplied him with ample
material "between truth and fable." Many phrases in the dialogue have the sound of authentic boatmen's talk; and the account of Mike's roistering in New Orleans, Mike's story about
old Jabe and the slicken's, Dr. Gravy's anecdote about his playing bear, and Jean Tisan's yarn about his wife are the stuff of
oral tradition.*

*The story as a whole has the form of a melodramatic novel of
the day—full of typical claptrap—wild coincidences, disguises,
sentimental characters, and maudlin maunderings. Despite all
these, it has some wonderful stuff in it. Note the passages recording the talks and the frolics of the boatmen and the trappers, the remarkable renderings of incoherent speech in moments of great stress (as at the time of Mike's death). Note particularly the scene, with undertones of symbolism, which shows
Fink, the boatman, confronting and refusing to yield to the
mechanical enemy of the keelboat—the steamboat. This is in a
class with John Henry's contest with the steam drill.*

Well, the writer has undertaken to write the history of Mike
Fink, and if it had not been his custom through life—somewhat
like Mike Fink himself—to get into the scrape first, and then to
make his arrangements for getting out of it afterwards, he probably would feel a little uneasy as to his task; for truth to say, undertaking to follow Mike, the devil only knows where he may
lead one. Fifteen years ago the writer listened to some stories of
Mike told by the late Morgan Neville, Esq., of Cincinnati, a
noble old gentleman whose pen had done much towards trans-
mitting to posterity the fame of the "Last of the Boatmen." In
Louisville, subsequently, many "yarns" respecting the early river
hero were repeated to the writer; and since that time, in New
Orleans, Natchez, and finally in St. Louis, anecdotes and stories,
and, above all, the actual facts which are to form the frame-work

of this history have reached him till, between truth and fable, he is amply supplied with material. The writer, though, is conscientious to a painful degree, and he wants to "fix things right"; above all, he is afraid of telling "tough stories," "stretching things out," &c., and therefore he intends to be very careful. After the story shall be written, though, he gives fair notice that he will swear to every word of it; when if anybody knows more of the matter than he does, let them meet the same test. Now, then for a good startling commencement.

WHEREIN MIKE PLAYS THE DEUCE WITH CERTAIN
FAMILY ARRANGEMENTS

There was a high time, one evening, in the fall of the year 179–, in a little settlement on the banks of the Monongahela, not far from where stands at present the bustling town of Brownsville. Old Benson's pretty daughter, Mary, was to be married, and as old Benson had the longest face in the neighborhood, talked slower, was tolerably well off as to farm and cattle, and, above all, as he had been the leading man in getting up the log meeting-house, old Benson, of course, was a man of influence and was called "Deacon." There was something a *leetle* queer about Mary's marriage, though, and not a few of the "boys" about, reckoned that "sights" would be seen when Mike Fink should come home.

Mike was the tallest, strongest, longest winded fellow in the section, carried the truest rifle, knew more "Ingin ways," was the wildest hand at a frolic, and, withal, was the greatest favorite in the country. He had been "buckin' up" to Mary Benson for more than a year, and, in fact, Mary was engaged to him; it was notorious that they were to be married that fall, when all of a sudden, taking advantage of Mike's prolonged absence off in the Alleghanies, old Benson changes his mind, and compels his daughter to marry a man from the lower country, one who was a perfect stranger to everyone except Benson himself, and who, moreover, even during his short residence in the neighborhood— less than a month—had contrived to set nearly every man, woman and child against him; to be sure the population was not of the densest.

Benson was an Englishman by birth, and had lived in New Orleans, and along the lower river.

Taggart, Mary's new suitor, was also an Englishman, had a sort of seaman air with him, and it was in the lower country that he had made acquaintanceship with Benson. He was a heavy, dark browed man, of thirty-five, while Mary was not more than eighteen. Whether it was a matter of mere liking, or of sordid interest—this change in the father's intentions—nobody knew, but he was a cold, severe man, Mary was to be sacrificed, and her pale cheeks and streaming eyes were of no effect in averting the doom. Mary was not beautiful exactly, in feature, but there was a mild charm in her feminine character. The western woods at that time contained many emigrant families from the east, but among them all there was not a girl of Mary's grace. They used to call her "the lady," and the term expressed exactly the unpretending refinement which entitles a female so to be considered, and which was the natural characteristic of Mary's mind, untaught as it was. The poor girl loved rough Mike very fondly, for he was the kindest creature in the world to her, but she had none of the heroine about her. She had early lost her mother; she dared not disobey her father, and now, though her heart was breaking, yet she came forward to the sacrifice.

As has been said, there was a high time in the settlement. The evening of the marriage had arrived, when, at the last moment, old Benson took it into his head to make another change—sending round excuses to all the neighbors, and announcing that the marriage would be a private one. It was understood, moreover, that Taggart would take his bride off with him to the south immediately. Jabe Knuckles' "store," a log tenement on the river's bank, was headquarters that night, for all the idleness, curiosity and indignation of the settlement. A barrel of whiskey was on hand, and other matters no less exciting.

"It's downright cruelty to the young!" cried out Jabe, filling a can, "and Mike Fink is jest nat'rally bound to make a widow of Mary, so as to set things agreeable agin!"

"And scalp Deacon Benson!" observed another.

"And raise h-ll generally!" suggested a third.

"Ingin Pete couldn't a struck Mike's trail," said Knuckles, "or he'd a bin here 'fore now. I sent Pete off towards the mountains more'n a week ago, when I first smelt out the plot. He knows Mike's huntin' grounds. Thunder, don't it set one's blood a bilin'."

Jabe took a vigorous swig at the can and the others followed his example. Midnight came and still the crowd remained, having rung the changes upon Benson's treachery and Fink's expected wrath, and growing more and more indignant every moment. Indian fights, flat boat adventures, river yarns, &c., succeeded, the grog passing more frequently after every one, when, between two and three in the morning, a yell without cut short a song of Jabe's; there was a heavy blow upon the door, and in stalked the long gaunt figure of Mike, followed by a wiry looking half breed,—"Indian Pete," mentioned a moment since.

"Mike Fink—and too late, by thunder!" roared out Knuckles.

"Mrs. Mary Taggart, and in bed at that, since nine o'clock!" shouted another.

Mike looked around, wildly, gave a spasmodic swallow, and then seizing a can, washed down his feelings, as well as he could, by a deep, long, fiery draught of the intoxicating liquid.

"Poor Mary," said Knuckles, "they forced her into it!"

"To be sure they did!" echoed half a dozen, "and it'll kill her yet!"

"She's ben lookin' like a ghost for two weeks!"

"And expectin' you would get back in time to stop it!"

Fink gave a perfect yell of rage and anguish.

"I'm in time, I tell you!" he cried, trembling from head to foot with the excess of his emotion. "I tell you I'm in time, and you shall see it! Who'll go with me to shake hands with the bridegroom?"

The brains of the whole company were half maddened, and Mike's proposal was received with a shout. "Hurrah! That's the talk! Give him a ride to the river; Deacon Benson, too, rot his picter. Mike Fink forever!" another "drink all around" and the crowd were on their way, with shout, and laugh, and savage jest, to inflict something upon Taggart,—what, they knew not.

A shout of hate and derision roused the inmates of Benson's house. It was a substantial log tenement, of two large apartments divided by an ample passage way, and with low garrets above lighted by small gable windows. Every thing remained quiet within, but it was a sort of boding stillness. Another terrific shout, and Mike Fink, advancing from the crowd demanded that Benson and Taggart should show themselves.

"To git married is a manly act, and one should be proud of it, not skulk to his bridal bed like a coward! Deacon Benson, show yourself with your son-in-law!" Still no reply was given, and amid a storm of reproach and derision, which arose from all hands, Mike stepped onto the rough porch running along the front of the house; at the same instant a shot from one of the windows struck him in the neck, and he staggered back among his companions! A loud shrill scream from within was taken up by the throng without.

"That shot came from Taggart!" "Kill him!" "burn the house!" "kill Benson, too!" &c.&c. A dozen of them actually ran to collect combustibles, while Mike was borne to a short distance, recovering as he was carried.

"A scoundrel like that, boys, can't carry off Mary Benson! Take her from him, and then give him an Ingin run for it."

Torches were already flashing about the house, and heaps of brush were thrown into the open passage way. A simultaneous rush, notwithstanding that two more shots were fired, placed them all under shelter about the dwelling; and now whirling smoke, and fierce crackling flames told that the work was going on too surely. Screams of terror arose from one of the apartments, and Mike, with Knuckles, dashing in a window, sprang through in an instant. Mary lay on the floor in her night dress, bleeding, and a man was in the act of escaping through the side window.

"That's Taggart, Mike," said Knuckles. Mike fired, and the man dropped from the window as if mortally wounded; and yet he was not so, for several other shots were fired at him, from without, as he jumped a fence and plunged downwards towards the river.

Mike bore Mary out in his arms, and saw that she was marked in the face, as if she had received a blow. He took a bitter oath to wreak full vengeance on the coward who had given it. The house was now in a bright blaze, and Benson came forward with his cold, repulsive calm "fairly smellin' out of him," as Jabe Knuckles said.

"You have ruined me, Mr. Fink," said Benson.

"You are a snake hearted villain, Benson," replied Mike, "and I'll see you hanged yet, if watchin' of your ways will secure justice to you."

MIKE DOES THE AGREEABLE AS A LADY'S MAN

Before we hurry matters forward, which it will be convenient to do, let it be known that Mary's husband, Taggart, was never again seen in the Monongahela settlement after the night of the fire; that Benson himself disappeared with his daughter within three days after that event, leaving no clue behind him; and, finally, that several weeks elapsed before Mike Fink so far recovered from his wound as to carry his head straight—a point which he was rather particular about in this early stage of his career. And now, then, skipping several years, here we are in the midst of a river crowd, at the "grocery" of old 'Siah Hodgkiss, mouth of Bear Grass Creek, Louisville.

Mike Fink was there with his crew, for Mike had been on the river for some time, having changed the hills for the streams, and he was already celebrated from Pittsburgh to New Orleans. Jabe Knuckles was there, too, one of Mike's "bowers," but Jabe, unaccountably, had softened down his character, considerably; he was now not loud, but learnedly disputacious and moral, and

philosophical, and withal, he preferred lying in the sun, thinking that he was thinking, and reading old almanacs, to pulling
his sweep with proper vigor. Yet, broadhorns would float down
stream, anyhow, and Mike, who loved Jabe like a brother, used
to call him a "tarnal lazy old turtle," and do his work for him.

Mike was "some" in the present crowd, and no mistake, and
he was enlightening a portion of it—Miss Mira Hodgkiss, by old
Hodgkiss, dam Mrs. Hodgkiss, as Mike used to say, especially—
with a few anecdotes of his "airly and tender youth!"

"You see, Miss Miry, I first see sunrise way off in eastern
Pennsylvany, whar thar wa'n't a hill big enough to cool off on,
or a river large enough for a strong swaller. Wall, the old folks,
too, hadn't more'n a three foot streak of land, and one cow, and
this yer cow finally settled my fortin—."

"Cattle's got more to do with one's luck than you know of,
too, Mike Fink!" solemnly observed Jabe Knuckles, shutting
one eye, and not being able to open the other! "A bull is one
of the signs!"

"Yes, and a sleepy old calf, with a whiskey tit in his mouth, is
another of 'em," sung out Mike, at which there was a great
laugh, and "Old Almanac" was requested to "shut up."

"Yes, Miss Miry," resumed Mike, "that cussed old cow driv
me over the mountains; for it had the orfullest holler hind its
shoulders you ever did see, and the old folks being petiklar careful about the crittur, they jest insisted that I should foller it
around in wet weather, and bail its back out, so I quit!"

There was another roar at this, and old Hodgkiss drew another
pitcher of whiskey from the barrel, and Miss Mira fairly sidled
right up to Mike, where he was sitting with his heels upon the
little bar, and Jabe moralized about hollow backs and young
women, and every body seemed comfortable except old Hodgkiss, who was about as careful of his daughter as the elder Fink's
were of their own one cattle, and who, moreover, had a great
fear of Mike, seeing that he made love to all the gals, and not
without a full share of encouragement either. The boatman now

squeezed Mira's hand, and began pouring out a love ditty—one, by the bye, which he actually originated:

"O, my love she ar handsome, she's not ver-ri tall,
But her modest demeniour, does far surpass all;
She's slim round the middle, her hair it hangs down;
She's a bright morning star, oh, she lives in this town."

The singer growing warmer in his demonstrations, pressed Miss Mira more closely with every modulation.

"Well, now, Capting Fink," at length ventured old Hodgkiss, in a quick, sharp, Yankee, somewhat anxious, but very civil voice: "You du sing your songs right straight through and through one, and that's sartin truth, and I allays said it to Mira —and Mira, there's that pesky bear's cub, neow, huggin that shoat ter death, and why don't you go, Mira?"

But Mike wouldn't part with her, and furthermore Mira declared that it wasn't polite to leave people "a singin' "; and besides, a bluff flaxen-headed, handsome little boy that called Mike "daddy," put after the cub with a sharp stick, and old Hodgkiss was kept in his anxiety. Mike went on, mischievously, and this time with his arm about the girl's waist:

"Pretty Pol-li, pretty Pol-li, your dad-di are rich,
But I aint no fortin' what troubles me much"—

Mike here slipped a gold piece into her bosom, notwithstanding his plaint about poverty:

"Would you leave your old dad-di and mam-mi, also,
And all through the wide world with yer darling boy go?"

This cool request Mike seconded by taking a kiss—and without hurrying the operation, either, and "dad-di" was compelled to come out again with a very funny sort of earnest expostulation.

"Capting Fink, there aint a family man on the river that don't jest make you one of themselves, and yeow know how much I care about you skylarkin' with Mira, but what on airth is the use of troublin' yourself to amuse her, when you see that she aint enjoyin' of it!"

"Why lor a massy, father," said Mira, "if I love a thing on airth, it is singin'. Don't interrupt the captain, now, really!"

Mike, with a loud laugh, followed his humor by pulling the complimentary young lady down on his knee, and singing away as follows:

"Oh, some call me rak-ish, and some call me wild,
And some say that I pretty maids have beguiled;
But they are all liars by the powers er-bove,
For I'm guil-ti of nothing but innercent love!"

This avowal of "honorable intentions" was capped by an embrace and kiss of the very warmest character. Mira blushed a little and looked flustered, and Mr. Hodgkiss "let right out—and had tu du it, tu!" as he declared.

"Taint that you don't sing right sweet an' handsome, Capting Fink, and 'taint that you aint jest the most pop'lar man on the river, neither; but galls is galls, and whisky is whisky, an' when they both git into the head at the same time, they're a leetle dust too hot for each other, that's all; and there's Mira, now, all white and red and shamed to death 'bout what you bin a duin' to her."

Mira recovered her composure, though, very suddenly, and begged to express her entire surprise that her father should go on so about the matter!

"Jest as if Captain Fink wasn't a gentleman! and jest 'cause Captain Fink always *will* sing and do things when he comes along!"

Mike ordered a fresh supply of peach, throwing a handful of silver at Siah's head, which the publican took care to pick up under the pretense of tilting the barrel; and now, during a temporary lull in the confusion, Jabe Knuckles made unsteadily for the door, his weather eye remarkably cloudy, and muttering as he went:

"*Virgo*, that's another sign! Yes, and twins—twins is another!"

"What's that you say, Mr. Knuckles?" called out Miss Mira.

"Pre-*prediction!*" replied the river worthy, disappearing with a "shear."

Others of the company were leaving, and one or two were asleep, or otherwise overcome, and 'Siah made a vigorous effort to get his daughter off to bed, when she "really begged" that her father wouldn't worry on her account, as Capt. Fink had just promised to give her the true and particular history of his little boy, "Carpenter," who was now lying asleep in a bunk, at the back of the grocery.

"And you needn't trouble yourself about sittin' up, nuther, old hoss," said Mike, "as this yer matter 'tween me and Mira is of confidential order, prehaps!"

MIKE GIVES MISS MIRA THE HANG OF HIS HISTORY

"You see, Mira, I'm tol'ble on the wrong side of thirty now, and not jest the hand for telling sure enough love yarns; but then you aint twenty yet, and moreover you're a female and take to sich things constitootianly by natur; and moreover agin, I've gotten su'thin to say to you at the end of this yer beginnin' and that's what I'm arter, so lay low and listen!"

"I was desappinted a good many years ago, Mira—poor Mary Benson was a better looking gal than you be, too,—and likelier behaved at that; howsomedever"—we need not follow Mike through his love story and its catastrophe.

"Well," he continued, "then it was I went on the river, thinkin', prehaps, I might hear of Mary, some day; but I didn't; and eventooally broad horns stuck out'r me all over, and I felt hired nat'rally to stick to navigation and be first cap'n, and so here I be—and like to remain at that price, I predicate. I'd made three or four trips up and down to Orleens, laden with corn, cattle, and other fancy stuff, and brought up, a foot, tall piles of the *large-John*—as the Frenchmen 'bout the old calaboose squar used to say—and I was going down on my first keel—*Mary Benson* I called her—when one of my hands, 'Ingin Pete,' who used to hunt with me in the old Alleghany country, got scent of pirates 'long Arkansaw, and 'twasn't long 'fore it was play snake, play possum, I tell you! You see, the half breed was a mighty sour lookin'-varmint, far as face went, and some of these Arkansaw spekylators got to feelin' his heart towards me, and he let on that he loved me 'bout as well as they did honesty, and they bit like young catties. Cuttin' my throat wasn't good enough for 'Ingin Pete,' he pretendin' to have all sorts of a spite agin me, and talkin' this way he soon cum to see the head devils in the business, and who should they be, but *Old Benson* and *Taggart*, that he had given his da'ter to! The hull hells-work of that matter was plain enough, now; Benson had been in the pirate business before he cum up to Monongahela to whip the devil around the meeting-house, and when his old crony, Taggart, made a call upon him for Mary, he had to give her up or do worse. They were now spekylatin' together agin, and expected to get me cheap, for certain. A big pile of money and a small chunk of revenge was their bargain, and this was the way they fixed it. Ingin Pete was to keep dark 'till on our way up from Orleans agin, after the cargo had been sold. He was to know all about the money, and on our return to the Arkansaw shore, he was to give the word, when arrangements would be made to catch us foul in the right place. He was to secure our arms during his watch at night, let the varmints on board and then kingdom come to us! All was settled among 'em and we put out jest as innercent as could be, I tell you! We did'nt work very hard that day, though, I reckon! That trip would a-sooted Jabe Knuckles, and no mistake, but he hadn't took to boatin' then. Dark cum, and we tied up only a few miles from Benson and his gang,—and now, old 'Siah, a little more peach and sweetnin', sense you will set up, and I'll tell you somethin' to keep you wide awake 'till daylight!"

While Hodgkiss mixed the grog, Mike crossed the apartment and saw that the little boy was sleeping comfortably; Mira closed up to him with deeper interest on his return, and the narrative was resumed.

"Without having learned their den exactly, Pete had the hang of their tracks, enough to git along with, and leavin' only a boy aboard the keel, nine on us set out to trap these river rats. We kept along the bank a few miles to a bayou which we had to ascend; but what should Pete, who was scoutin' discover, as he neared the place, but two men pushing out into the Mississippi, one on 'em Taggart, as he thought; and now wa'nt they *watchin' us*, and which was the smartest, that was the question? I stepped out in the starlight, hailed the skiff, and commanded the men ashore, but they fired a signal shot and only pulled out faster. The thing was out; I cracked away—tumbled the one that Pete called Taggart into the bottom—must a shot him through the head—at the same minute the skiff took a whirl against a sawyer and over she went, leavin' the live rascal hanging onto the branches. All we had to do was to make a rush up the bayou and lose no time about it; and up we went, and across two clearings, and through a belt of timber, and on to a lake, in all about two miles, but here we were stopped. Pete was ahead, and just as he made a sign that all was right, there cum a shower of balls, wounding two on us, and killing Pete outright. Another rush, and we were over a ditch and levee, and down upon a right smart log castle! We heard the sound of horses dashing off through the woods; no more fight was made, and in we marched. There was an old nigger woman and two or three little snow-balls, in the first room, but we could get nothin' out of them; and, I tell you what, tremblin', and feelin' sick as to what I might find, I went into the second. Simple stories is best, I reckon; *there was Mary Benson!*"

Mike wiped his eyes and paused for a moment.

"Well, when I tell you she died in my arms, that night, I need'nt say how I found her! I knew her, though, spite of sickness, and suffering, and she knew me! Taggart was dead, her father was a cut-throat, and her child—that boy—so like herself, now, as I look at him, she gave him to me to bring up to ways of honesty."

"Mira," continued Mike, and his voice was full of feeling, "you are young and foolish, and it may be I am wild and wicked. *I never mean to marry!* and I've told you about poor Mary so as to let you know I'm in airnest! If I've trifled with you, it's bin because you're foolish; and I stop it now, you see, 'cause I think it might be to my shame, and the worse for you!"

The girl drew off slowly and incredulously as these unexpected words were uttered. She looked in Mike's face, but every trace of liquor, excitement, or nonsense, had vanished, and she knew what he was when he chose to be serious about matters. A flush of anger and vicious feeling now passed over her features; anon, succeeded by a few hysteric sobs, when, suddenly conquering her emotion, she gave Mike a strange, half reproachful, half reckless glance, and withdrew.

The father had watched the scene with trembling interest. Mean and sordid as he was, he loved his daughter, and dreaded her wilful temper and ungovernable impulses.

"Capting Fink," cried he, as soon as the girl had disappeared, "Mira isn't good enough for your wife, though her own father has to say it! You deserve a princess, you du! Let me shake your hand, Capting; if I didn't think you was going to take Mira away, I wish I may be shot! Only kin on airth, too; an old, lone man," and here the ancient 'Siah gave way to a most infantile boo-hoo—as he would have said himself. Fink drew from his bosom a rude locket, kissed it fervently, breathing the name of "Mary," shook the old man heartily, honestly by the hand, and then casting a glance of kindly interest on the sleeping boy, and saying he would come for him in the morning, withdrew to his boat.

MIKE TELLS A YARN ABOUT A "MADMAN"

There was water enough on the "Falls"; it was a bright day in spring, and at an early hour, all hands at their posts, Mike was guiding his clean and trim built "keel," the *Mary*—he still adhered to the name, and it had always been a charm to him, he said—through the rapids, below Louisville. There was not much peril in the passage, at the moment, and the exhileration was only of the pleasant kind.

"That's like a lady!" cried Mike, as, under the bold and skillful guidance of his sweeping stern oar, his craft a moment yielded to a powerful eddy, and then drew out again with a graceful curve.

"See how she puts her feet out! Dances like a fairy, by gracious!"

> "As we go—as we go
> Down the O-hi-o,
> There's a tight place at Louisville,
> You know boys, know."

"Jabe Knuckles!" shouted Mike, "one of them Philadelphy noospapers you've got sorted away, tells about a York feller that's got a steam fixin' to take boats up rivers without hand, hoss, or hawser! I reckon he'll never try 'ginst this water, eh?"

"I reckon!" echoed some half a dozen; but Jabe was rather proud of his literary collection and to doubt anything which he had "read," was almost equal to attacking his own veracity.

"I reckon he *will*, and do it, too—if he keeps goin' on!" said Jabe; perversity, for once, making a prophet.

There was a terrible laugh, of course, at Jabe's expense, one negro hand declaring that it was "jess like de talk 'bout lightnin' rods! Bress de lor," he continued, "I nebber had de fuss one 'bout *me*, an' I got to be struck yet!"

"Ha, ha, ha! shut up, now, Jabe," roared every body.

"Well, boys," said Mike, "I don't know whether it's true or not, but when them things cum about there'll be no Mike Fink left, I guess. I remember when I warn't more'n twenty or so, I was on a long tramp down the Ohio, when a stranger cum along in a skiff, and took me aboard, nighly a hull day with him. Well, he was mad, and looked mad, and talked mad, yet I wish I may be shot ef I didn't like and love him, and remember him to this day; and something of this blasted steam nonsense must a done the mischief to him, too! Why, he pinted out to me half a dozen large cities, that he said he *saw*—places whar a tree ain't been cut yet! and he talked of deepening the river channel for its commerce, and he'd bin to Louisville, before, and spoke of these falls, and a canal that would one day be built, and all this was to be done by steam! He told me to remember his talk when I'd be older, and then he'd be quiet awhile, and sigh; and then launch out again about coal, and timber, and towns, and farms, and hills echoing the song that was crazing him; and, finally, he wept like a child and longed to be buried on some river knob or other, that his sleep might be lulled by the sounds he spoke of! He was turned of fifty, and his hair was white and his face wrinkled, but his eye was like an eagle's—only wilder, as he spoke, and he kept my heart aching all the while, and cuss me if I know why yet! In the afternoon a squall came on and we put ashore, and there, as we stopped under a rock, he took out his knife, as if he waan't knowin' to it, and began cuttin' his name, I suppose, in the stone.

"What on airth was it, Mike?" inquired several.

"John Fitch;—and right under it he cut somethin' like a 'keel,' with a sort of paddles at the sides, and a smoke-pipe, and this he said was what was goin' to do all the wonders!"

"Well, that's a steam boat!" cried Jabe, rousing up a little, "and it's a good many years since you were twenty, and they only just invented it now in New York!"

"Don't know," said Mike, "but Fitch ef that war his name, told me he'd run one for a hull day, and made seven miles an hour, on the Delaware, ten years before!"

"Now that I *don't* believe!" remarked Jabe Knuckles, with great firmness; nor did he—or he had never "read it." The thousands now alive, however, who *know* it, feel as little interest in doing justice to the memory of genius as Jabe did.

They were clear of the rapids, and gliding along some two or three miles below, little "Henderson"—Fink had named the little boy after a lost friend of his youth—who knew already how to handle a rifle, cracking away, occasionally, at the tarrapin, as they lay sunning themselves upon the logs, and his "daddy" encouraging him, when a canoe suddenly shot out from the Kentucky bank and made toward them. A single Indian handled the short paddle—a squaw—and a few moments brought her alongside. The forest children were not so scarce along our Western waters, forty years ago, and it was common enough for a canoe to make fast to a 'keel' or 'flat,' and so save themselves the labor of propelling it for a time. The squaw was anything but attractive in her appearance, her garb being soil'd and ill-arranged, and a bandage covering a portion of her face, as if she had received a severe injury. To the rude questions and jests of the men, she replied but by signs, and kept her place in the canoe with characteristic equanimity.

"Jabe! go and convart that heathen," said Fink, as noon came around, and the men were gathered in groups about their meal. "She's a yearnin' for the truths, about now, I reckon!"

Jabe made an offering of some of the fruits of civilization, not forgetting to include a can of its happiest results; but the squaw showed that she did not lack for provisions, of her own rude kind.

"The poor, benighted critter!" sighed Jabe, "she aint got any more taste in feedin' than in prayin'—parched corn aint Christianity, no how!"

"Lost, soul and stomach!" said Mike. "What nation?" demanded he of the squaw, making a sign at the same time. She appeared to understand him and replied:

"Choctaw!"

"Why, what on airth be you doin' up here then?" inquired Mike. "'Low you've bin on to Washington!"

The woman simply pointed south, and said, "Yazoo."

"Just to think how these she varmints do ventur!" said Mike. "Too cussed ugly, too, for a cabin passage!"

MIKE CONCLUDES TO "MAKE A NIGHT OF IT"

Fink, at the head of his boat's crew, generally "regulated the town" upon each visit to New Orleans, and on this occasion he had been particularly active in the discharge of this duty! He had cleared three French ball rooms, had two levee fights with *gens d'armes* sent to take him from his boat, paid a fine to the city, and, as a crown to his triumphs, he had broken "a bank"! These were Mike's relaxations, but, at this time they were unaccompanied by insult, or outrage—further than the excitement of "spreeing" begat. There was nothing malevolent about Mike's heart. His huge frame was animated by a nature warm, generous, impulsive—full of the milk of human kindness, and only terrible and dangerous when roused by treachery and wrong. At this time, too, intoxication had not become a vice with Mike; his powerful constitution bade defiance to all assaults, and whilst he was the wildest, most reckless, and, consequently, renowned boatman on the river, he was at the same time one of the most keen and business-like in his serious operations. There was no taking him at a'vantage. "Wide awake" was his watchword even on his frolics.

In the highest spirits, on the night previous to his departure on his return trip, Mike was at a noted dance house in "the swamp"—as the back part of the city, very naturally, used to be called. It is hardly necessary to say that the haunt was one of vice, and even of crime, but it was a usual place of resort for boatmen, nevertheless, and there Mike Fink was ever King of the crowd;—the awe of the men, and the hero of that class of females by whom they were surrounded. On this occasion he was accompanied by Jabe Knuckles, and a man by the name of Talbott, with whom he had had some business on the Levee, and whom he took a fancy to for the reason that he was the "ugliest white man yet." Some dreadful accident or other had disfigured the man. The flesh appeared to have been cut away from under each eye, leaving the balls exposed and horrible to look at, while the upper part of the nose was gone altogether, leaving a frightful gap between the brows and the extremity of the nasal organ. This gap was partially hidden by a patch, but the face altogether was hardly human in its aspect. The injury had destroyed everything like character of expression. The eyes seemed ever glaring, and the mouth lacked their aid in the illustration of meaning and emotion.

"If you're determined to stay, I must leave you, Captain Fink," said Talbott, "it's late."

"You can slope, old crawfish," cried Fink. "Here's Jabe; my other shirt. Its all right by his almanac."

"Pshaw! you've danced enough, and drank enough, and there's not a girl in the house but you've had a two week's acquaintance with."

"Hush! lay low; I'll know more about that in the morning," said Mike, with a chuckle of exhilaration, "As for dancing, the thing can't go on while you're about, old hoss; your face is certain death to a breakdown!"

The ogresse who was known as the head of the establishment, now approached Mike, with a grin, and whispered something which seemed to afford him great satisfaction.

"I'm thar! old eelskin; I'm thar, I tell you! Young, tender, and white, at that —hi-i-i"; and he gave an Indian yell that made the bottles ring.

Talbott shook his head, bade him goodnight, and departed; but, within an hundred yards of the house, he turned into an open lot, and was there joined in a few moments by another figure.

"How does the chance look?" inquired the new comer.

"It's all right!" was the reply. "The new girl catches him. He'll stay the night. I shall sleep at the 'Orleans,' to be clear of the matter."

"And he still carries everything about him?"

"All! his sales, and the bank into the bargain. We can get it all back at a single rake!"

"D———m him, and revenge besides!" muttered the stranger. "Old Pauline will be careful to sweeten his night-cap?"

"No fear, she's got the stuff. The room is all fixed, and the girl knows nothing."

"Good night, then!"

"Take it easy—stop. You are still certain that he never saw you when he came to gamble?"

"I have avoided him for five years," said the stranger. "If I shun him after tonight, though, he must come as a ghost! Good night!"

"Good night!—at the Caffe Marigny!—breakfast!"

They separated.

In a chamber of the second story, opening upon the back balcony and furnished rather handsomely, with a large bed draped with gauzes, &c., in the creole style, sat a young girl, listening anxiously to the sounds which came up from below, and thrice intently as Mike's voice ever and anon was heard. Presently, heavy steps without, and a snatch of a song startled the girl to her feet:

> "He war crooked backed, hump shoulder-ed,
>   And with thick lips is blessed;
>   And for to make him ug-i-ly,
>   The Lord had done his best!"

The door was thrown open—instantly closed again by the girl, as Mike passed in, and now, turning the key in the lock, she suddenly faced her visiter.

"My God!" exclaimed Fink, actually staggering. "You, Mira—and *here!*"

"There is no danger to a young girl in your company, Captain Fink!" said Mira Hodgkiss, for it was she, sure enough.

"Oh, my God! this airth is gittin' too bad!" cried Mike. "Oh! you lost unhappy gal; hell-bent and no savin' on you! Come to this, and so soon, too!"

"Many thanks for your pity, Captain; but we're here about the same time I reckon, and lucky for you, too, perhaps! Sinner or saint, I am not here to ask favors, but to show you that all women didn't leave the world with Mary Benson! I laugh at your thoughts, and scorn explanation till my heart may soften again. At this moment I'm here to be revenged!"

"Your poor father!" cried Mike bitterly. "For you—you always had the devil's drop in you!"

The girl's whole frame trembled with passion.

"Oh, you're a keen headed, true hearted hero, with your *Mary Benson!* I'm not so good looking as *Mary Benson!* So well behaved as *Mary Benson!* Ha! ha! ha! I'm not fit to be the wife of Mike Fink! Ha! ha! ha! And now, here I am with Mike Fink under my foot, to do with him just as I please; ha! ha! ha! To say go or stay—live or die, as I like; ha! ha! ha!"

"The gal's head's turned!" muttered Fink, in astonishment.

A burst of hysterical sobs, and finally tears, calmed the girl, somewhat, when she again spoke:

"I tell you Mike Fink, I've followed you in spite more than in love! I never knew what gall and anguish was until you made me feel what contempt was. Go down on your knees, Mike Fink, and kiss that floor before me! Without one word to tell you how I came here, feel in your heart that I'm more of a woman—a *better* woman than your puny *Mary Benson* ever was, and then this gnawing in my breast here may leave me! Quick, Mike Fink you've not long to spare!"

The girl had worked herself into wildness again, and Fink actually thought her crazed. He debated within himself whether or not he should carry her off, forcibly, and make a proper disposition of her until he could return her to her father.

"Poor misdirected creetur," muttered he, "I oughtn't to leave you to your fate!"

"A devil whispers me to leave you to yours, Fink!"—she struggled terribly with her feelings.

"Listen! I have but to detain you here a few minutes longer and you will be unable to quit a danger that's near you!"

This did not sound so madly, and Mike was instantly on the *qui vive*.

"What do you mean, Mira?" said he, advancing, and taking her hand; the girl trembled with emotion. "I do not despise you. It will be your own fault if I do not love you like a brother!"

Subdued, and shedding a torrent of tears, she threw herself upon his breast.

"I am here to save your life!" sobbed she. "You drank some liquor with the old woman, as you came up?"

"I did not," said Mike; "to play a trick on one of the gals, I poured it into her drink, and she swallowed the whole mixture."

"Thank God, then!" fervently exclaimed the girl. "You are safe and free, and quit the house this instant!"

"Speak on, Mira; give me the hang of it!" cried Mike.

"Well, then—you have won large sums of money, and you carry it about you. You have been to this place frequently, but have never passed the night, and they have been afraid to attack you awake. At last they laid me, a young new-comer, as a bait for you; you were to stay through the night, and they were to have given you a drink to stupify you!"

"Wall, if that don't beat ingin," laughed Mike, "I'll gin in! And how did you find all this out?"

"I've followed you to this house every time you've been to it," replied Mira.

"But how came you to larn the plot; and how kem I not to notice you?"

"I was disguised as a ragged Indian girl!"

Mike's breath was fairly taken away from him! Overwhelmed by remorse, and running over with gratitude—a perfect Ohio river rise of sensibility—he was about bursting into extravagance, when Mira laid her hand on his arm, and made a signal of caution and silence. The single light had been so disposed as to throw the whole chamber, nearly, into shadow; and now drawing Mike into the deepest part of it, Mira spoke to him in a low whisper.

MIKE PERFORMS CERTAIN MARRIAGE CEREMONIES

Time may be saved by giving certain explanations in our own way, and therefore we do so.

The idea of following Fink, and watching an opportunity of revenging the slight put upon her in some way of her own just suited the warm passions and wilful temper of Mira, and she put it in execution, as has been seen. She continued in the neighborhod of the "keel," sometimes before, sometimes behind, for many days. Sometimes she even went on board, and contrived to attach little "Henderson" to her, and all without suspicion. She knew the boatmen, and how to humor or repel them. Even after passing the Yazoo, she continued near them, only shooting ahead when near the end of the voyage, so as to land in New Orleans before them. She kept up her acquaintance with the boy, and managed to follow Mike to all his haunts. At the house of old Pauline in "the Swamp" she overheard one day a discussion of plans to entrap Fink. The suggestor was an old, snakish-looking man, and Pauline, the hag, was to receive a large sum, and be held harmless for lending the use of her house. Many plans failed, and the time arrived for Fink's departure, when the old beldame proposed to tempt him by promising to introduce him to a beautiful young female, fresh on the town, and new to vice. Such a one she would procure. Instantly Mira departed, resumed her proper garb, presented herself to Pauline, as an unfortunate who had just been driven from her home; and was seized upon eagerly as the object desired. By close attention, she soon learned the further plan of overpowering Fink by a drug, and of entering the chamber through a door situated behind, and affording entrance through an armoire that stood near the bed.

"An old man!" said Mike. "Wall I allow he's not an old enough fox to save his tail this time! Mira! I take all them rash things I said to you down at a gulp; and, now, keep shady and you'll see sights. The boys are pooty near all back at the keel by this time; Jabe Knuckles went 'fore I kem up here. Let me jest drap you over the railin' outside; rouse the reg'lators; bring 'em back and place 'em round the sheds, and fences, and then wait 'till you hear Mike's yell, that's all!"

Mira put on a dark dress that hung in the room; wrapped a black veil round her head, quadroon fashion, and was ready in an instant. The sounds below had gradually died away; the mischief was within, not watching without the house; and after, through an uncontrollable impulse, opening his arms to the girl and embracing her with a ferocious warmth that more than repaid his ferocious coldness, Mike stepped out on to the gallery, passed Mira over the rail, and dropped her to the ground, she at the same time feeling the buoyancy of a feather.

"She'll have to run up pooty nigh to Bienville street," said Mike, "ten minutes—and then back. Reckon I can't go to sleep jest yet."

Within an hour or so of this time, the shriveled wretch, Pauline, and the old "Banker," rose from their seats in the front bar, below, now closed and fastened, and proceeded towards the back apartments.

"You, now, go to bed," said the villain; "I shall kill them both, the girl first—for Fink is secure! I will then throw open the window on the balcony, and it will all pass as a murder through jealousy or revenge. Fink's character is well known for woman scrapes."

He mounted the stairs cautiously; crossed the room above, to a door in the opposite partition wall; placed his light on a chair, and then knelt down to listen—affording, of course, a very pretty murderous picture, and one which has been presented tolerably often in the melodramas. A snore, like that of one of our latter-day asthmatic steamers—an intermixture of snort, blow, and whistle,—could be heard distinctly; and, now, after a great deal more murderous pantomime, in trying the handle, &c., the hoary ruffian blew his light out and pulled the door open, towards himself. His course was still stopped, but after listening again to the now very audible "blow," and feeling about a moment, another door—or panel—yielded before him, and the stealthy creeper found himself in a close square closet; this was one of the customary divisions of the armoire. The snore was now tremendous, and after a moment, to take another turn on his nerves, the murderer prepared to let himself in upon his victim.

At this instant, while fingers were on the bolt, he became conscious of a strange sort of movement on the part of his prison, and before he could collect his thoughts, himself and closet were whirled with stunning, shattering violence upon the the floor—the whole house shaking, and a loud, long, shrill cry rising over all, that might have been a summons for all the savages that ever danced at a torture!

"Hi-i-i-i-i-i-i-ho-wah!" yelled Mike.

"Hi-i-i-i-i-ow-ow-ow-who-whooh!" in every variety of devilish echo arose from without.

Mike fired a pistol into the bed and mosquitoe bar, which latter in a moment was blazing, and, at the same time, half a dozen heads were thrusting in the window, and bursting through the door, from the balcony!

"Wake, snakes!" shouted Mike, "tree's down and now for honey!" At the same moment he jerked open the panel in the back of the armoire; pulled out the entrapped one as though he had been a rat, held him up to the light and dropped him again as though he had been a serpent.

"Old Benson, by G—d!" cried he.

The detected monster, ghastly, and trembling, looked around the room, now full of Mike's friends, despairingly, but was unable to articulate.

"Poor Mary's father, too!" muttered Mike, as a pang shot through him. The remembrance of the dead, however, could not excuse the living, for Benson had known Fink all along, and had crept hither, at midnight, to murder him.

"Why that's old double O, that keeps the table, on the Levee!" cried several. He was known to others, though he had always kept out of Mike's way.

"Hang him to the bed post!" "Ride him down to the keel!" Several similar suggestions were being offered, when Jabe Knuckles entered the customary door of the chamber, holding out at arms length, between his finger and thumb, as it were, in the same way in which he might have handled a vicious craw-fish—the scarcely less active Pauline! The shrivelled little monster struggled and scolded and blasphemed, but all in vain. Jabe held her up a moment, that all might have a good laugh at her and then deposited her upon the prostrate armoire.

"There's a pair of signs for an almanac," said he. "If them two aint old Scorpio and the Crab, I'll never agin look in the book for sunrise!"

"A pooty pair!" cried every one jeeringly.

"A pair, and a *match*, too," shouted Fink, "and cuss me, boys, ef we don't marry 'em!"

The suggestion was received with a hurrah, when an incarnation of darkness known on the keel boat as "Gravy," from his office—he was cook—and who has heretofore been mentioned as delivering himself of a fixed opinion with regard to lightning rods, stepped forward from the crowd and requested that he might have the honor "ob tyin' up de young couple!"

"Aye! aye! aye! aye! Dr. Gravy for parson" screamed everybody.

"And I'll stand up with the groom!" cried Mike.

"And boys, we'll all stand up for the maids," said Jabe Knuckles.

"Captain Fink," at length said Benson, spasmodically, with the face of a corpse and the soul of a craven, "*only spare my life!*"

"Granted!" said Mike, and his loathing almost took away his stomach for the frolic. The old woman now, also, began to beg, and remonstrate, but all in vain. Benson was taken out on the gallery, and in an inconceivably short time had received a full *plumage* with the accompanying tar; the "maids" had, also, decorated the bride as fantastically as taste could desire, and, now, the Rev. Doctor Gravy, having robed himself in a sheet, and powdered his clerical phiz for the occasion, advanced between a row of candles to perform the ceremony.

"Brudder Knuckles," said the doctor, "I trouble you for de good book!" and Jabe incontinently handed forth his almanac, observing that "a change might be expected about this time."

"Which am de young couple?" demanded the doctor, with a roll of the eye that set the crowd shrieking. Mike and Jabe, literally, *supported* their respective parties.

"Nobody don't say nuffin 'ginst de comfitability ob dese young people, I reckon?" inquired the doctor.

"No!" was the thundering response.

"Nobody cares much what dar captissimil condominations was, nuther, I reckon?"

"No!"

"Den nebber after hole you peace, de hull on you!" solemnly proclaimed the doctor. "And now, den, bofe take hands." The trembling wretches obeyed, actually imbecile, through terror.

"You take dis woman fo' you true unlawful wife?"

"Well, he does," said Mike, making the response.

"You take dis man fo' you true unlawful husband?"

"And two better," said Jabe.

"Den," concluded the doctor, "I pernounce you bone ob one bone an' flesh ob one flesh, ony take care ob de tough parts. Saloot you bride!" A whirlwind of mirth and frolic hailed the conclusion of the ceremony.

"And now, boys, a health all round, and we'll wish the young couple good night. There is a bar below, and—where is that love-draught you prepared for me, Mrs. Bride?"

In vain the terrified beldame protested innocence and ignorance; the draught was produced, and a large glass was poured out for herself and the groom.

"All at a swallow!" They drank with a shudder, and the effect, from the powerful dose, was almost immediate. At this moment, the doctor ran up from below, where the crew were emptying the bar, to say, that *"de Jonney be dams was a comin'!"*

"Let them come!" cried Mike, raising his shrillest yell, and rushing down to the street, with his crew at his heels.

"Aboard, and fend off," shouted he. A charge was made upon a party of the *gens d'armes*, who were approaching with their drawn sabres, but the civic heroes fled at sight of the formidable band which presented itself.

As Mike turned down towards the *levee*, he saw Mira waiting for him. Catching her in his arms, he bore her off with a hug of triumph,—and, here, leaving both in this state of high enjoyment, we think fit to close the chapter.

A SWEET YARN, AND A CASUALTY

If our readers please, we will now jump onward a short lifetime—there or thereabouts—and alight on the deck of a keel boat which, in the fall of the year 1822 was descending the Mississippi, a short distance below St. Louis, bound from that

city to New Orleans. It was an afternoon of the "Indian summer"; the air was calm, the skies were full of softness, the
foliage afforded the usual rich variety of autumn tints, and the
keel itself, with its characteristic groups, made the central object
of a picture which the pencil of Bingham is now rendering
familiar to the world.

It was an open reach of the river and the keel was gliding
down the centre of the current under the simple guidance of a
tall, well favored, yet rather lounging looking youth who managed the stern oar. He was some twenty-one years of age; had a
quick yet somewhat sly glance; a broad, manly under jaw, a wide
expressive mouth and "chawed tobacco" of course. His whole
appearance spoke of the woods, and streams and the reckless
spirit of freedom which they foster. The hands were listlessly
distributed about the boat, idle, as might be, but immediately
beneath the steersman was gathered a group, apparently laughing at a large, lumbering, dissipated looking man of fifty or so.
Loudest among the laughers was another elderly man, probably
about forty-five. The voice of this character was loud, and, although not in anger, it conveyed something of the absolute and
overbearing. His eye, too, had a mingling expression of wicked-
ness in it; and the manner in which the tobacco was masticated,
rather than anything else, betokened a nervous restlessness. This
man, also, had a broken, debauched air about him, and altogether, his appearance was as unprepossessing as remarkable.

"That's a fact!" roared he. "Jabe Knuckles, there's, gittin'
pious! want's to quit boatin' and settle in St. Louis, and all
sense he got goin' down to Frenchtown to play loto with old
Madame Tisan. Ha! ha! ha! Old Louisville yet, for Mike Fink,
by thunder!"

> "Adieu to Saint Louis, I bid you er-dieu;
> Likewise to the French and the mers-qui-ters too,
> For of all other nations I do you disdain,
> I'll go back to Ken-tuck-i nd try her er-gain!"

"I tell you what, daddy Mike," sung out the young steersman, "you've bin wrathy 'ginst St. Louis, ever sense they fined

you for trimming off that nigger's heel, of the old man's, with yer rifle!"

This reference to a well known piece of deviltry on the part of Mike (it has already been told in the Reveille, by *Solitair*)[1] appeared to stir that worthy very pleasantly.

"Well," laughed he, "the nigger's heel stuck 'way out over the bluff, and I did redoose his measure about two sizes, that's a fact. Boys!" roared Mike, "all come aft, and I'll tell you about Madame Tisan and Jabe Knuckles's pup slickin's!"

"That's all a d——d no such thing, Mike Fink," said Jabe Knuckles, opening his sleepy eyes, and apparently not relishing the story; "I didn't swaller the first mouthful, and you know it!"

"Well, hoss, I seed you pullin' har out of your teeth for a week, any how!" laughed Mike.

"Give us that yarn, daddy," said the steersman.

"Old Jabe and the Slicken's!" sung out everybody.

"Well—keep her out more in the stream, Henny. First time I kum to St. Louis—Jabe was along, of course—it was cold weather, and just 'fore fast time—or just after it—one or other; greasy Tuesday, or something—they call it *mardigraw* down in *Orleans*—and a raft on us went down, night-time, to a dance doins at old Madame Tisan's—that Jabe's sweet on, now. Well, there was a awful pollyvooin' and French fashions, you know, but the galls was mighty pe-art lookin' as French galls allays is, and it was 'wooly voo dance Miss?' and 'wee Munsheer!' and dosey-do, and shassey, and toe-nail, and break-down, I tell you, jest as if we'd bin all 'quainted all 'long, ony there was a hull lot of French pups about, and they kept puttin' in their *ki-i-i* into the rest of the lingo, every now and then, when they got trod on, and then Madame Tisan would go on jest as if she'd pupped 'em herself, and felt a nat'ral affection for 'em. Well, some cake doins was to wind up the ball—a sorter slap-jack party, and right over the fire was an almighty big open kittle, full of molasses slickin's, and grease, to pour over the slap-jacks; and it was a bilin' and creamin' up beautiful, I tell you, when jest 'bout then

1. See p. 87 of this book.

I broke one of the cussed puppy's legs, and Madame Tisan mounted me in the most onairthly kind of loud French, pre-haps! The he pallyvous took it up, too, and were might sassy and fighty—to one another, I reckon, for I didn't take the trouble to ask 'em what they said, and they knew better than to cuss me in the vrenak'lar, I predicate, and arter a while, jest to prevent mischief in futer I picked up a couple of the pups—they were all over curly, I tell you—and, in the row, I popped 'em careful into the kittle!"

"Good again, Mike!" "Don't squirm, old Jabe!" "Dog candy by thunder!" &c., &c., &c. The auditors were in high delight, all except Knuckles.

"Well," continued Fink, "down they went and like the sweet-nin', I reckon, for they didn't come up again, and the kittle went on bilin' and bilin', and bimeby, boys, it was *cake time*."

"Oh thunder!" "Well, that takes *me!*" &c., broke forth the whole crowd, roaring with laughter, in anticipation of the fun.

"It was cake time, old Jabe! D'ye hear?" cried Mike, "and the way the slapjacks kem in all smokin' in French, and the way the plates rattled, was a caution, and every pollyvoo as he got his 'lowance chassy'd up to the fire place, and old aunty Tisan jest ladled out a reg'lar rise of sweetnin' over his plate and then he went to work swallerin'. Wall, it all looked mighty temptin', and went mighty fast too, and bimeby old Jabe takes his chaw out'n his mouth, chassy's up with a plate, jest like the rest, and then I gin to wink to the boys and they lay low for the laughin' time. Aunty Tisan was gettin' tol'ble down in the kittle, 'bout now, and first thing Jabe did was to begin pickin' his teeth and spittin', but it was right good for all that, and he took another turn at it. The pollyvoos, too, began feelin' their teeth, and the old woman a stirrin' up faster and faster, and then there was all kinds of nasty faces and next all kinds of sakry damnations and monkey doin's, and last of all old aunty ladled up one of the pups, safe and sound, *all but the har!* Oh, jehu mariar, wa'an't there a squeal! 'Sakry 'mericaine' was the fust thing sung out, and I jest gin old aunty an idee that Jabe was the man, and lor didn't she comb him! He aint got the creases out'n his face yet! The ball broke hellniferous, I tell ye; old Jabe has bin ever since playin' loto with the wider to make up, but it aint no use, boys, for that pup slickin's still sticks in his teeth and no mistake!"

Amid the scream that followed, Knuckles appeared to be very unhappy; the sluggishness that had for years been settling upon his passions seemed to rise a little, and, with something like temper, he retorted:

"I reckon, Mike Fink, Aunty Tisan don't stick in my teeth half as much as Mira Hodgkiss does in your'n!"

As if he had been stung by a rattlesnake, Fink sprang to his feet! His face, first livid, grew suddenly purple, and in another half instant he had grappled Jabe by the throat, plucked him from the deck, and was in the act of hurling him overboard, when the youth Henderson left his oar, the hands gathered round, and Fink's first impulse cooled a little.

"Mira Hodgkiss! you dar to say Mira Hodgkiss, you blasted old sarpint, you! Man and woman, child and parent—years and years gone by, too—and all only waitin' for a chance to stab me! The devil in hell will be the better for it! Keep off, all on you— you too, you cussed imp of a black hearted—never mind. There's a streak of an angel in you still, I hope, or ought to be."

Fink addressed the latter words to the youth, Henderson, his son by adoption, playing, at the same time, convulsively, with an immense knife which he wore in his belt, and his features distorted by the workings of rage, hatred and malignity. Knuckles lay gazing at him in stupid amazement; the youth Henderson was shocked and grieved; and the hands, generally, accustomed as they were to Mike's "ways," were completely dumb-founded.

After further raving, Fink suddenly paused an instant, took a fresh draught of whisky from the can which he had been using, and then called to Henderson:

"Take your rifle! Go forward! If your heart is true to me, I'll know it by your shot; if not, the devil is near, and God forgive you!"

As if from a habit of mechanical obedience, the young man took up his piece, went forward to the very bow of the keel boat, and took his position. Fink again filled the can to the brim, placed it on his head, and with a savage, reckless laugh, cried 'fire!' Crack went the rifle, and the ball dashed through the tin sides so rapidly that the liquor spirted from the holes, over Fink's head, leaving the cup itself still standing! The crew gave a loud hurrah; Mike met Henderson, half-way, with a grasp that almost wrung his hand off, and then, approaching Knuckles, was about to speak more kindly, when a half a dozen voices called out, sharply,

"Steam boat!"

There she comes, yonder, round the point, and every eye and thought is directed towards her, to the oblivion of all else; for in those days a steam boat was no every day object, and while the rival craft—Mike had not yielded his supremacy—approach each other, we shall take the liberty of jumping as far back as we lately jumped forward.

The reader is sufficiently acquainted with the headlong, reckless character of Mira; Mike was at least a demi-savage, as far as the conventionalities of society went, and after a few weeks of passion, fiercely indulged and thoughtlesly regarded, they "settled down," as the saying is, into as careless a couple—happy, in their own independent way—as any of the advocates of the social system might desire to see. Mira had taken her course, assumed the responsibility, and teazed Mike with no idle importunities; in fact, the propriety of a more regular partnership in Mike's domestic arrangements hardly entered her mind. She loved him; would "go her death" for him if necessary, and in the full faith that he thought her the "greatest woman alive," she stood his whims, humors, and occasional violence. During his stay at Natchez, Mike, unsuspectingly, renewed his acquaintance with Talbott, who had kept entirely behind the curtain in the New Orleans affair. He took him on his keel up to Louisville, the man's hideous features, at first, affording a subject of mirth, but soon, in connection with his repulsive habits, rendering him an object, to Fink, of disgust and abhorrence.

"Cuss me if a dog should lick my hand," said Mike, "who could lie at the feet of that old fiend-face!"

They parted, but the acquaintance had been made, and after some months they met again at Natchez, but this time to Fink's sorrow. We must be brief. Ever a creature of wild impulse, Mike became infatuated with a female from the east— passionately, helplessly so; and Talbott it was who made the matter known in its worst light to Mira. Fury on her part led to scorn on the part of Fink, and phrenzy brought on the catastrophe. The same reckless indulgence of spleen which led her to follow Mike now drove her to abandon him and her momentary hatred prompted even to a more desperate step. Talbott was the abhorrence of her lover and through this hatred of his she saw her fullest revenge. The man was a monster to her, yet she married him!

It is not necessary to describe the scenes of violence which followed. A prey to passion, remorse, and a quenchless thirst for vengeance, Fink from that moment became less a man. Years wore on, and at the battle of New Orleans, he with his crew did gallant service, their rifles pouring death into the ranks of the enemy. Pursuing the British, too, on their retreat, at the head of a small scouting party, Fink met Talbott, and in such a questionable situation as led to a belief that he had been, and still was employed against the American interest. They had a bloody personal encounter; Talbott was nearly killed, and so they lost sight of each other. The name of Talbott, or of Mira, was never breathed within the hearing of Fink, those who knew him carefully avoiding to rouse the fury which of late years never wholly slept within him. Excitement, violence had become necessary stimulants to him, and under these evil influences, young Henderson had grown up to manhood, another Fink in his natural generosity, and, alas, in the promise of his career.

Mike had lived to see realized, partially, the dream of John Fitch. Steam boats were rapidly driving "keels" from the Ohio, and for the last few years he had been employed upon the Missouri and upper Mississippi, in carrying between the military posts on those rivers and St. Louis. His present trip was to New Orleans.

"Captain Mike, shall we give her the channel?" said the steersman, Henderson, as they neared the approaching boat. Fink's reply was to set his teeth, give a fierce snort, and grasp the heavy sweep himself. There, standing erect, he fixed his eye upon the steamer, while every muscle hardened, as it were, into granite. He had made an ineffectual attempt to reconcile matters with Knuckles, and the latter, dogged, sullen, and hurt, had gloomily held off. Mike was "*dangerous*" as the hands remarked.

"Guess ole man Jabe hasn't got shook up dat way his hull life afore!" said Doctor Gravy, who was still alive and "just as natural!"

"Ef he ain't a cryin'!" said another.

"Bin a-growin' childish ever so long!" was the remark of a third.

"Well," cried the doctor, "foolish or no, ole man Jabe was de fuss I hear say dat dem tings (pointing to the steam boat) would trabble up 'ginst strong water, one day, ef day kep' goin' on, and guess his olmynic was right dat time! De debbles hot water in dem kittles, I reckon! De patent double barrel navumgation system, *dat* is! Dis child doesn't see no use ribbers tryin' to run down stream no mo', no how!"

"Going to take the bank, aint she?" enquired Henderson, looking at his captain.

"If she does, I'll sink her!" said Fink, setting his jaws more firmly.

The were now in a bend of the river, the water was quite low, and a bar from the Illinois shore threw the current close over to the Missouri side. The steamer was laden deeply, appeared to struggle greatly with the stream, and sure enough was about to take the inside. Fink steadily held his course, swerving not an inch, either way; his keel was a very large one; he "despised a steam boat any how," to use his own words; the wicked spirit was roused within him, and without any question of courtesy or river regulation being involved in the matter, it simply suited his morose humor, at the moment, not to stir "out of his tracks!"

The ascending steamer was a small, old fashioned, "lower cabin" affair, and had a good many passengers. On her deck appeared one group that was somewhat remarkable. By the side of an old man of grizzled locks and hideous aspect stood a young girl of fifteen or sixteen—of pleasant, attractive features, of modest sensitive manners, and seated on a bench close by them was a plainly dressed and sickly looking woman, who from her worn appearance might have been forty-five, but who actually was nearly ten years younger. As they looked towards the approaching "keel," a pleasant spoken and well dressed young man addressed them.

"Captain Talbott!" said he, "times are changing on the rivers. *Cordelling* a boat like that which comes yonder against a current such as this must have been severe work! How would you like me, Miss Jane, to be on the bank, now, with a rope over my shoulder, dragging you on your way to St. Louis?"

The girl smiled with a very pleasant expression, and hoped that steam had forever banished such hardship; the elderly woman sighed heavily, Talbott at the same time giving her a glance of harshness and impatience.

"Poor mother never wants to hear talk of the river!" whispered the girl to the young man, and he, in return, gave her a glance of sympathy and interest.

"That keel will be into us if they don't mind," growled Talbott, at the same time walking forward to join the pilot of the boat, who just then was turning out into the stream.

"You've put her out too late; she'll strike us!" said Talbott.

"D———n! That's Mike Fink, or the devil!" cried the pilot.

All was confusion in an instant. An attempt to correct the error just committed hastened the catastrophe, and while a thousand orders, cries and execrations arose from the steamer, Fink, the enormous sweep firm within his grasp, stood erect at the stern of his keel, and came terribly down upon them! A crash that hurled the chimneys overboard, that tore the larboard guard and bow to pieces, and sent the water pouring through an hundred gaping seams, told the weight and force of the collision. Ropes were thrown from the steamer to the recoiling keel, but the former was already sinking. The deepest part of the channel, and, look!—down—down—and, now, a sudden lurch, and from the shelving deck every soul is swept into the stream! Among the cries, one call for help is doubly answered to. A youth plunges from the keel, with superior stroke dashes past a second youthful swimmer, who strives for the same object, and in another moment is making triumphantly for the shore with a fair burthen!

"Keel's sinking, Mike!" roared a dozen throats around that grim steersman. With a savage smile, he was directing the bow towards the bank, but a great portion of his freight was lead, and another moment would complete the disaster.

"Shore, all!" cried Fink, and instantly the fated keel was deserted by all save one. Giving a glance back, as he swam, Mike saw Jabe Knuckles sitting on the deck in the same gloomy abstraction.

"Ashore, Jabe, she's sinking!" he cried out.

Knuckles raised his eyes, fixed them reproachfully upon his old companion, friend and tyrant, crossed his arms upon his breast, but still kept his position.

"Are you going to drown, you old fool?" cried out Fink.

Jabe did not answer, but there was a movement in his throat, his lips worked, and his eyes seemed to say, "Fool or dog, Mike Fink, I have a heart to be stung by outrage from an old friend," and even so did that old friend interpret it. Wrung with remorse, Fink turned back to snatch Jabe from his fate, but even as he struck out his bold arms, the boat with its sole tenant vanished from before him, and, just beyond the spot which it had occupied, as though he was the sport of witchcraft, he saw a pale wild female face that filled his soul with horror! 'Twas real!—the eyes were turned upon him! A ghastly smile yet a familiar one flickered as it were upon the water and all was calm again, without a ripple!

"Mira!" screamed Fink. Alas, the depths of that dark stream now couched a brain ne'er more to be distraught with misery. Self infliction, outward wrong, she never more should know. Guilt, violence, despair, had wrought their work upon her, would that there were not still at hand another victim.

MIKE SETTLES A LOVE AFFAIR

Another dash forward with our story! Ascending the brown Missouri, pause at the mouth of the Yellow Stone, where, at the time we write of, the American Fur Company already had an important station.

After his wreck, Fink, grown thrice reckless and desperate, goaded as well by his own accusations as by the doubts and cold looks of those with whom he had had connections, loitered about St. Louis for a time, sunk in dissipation, and careless for the future. He was "flat broke," and, finally, he engaged himself and his "boy," Henderson, to General Wm. H. Ashley, then actively employed in the fur trade, to hunt and trap for the company, on the usual terms. Fink made his way up to the Fort, and the fire about his heart may be imagined, when almost the first man he met there was Talbott! This man had likewise been engaged, as gunsmith—a business which he had unsuccessfully pursued in Louisville, and it was on his way to this employment that he had again, after years, encountered Fink, and fatefully as usual. His wife, the wretched Mira, had been released from a load of life through the reencounter, his daughter, Jane, barely snatched from death, been thrown on his rude hands, thence to draw all she was likely to gain, wherewith to deck her mind.

If the meeting at the fort, however, was poison to Fink and Talbott, to Henderson it was quite the contrary; for the fair young creature whom he had rescued from the stream—triumphing in doing so over the more polished youth who had been her immediate companion—he now saw daily, and with a feeling powerful as new to him. Young Edwards, Jane's travelling friend, was a clerk at the post, and under all circumstances, it was very natural that himself and Henderson should be rivals. Edwards cursed the fortune which had made him second in the rescue of Jane, and Henderson gnashed his teeth, as he thought of his inferior position, and lack of the usual recommendations in female eyes. A dark cloud of passion and violence rested, as ever, above Fink and all connected with him, and for himself he roamed about with scorpions in his breast. His temper grew to be unbearable; he was a terror to all in the fort. The commanding officer, in the loose state of discipline then customary, found him unmanageable; and for the quiet ones, generally, they wished him at the devil. Henderson, too, had his disturbances, and finally Fink, in a fury, withdrew from the fort altogether, prepared a rude sort of cave in the neighborhood for his winter's den, and dragged Henderson after him to share his gloom and bitterness. All was not harmony, even between Fink and "his boy," as he called him. The former had intentionally avoided the sight of Jane—Mira's child, by the man whom, of all earth, he most abhorred; and, apart from this consideration, there was something in the idea of the offspring of Mary Benson and Mira Hodgkiss coming together, which made his blood creep! True, there was no bar of blood, but that of circumstances seemed to him equally forbidding.

"If you love me, Henderson," Fink would say, "you won't sting me by giving your heart to the flesh and blood of a domestic poisoner, and a traitor to his country. I'd rather see you dead, Henderson, and then die myself on your grave, than you should take that gal!"

The youth was silent and gloomy; Mike tetchy and suspicious, and thus, by themselves yet unsympathising, they lived together.

It was a fine bright day in January, and Edwards was walking with Jane without the fort, on a path which led towards the river. He loved the mild and friendless girl with all his sole, and looked forward to the time when he might place her in a more proper sphere, away from the rudeness and heartlessness of her father.

"But you are kind, and encouraging in your manner to Henderson," said Edwards. "He thinks you are in love with him, and, perhaps, Jane"—added he, hesitatingly, "he may not be indifferent to you?"

The girl looked at Edwards almost tearfully. She was timid, and evidently much distressed by this turn in their conversation.

"He saved my life, William, you know!—though you, you William were near me; and would have rescued me, I know it!"

"The deuce take his fortune!" cried the youth, with a swelling heart. "Of course you should be grateful," continued he, "and I own that he is a better swimmer, and better shot than I am, but—"

"He hasn't got a smooth tongue, and a mean town heart, to talk 'ginst people who haven't a chance to be heerd!" cried Henderson, advancing, rifle in hand, from a clump of trees and brush through which the path wound. Edwards drew a pistol from his belt and stood on the defensive, Jane at the same time clinging to him in terror.

"Oh, indeed, Mr. Henderson," said she, quickly, yet trembling. "Mr. Edwards never speaks of you disrespectfully. He would not do so. He is too good—too noble—"

"Oh, ha, ha, ha! That's right!" mockingly said the young demi-savage. "He's too handsome, too!—and keeps himself too nice, and sweet, and combed out; and is too fond of love-walks and—*lyin'*!" The last word was yelled out under the impulse of growing rage, and in another second both weapons were levelled, when a rifle crack was heard, and Henderson dropped the muzzle of his piece, as if he had received a sudden twinge.

"I've only creased[2] you, Henny," said Mike Fink, advancing from the other side towards the path. "Sarved you Mustang fashion, I reckon!"

2. The well known prairie feat of tumbling a wild horse by touching a nerve at the back of the head with a ball. *Sometimes* the shot is too low, however [Field's footnote].

The young man put his hand to his shoulder, and stood looking, first at Edwards and the girl, and then at Fink. He was boiling with rage, but the novelty of the check he had received and his habitual awe of the boatman restrained him.

"Young man, you'd a bin a goner in another half shake," said Mike to Edwards; and now, for the first time, he took a look at the girl. His gaze became riveted for a time, but at last his eye moistened, and he turned away.

"She's like her!" he muttered, "I'd a know'd her, poor thing; ony she's not got the same fire in her eye—nor her heart either, I hope!"

"Gal!" said he, advancing suddenly, and with over forced harshness, "these boys, yer, will shed blood on your account, ef you trifle with 'em! Tell my boy, Henderson, right off, that he's nothin' to you, and never will be!" Henderson started, and again raised his piece.

"Down with that rifle!" shouted Fink, in a tone of thunder. He was obeyed.

"Now, gal, speak." More dead than alive, the young creature turned from one to the other, incapable of utterance; at length, fixing her eyes upon Edwards, she sobbed out: "Oh, William, William, you will be killed on my account!" and buried her face in his bosom.

"Well, that's better than talkin'!" said Fink. "God bless you, gal, and make you happier than—your mother! For you, Henderson, never cross their path agin, or, my own boy as you are, you make me your enemy. Come!"

A HEART-THAW AND ITS CONSEQUENCES

Gloomily went the winter with "old Mike" as he was now discourteously called. Shut within his den, he was haunted by phantoms of past times. Mary Benson, her father, Taggart, Mira, Jabe Knuckles, and worse still, the thought of Talbott, living within reach of him, and poisoning the very air with his presence,—all combined to drive him further down the road which knows no turning. He made but one visit to the fort, and that was marked, as usual, by an act of recklessness and defiance. The regulation with regard to spirits was enforced as far as possible at the post, but still whisky found its way there, and on Mike's burrowing for the winter he had laid in somewhat of a store, for the solace of his solitude. This ran out, though, when taking his rifle he marched up to the fort, looking more like a grisly bear than a human being, gave Talbott, who stumbled upon him, a thorough start, and entered the store room. He demanded a supply of the liquor which he knew was there and was refused. At the farther end of the apartment were a number of barrels, kegs, &c., containing stores. Selecting one, he deliberately raised his rifle and drove a ball through the head of it; from the hole spirted a stream of refreshing clearness, when, taking a capacious vessel, which stood at hand, he walked across, placed it beneath the jet, and reloading his piece, cooly waited 'till it was filled.

Henderson's time passed scarcely less heavily. His thoughts still set on Jane, yet forbidden by his pride and spleen from importuning her, he was further exiled from the fort by the commands of Fink. He was heartily weary of his bondage to his old protector, and only waited the advance of spring to bid him adieu forever. Sympathy, confidence, was not to be restored between them, and constraint and coldness threw a deeper gloom round their wild quarters.

At the fort things went comfortably enough. Compelled to know her own feelings Jane had since learned to confess them, and Edwards was the happiest youth that ever posted up trapper accounts in the wilderness. Talbott selfishly saw an advantage to himself in the match, (for the young man was not without influence,) and his only dread was that Henderson might yet attempt some violence, urged by love, or that Fink might do as much impelled by hate.

While matters were in this state dark rumors began to spread concerning the two tenants of the cave. No one could exactly define their shape, or trace their origin, but they grew darker and fouler; whispers of crime, insinuations of vice, nameless in its character, and finally, through an officer at the post, they reached the ears of the suspected. Still, so artfully had the slanders been spread, that at one moment Fink himself would seem to have given birth to them, and anon Henderson might have been thought guilty. The effect on each was of course to widen the estrangement, poison thought, and fit the heart for deeds unnatural. True, Fink and Henderson both felt that their enemy, Talbott, had much to do with the matter, but they had grown to have nearly as little confidence in each other as they had in him.

Spring had come; the returning sun loosened the streams, filled the heavens with brightness and the earth with balm. Parties of trappers had returned from the mountains, everything was brisk and gay, and one day it was resolved that "all hands" should go down, in a body, and "rouse out" old Mike from his torpor. A keg of the *forbidden* was procured, and there they all were round the "Bar's den." There were trappers from the mountains; the regular hunters of the post; a number of half-breeds; half as many whole breeds, with their skins and blankets; old Jean Tisan, down from the head waters of the Missouri for the first time in three years; and last, not least, there was "Dr. Gravy," his wool full of dangling feathers, and his face painted, come to surprise "de ole hoss." "Gravy" had accompanied Mike to the fort, but had been away all winter in the mountains.

"Three cheers for old Mike Fink!" Roar after roar went up, filled the air, vibrated through the dull abode of the boatman, and finally touched the slackened strings of his own heart. True, the sounds awakened were rather of an equivocal character, but they roused him from his lethargy, and he came forth.

"De Lor! Cap'n Mike," cried the doctor, "I kim 'long down to gib you a scare; whew! arter seein' you I go right 'long take de paint off!"

Fink was indeed an "awful pattern" to look at. He shook hands with his old friends, however, and Henderson arriving from a hunt, he even felt a reviving warmth, as he looked at him. There was a fount of feeling in his heart not yet exhausted.

The keg was broached, the spirit was freely circulated, and the occasion and the season were worthy of each other—sunny, and promising still better things. "Yarns" were spun, too, of every variety; river songs were given, and, finally, "the doctor" told how he had "played bar," on one occasion.

"You see, Cap'n Mike, we was 'camped 'way off, arter makin' a *cache* near de ribber, an' dis child ob science, myself, was on de ground, an' ole *Jantisan*, dar (Jean Tisan) was close up wid him feet to de fire, an' him mouf, tudder end, wide open, an' up comes little cap'n major dar, wot'd made a bet wid old Jan 'bout gibbin' 'im a scare, and major ses—'Doctor,' ses he, 'put on dis skin'; we'd killed a 'grisly' dat same day,—'an' git right over old Jan an' grin, an I'll gib you big chunk o' 'bakker!' Well, I goes an' tries to it on, an' felt bar all over, and over ole Jan I gits, and fuss ting I gib a growl, and den I grin like the debbil—and wot you 'spose ole Jan done?"

"Tell it out," was the cry.

"Wy he ups and gibs me two poun' of snuff right in the eyes, an' bress de lor, it make 'em smart so I nebber see dat chunk o' bakker ob Cap's dar, yit!"

There was a hearty laugh, and the "Cap'n Major" spoken of promised the tobacco once more, and now Jean Tisan became the hero. He was a little weather-stained, wind-dried Frenchman, over sixty years of age, yet still one of the most active, as he was one of the oldest trappers in the employ of the company.

"Aha!" said the veteran, taking a big pinch from a special side pocket, "I was get dat trick from someting dat scratch more as grisly bear, good deal, bidam, two bettare!"

"Tell it out! Give us the yarn!" cried several.

"I get him from Madame Tisan, my wife, bidam!"

"Not old Madame Tisan, in St. Louis?" enquired Fink, who had gradually thawed into sociability, if not merriment.

"Oui, Madame Tisan, St. Louis," said the trapper. "I was no see her more zen fifteen year,—St. Louis, too, bidam! St. Louis all Yankee, and Madame Tisan all hell, vat you call, an' I say good bye to all de two! I was make St. Louis myself, wis La-

clede, mais, first ting, I marry and bring Madame over from
Caho, and next ting, contree belong to Yankee doodele, and we
have freedom, bidam, wis de constable and de jury, and tax, and
dey all help Madame Tisan to faire come ze debbil in my maison.
She make balls for de stranger, and I stay way hunt and nevare
come back, and ven I do she scratch my face to drive me away
encore, and so one time bidam, ven she give me some cuffs in
de nose, I gives her some snuffs in ze eye, and evare since she is
veuve—vat you call, Weedow Tisan!"

This *souvenir* of Mike's old acquaintance put him in great
glee; the whisky, too, was operating, and he replied to a call, by
telling several stories himself. Henderson was also in great
spirits, and when he made the first advance towards a reconciliation with his old protector, by calling on him to sing "Neal
Hornback," Mike's heart quite opened towards him. He gave
him his hand, took a "big drink" with him, and complied.

"Ye see, boys," said Mike, "Neal was boatin' up Salt river,
and Tom Johnston and me stole three kegs of whisky that he
was mighty chice about, and he went about lamentin', and
tellin' me how it was Johnston and Macdannily, and I never
lettin' on nothin'. Well, you see, it made all sorts of a larf, and
I jest made a song about it.

NEAL HORNBACK[3]

My name it are Neal Hornback
  I sail-ed from Mudford shore,
And ven-tur-ed up the Poll-ing fork,
  Where Indians' rifles roar.
Oh, the matter it are conclu-di-ed,
  It are hard for to unbin-d,
I waded the forks of Salt riviere,
  And left my kegs behind.

An hour or two before day,
  I pick-ed up my gun,

3. Neal Hornback is a veritable Mike Fink ditty, composed by the boatman himself. Col. Charles Keemle, of the *St. Louis Reveille*, took down the
words from Mike, on the Missouri, the year that Fink was killed. Fink used
to sing the song with a rich sobriety, enjoying the burlesque of it fully
[Field's footnote].

Returned to my periogue,
    And saw the mischief done.
I laid it on Tom John-sti-on,
    Who were innercent and clear,
But for to destroy my charac-ture,
    It plainly did appear.

I call-ed my friends er-round me,
    And thus to them did s-a-a-a-y,
Macdannilly and Tom John-sti-on,
    Have stored my kegs er-way.
Oh, if they are the lads whot stoled your kegs
    They have done the verri thing,
And if your kegs are miss-ing,
    You'll not see them er-gin.

Neal's body it were enormer-ous,
    His legs were long and slim,
Good Lord, it would make you sor-ri,
    Was you to look on him.
He were crook'd back'd, hump'd shoulder-ed
    And with thick lips is blessed,
And for to make him ug-i-ly,
    The Lord has done his best.

A storm of applause followed the song, and Mike once more was in his glory!

"Henny," cried he, seizing Henderson by the hand, "swop shots and be my own son agin'!"

The proposal called forth three cheers; cups were filled, rifles were seized, and the two best shots in Missouri took their stations one hundred yards from each other. A scene of this kind has already been described. Shooting objects off his boy's head was one of Mike's earliest feats on the river, and, in time, the boy grew to be no less expert. It was Mike's boast that their skill, nerve, and trust in each other might be thus tested, and at any moment. They stood ready, with their pieces.

"Look out, old Mike!" said one of the men from the fort, "he'll pay you now!" The words meant nothing, but they caused a shade to fall upon the brow of the boatman.

"Fire!" said he. Fink felt a quick, partially stunning blow on the top of his head, he raised his hand and his matted hair was wet with blood—the ball had torn up the scalp and glanced off; at the same moment, looking from a clump of trees, some distance beyond Henderson, he saw Talbott! Fink's heart was on fire; his hand trembled; could his "boy" have meant to harm him? His eye wavered.

"Henderson," said he, "I taught you to shoot better than that!"

He raised his rifle, fired, and the ball crashed through the forehead of the young man, who, falling to the earth, was immediately surrounded by the crowd.

"That job was a pretty plain one!" said Talbott, coldly as he sauntered up.

Fink, on his knees beside the body, heard not the foul insinuation.

"LAST SCENE OF ALL"

The breath of May stole wooingly along the earth; a velvet sward invited the footstep, and the pleasant shadow of the young leaves fell as an airy mantle around Edwards and his fair young Jane, as they left the fort one morning to visit "poor Mike Fink,"—for, spite of all—violence, even the suspicion of blood foully shed—there were those who still followed him with thoughts of kindness and forgiveness. The young couple whom we speak of certainly had cause to remember the boatman gratefully.

"Your father is very wrong, Jane, in his persecution of Fink. He is a crushed and broken man, and his despair and desolation since the death of Henderson, should convince all hearts and soften them, too. The act was not a malicious one."

"Oh, no, no," cried Jane; "my father himself cannot think so; but their enmity has been so bitter!"

"He calls him, publicly, a murderer, Jane, and the faithful negro who alone has clung by Fink, or been permitted to do so, says that the unhappy man is wounded to the soul by the imputation."

"Shall we be safe in approaching him," enquired the girl, "or shall we not offend, rather? He shuns every body."

"We will see 'the Doctor' as he is called, first," said Edwards.

At this moment the negro appeared a short distance before them on the path, waiting, as it would seem, for the young man.

"How is he this morning?" asked Edwards.

"Dyin' for sure! Massa Ned," was the reply. "He won't drink de whisky you sent down—not de fuss drop," continued the negro; "an' you know, Massa Ned, it's bref in de mouf to dem as had drinked like Cap'n Mike."

Fink, had, indeed, not tasted spirit since his unhappy act. With a firm will, 'though it was, in his case, the only means of sustaining his shattered system, he put it from him. Food was almost an equal stranger to his stomach, and so was he rapidly and knowingly sinking to the grave.

"He don't sleep, nuther," said the black, sadly, "no mo' dan a wolf! Soon as night come, he go out on de grave, and dar he lay 'till day, and den he goes back in de dark agin. He's on de grave, now," added 'Gravy,' "an' reckon it's kase he can't git up. I bin to him, but he tells me 'no, go 'way.' He want to die dar, for sure!"

The black led them towards a gully which sloped to the river. The upper part of this was tolerably smooth in its descent; one side was higher than the other, and a natural cavity here had been enlarged and arranged by Fink, for his quarters. There was an easy ascent of a few steps from the cave to the top of the bank, which was finely shaded by trees; this had been the scene of Henderson's death, and there, now, was his grave.

Passing round the head of the hollow, Edwards and Jane entered a thick grove of trees, the underwood serving further as their screen, and from this spot they obtained a sight of him whom they were seeking. The grave was at the foot of a tree, and here Fink lay prostrate, his head and breast upon the mound, and his arms thrown across, as if embracing it. He was so still, so motionless, that he seemed already dead, and Edwards thought he was so. The young man stepped forward hastily, but the noise at once roused Fink who raised his head, gave an impatient cry as he saw that he was intruded upon and staggered to his cave. His appearance was frightful, unearthly; his features were hardly distinguishable amid the mass of hair which spread over his whole face, but the light from his dark, deep, sunken eyes streamed forth, nevertheless, showing that vitality was still strong within him.

"Poor Mike Fink!" sighed the young couple, as they continued their walk by another path.

It was noon; the few persons left in charge of the fort (the main force was again off toward the mountains,) were employing themselves carelessly about, when Fink, his rifle across his arm (when did he ever move abroad without it) entered the gate, crossed the area, and disappeared within a doorway which led to the armory. This apartment was the last of a suite of store rooms, &c., remote and somewhat private in its character. Talbott, suddenly raising his head from his work, saw Fink advancing, with his rifle, as described, through the outer division. Snatching up a loaded piece he called to him:

"If you come nearer you're a dead man, Fink!"

"I'm come to speak to you, Talbott," said Mike, "about old matters; about my boy!"

The gunsmith had been taken quite by surprise; he was himself treacherous and vile, and he saw in Fink's visit only an attempt to take a vengeful advantage.

"Don't cross that door, Fink," cried he, nervously, "don't; I give you warning!"

"I must speak to you about Henderson," repeated Fink, still advancing.

"Another step, and by—"

The step was taken, but it was Mike's last. A sharp report rang through the apartment, and the boatman fell heavily, holding his rifle up as he struck the ground, but making no attempt to use it.

"Well, now you feel safe," said he, with more of sadness than reproach, "and can listen to me for a minute."

The gunsmith, in his dastardly nature, could hardly trust his triumph. He was even more nervous than before, but Fink was, evidently, at length his victim, and soon his composure and venom returned together.

"I've saved you from the gallows, that's all that can be said!" cried he, exultingly. "Mike Fink, the Boatman! Ha! ha! I felt a day was coming, ha! ha! ha! Old scores will be paid at last. Mira, Natchez, New Orleans, Mississippi river, and some other accounts! ha! ha! ha!"

"God forgive my share of all of them!" said Fink, fervently, as, without attempting to staunch a wound in his breast, his hands still sought his crimsoned bosom.

"And some other accounts!" repeated Talbott. "D'ye remember Benson, and the dance house in the swamp? Benson died in the chain-gang, finally, but I first planned that matter! And do you remember Mary Benson's wedding night? Talbott has owed you something of a grudge for that; but there's another hasn't forgotten it—Taggart, and he stands before you!"

"My God!" said the dying man, as a stream of ghastly light seemed to flow in upon him. "Taggart! you, Taggart? Yes, there couldn't a-bin two such!"

"Yes; Taggart, whom you drove from the side of his bride— from Mary! whom your rifle rendered a fright and a monster for life, on the shore of Arkansaw; whom you have never known, save as another, yet hating and being hated in return, just the same!"

Fink, partially raising himself, had fixed his eyes upon the man with deepening horror.

As he listened, big drops of sweat beaded upon his forehead; his frame shook; a groan burst from the very depths of his bosom—but suddenly, like on the dispersion of a storm, a smile beamed forth; his air became calm, and with a sad but grateful voice he cried:

"My heart, after all, did not deceive me! A man aint lost entirely whose soul always whispers him when the devil's near! Taggart, Henderson, my boy, whom you've accused me of mur-

dering, was Mary's child, your own son! And you—you, yourself, with your lies and slanders caused his death, for doubt of
treachery unnerved me!"

The gunsmith stared in surprise, as he listened, but spoke
not.

"Jane, too, your other child—Mira's child! Henderson was
mad arter her; but my heart was still right! Mira seemed to
warn me! Thank me for saving you that sin and anguish, Taggart. Your gal, with an innocent hand, may yet—smooth your
death pillow—God—bless her!"

Loss of blood, excitement here overcame him; his brain
turned; his eye glared, and his mind began to wander.

"I'll bring back your daughter, Hodgkiss," murmured he. "It
was my fault, poor gal!—and little Henny—no mother, and no
friends,—laid in the earth, too, cold and bloody, and his face
turned from me."

Edwards and Jane had returned to the fort, and, more by
accident than design, now entered the armory. Shocked and
horror-stricken, they sought to render the dying man assistance.
Fink, recalled a moment to his senses, seemed to recognize
them, and making an effort to join their hands, his last words
were:

"I didn't mean to kill my boy!"

Thus died Mike Fink, and, as if fate had but one end reserved for all those who through life had been woven in his
chequered history, Talbott—or Taggart—a few weeks afterwards, driven from the fort more by his guilty imagination than
by any fear of arrest, was drowned in an attempt to cross the
Missouri.

A tender shoot alone remained of these wild, gnarled forest
plants, and in June, nature seemed kindly bent on recalling the
species to beauty, grace and order. Years have passed, but still,
in a fair town on the Missouri bank, resided a couple, who,
blessed with all that can make home serene, recall, at moments,
earlier, ruder days, and drop a tear to poor Mike, "The Last of
'the Boatmen.'"

Lige Shattuck's Reminiscence of
Mike Fink (1848)

N̲O̲ ̲N̲A̲M̲E̲ ̲W̲A̲S̲ ̲S̲I̲G̲N̲E̲D̲ to the following anecdote when it
appeared in the St. Louis Reveille, February 28, 1848. The
general pattern is a long-time favorite in American humor: a
rustic or frontiersman tells an impossible story to a visitor, and
the visitor is taken in. Mike Fink, it happens, is featured in the
story; but the tall tale might have concerned any hard-drinking
frontiersman, and all frontiersmen were then reputed to be hard
drinkers. There is no evidence for or against accepting this as
part of the oral lore about the famous keeler. Interestingly,
about a hundred years after it appeared, Van Wyck Brooks
appears to have taken this stretcher seriously. In his book, The
World of Washington Irving (New York, 1945), he says
solemnly that Fink "was supposed to have eaten a buffalo-skin."

A New England passenger on one of our steamers was inquir-
ing very anxiously for an introduction to an old Mississippi
boatman, one who knew something about Mike Fink. The clerk
informed him that an introduction was unnecessary; if he would
go up and talk to the pilot he might learn from him the whole
history of the old boatman. Up went the Yankee, and after
circuiting round Lige two or three times, he spoke:

"How d'ye dew, pilot—they say yeou are an old friend of
Mike Fink's."

"Knew him like a brother," said Lige.

"Well, now dew tell me something about him, some anecdote," requested the New Englander.

"I don't know as I recollect any real bright one just now—I
do recollect his taking a prescription once."

"What was that?" eagerly inquired the stranger.

"Why, he eat a whole buffalo robe," answered Lige, with the greatest gravity imaginable.

"Well, dew tell! What in patience did he masticate that for?" further inquired the stranger.

Lige turned round to the other pilot, and, winking his eye, observed: "He's sold, ain't he, Jim?"

"You ain't told me what he chawed the buffalo robe for," continued the New Englander.

"Why, the fact is," says Lige, "the doctors told him he had lost the coating of his stomach, and as he drank nuthin' but New England rum, he thought he'd dress his insides up in suthin' that 'ud stand the cussed pizen stuff, so he tried buffalo with the har on, and it helped him mightily."

The anxious inquirer was satisfied.

Mike Fink: A Legend of the Ohio (1848)

EMERSON BENNETT

EMERSON BENNETT, born on a Massachusetts farm in 1823, wandered around for a time, then tried his luck as a writer. In New York and Philadelphia he was unsuccessful, and after a love affair had ended unhappily, he headed West. About 1844, in Cincinnati, he was barely existing by selling linen-stamps and peddling magazine subscriptions. One day in a cheap restaurant he heard two men talking enthusiastically about a story in the Cincinnati Commercial. Recognizing some of the details mentioned, he asked to see the newspaper. He found that the story was one which he had submitted, without success, in a Philadelphia contest.

The incident was a turning point. He was hired by the Commercial, and he started to turn out one thriller after another about the West. Serialized in newspapers, some of these hoisted circulation; when issued in book form, they also sold well—some as many as a hundred thousand copies. Within a few years he was a rich man, banqueted by many admirers. He lived in a mansion, hired several servants, and drove spirited trotters.

Mike Fink: A Legend of the Ohio, published in 1848, went through at least three editions. This, like other books by Bennett, was a sort of a primordial dime novel, although it sold for a larger price. It does not, its author admits a bit sheepishly in the Preface, "give a veritable history of Mike Fink, as some might suppose from reading the title page." Such a history might, he goes on, be interesting but it would be inappropriate for a romance. Moreover, he questions that a "strictly authentic" account is possible, "from the fact that I have myself made thorough inquiries of such persons as were thought to know something of his history without being able to glean any thing of him beyond a few vague unsatisfactory suppositions, and occasionally some spicy anecdotes which . . . were very foreign to the purpose. I have also searched every record concerning him that has come to my knowledge, with no other result than to learn his general characteristics, which I have faithfully endeavored to transcribe. . . ." This seems honest enough, though from what appears in his book, it is probable that even this modest statement exaggerates his research: he seems to have found whatever material he used in the 1828 sketch by Neville and the 1829 sketch in the Western Monthly Review. But he made the most of what he knew, doing quite a job of building up suspense when he told of Mike's shooting off the Negro's heel or shooting the cup.

Also, as one would expect of so prolific a novelist, he showed some powers of invention. For one thing, he invented dialogue quite in keeping with Mike's character—some of it excellent. For another, he hit upon the happy idea of getting Mike and his crew into a tangle with the legendary outlaws of Cave-in-Rock. The river pirates who actually operated from that base had been opponents worthy of Fink, and though they had never had quite so bloody and picturesque a chief as Bennett's Camilla, Camilla was not so unlike such historical chiefs as Mason and the Harpes as one might suppose.

In the fashion of the day, Bennett dealt in most of his novel with a pair of pretty and sugary lovers, Maurice and Aurelia. Typical of their kind, they caused a great deal of trouble by getting captured by the outlaws and being unable to help themselves. In addition they had all sorts of problems to solve and many sappy love scenes to go through. Lacking space for the whole novel, we have omitted from the condensation which follows these and much of the sentimental melodrama, concentrating on Mike and his crew and their adventures. The various headings are adapted from Bennett's.

THE BOATMAN • THE FORTUNE-TELLER

It was on a beautiful spring morning, in the beginning of the present century, that along the river at Cincinnati, which at this period was only a small town, containing less than a thousand inhabitants, lay several keel-boats and broad-horns,[1] the crews of which were busy in loading them with freight of different kinds for the up and down river trade. Of these boats, only one, and this of the former class, seemed completely laden, and ready to push into the stream; on the deck of which the crew, some six or eight stalwart fellows, were lounging about in careless attitudes, apparently awaiting the arrival of some person or persons who were momentarily expected, judging from the manner in which they from time to time glanced almost impatiently toward the main thoroughfare of the village. Three of the individuals in question were separarated from the rest, and were conversing together near the bow of the boat.

"Well, ef they don't show themselves right soon," said one, "hang me up for bar-meat, ef I don't push off without 'em— that's the way to say it."

The speaker was a tall, powerful man, some twenty-eight years of age. His stature was rising of six feet, and his frame and limbs, though perfectly symmetrical, were very muscular, denoting one of great strength. His hair was thick and coarse, of a coal-black, and his complexion very dark, owing, probably, to long exposure to the weather in all its various changes. His features were rough, and rather coarse, but expressive of some intelligence. He had a light gray eye, which, though it never sparkled under any circumstances, sometimes softened from its naturally cold, stern expression to one of quiet humor. His cheek-bones were large and prominent, his nose very long, his mouth and chin well-formed, thereby adding a look of firmness and decision to the whole countenance. In pleasant repose, there was something about his physiognomy rather attractive

1. More commonly termed flat-boats [Bennett's note].

and calculated to inspire confidence and familiarity; but at the same time it was plainly evident that the lion was there and that when once angrily aroused he would become a dangerous being to trifle with. His dress was somewhat singular, though characteristic of the time and his profession. Next to his body he wore a red flannel shirt, open about the breast and neck, over which hung a loose blue jerkin barely extending to the upper part of his hip. Coarse linsey trowsers were secured round his waist by a leather belt, to which was attached a sheath, concealing all but the handle of a long hunting-knife. Upon his feet he wore moccasins, and on his head a singular-looking cap, roughly formed from the untanned skin of some wild beast.

The two companions to whom the individual just described addressed himself, though bearing no manner of resemblance to him, were still very far from being refined specimens of humanity. One of them was very tall, gaunt, ill-proportioned, with long bony limbs, a sharp thin face, small blue eyes, light delicate eyebrows, a peaked nose, a tremendous mouth, thin lips, sloping chin, sandy hair, and freckled skin, whose age might be thirty-five, and the characteristic expression of whose countenance was humor and drollery. The other was his opposite in every particular. In height he would not exceed five feet, was square-built, had a large long body, and short legs, that caused him to waddle whenever he walked or ran. His arms were long and brawny, and his head, barely raised above his shoulders by a short bull-neck, was enormously large, whereon was a countenance the general expression of which denoted the predominance of the animal over the intellectual and, to a stranger, would have been exceedingly repulsive. His face was wide, with a broad, flat nose, and one small black fiery eye; the other having been gouged out in a fight some time previous to the date of our story, and was now covered with a brown patch. His eyebrows were dark and shaggy and, joining in the center, extended across the nether portion of his low, retreating forehead, and added a look of sullen fierceness to his otherwise unpleasing countenance.

Yet, notwithstanding an aspect so unattractive, the individual in question was not so bad at heart as many another of an exterior more polished, an air more refined, and a countenance more smooth and smiling. He had some peculiarities which, though not intentional on his part, were ever productive of mirth at his expense. He used tobacco in every form, and could seldom be found without a large quid between his capacious jaws; besides this, he stuttered exceedingly and was in the habit of using high-flown words with but little regard to their proper signification, which not unfrequently produced an effect extremely ludicrous. He was known among the boatmen by the sobriquet of Jack Short, though doubtless this was not his original appellation.

"So y-y-you think you'll disembark, eh! Mike?" said Jack, in reply to the first speaker, who was none other than the veritable Mike Fink himself. "Think y-yo-you'll move on to-to the flu-fluctuating current, eh?—for a more s-s-salu-bri-brious clime, eh? W-w-well, g-g-go your death on't, ef you s-s-plit on a sandbar, M-M-Mike"; and the speaker gave the quid in his mouth an extra turn, and expectorated very freely.

"Why," rejoined Mike, "I don't think thar's any use in our sunning ourselves here much longer like alligators on a mud-bank, unless we can git up a row to keep our j'ints from being marrow dried. What say you, Dick Weatherhead?"

"Why, I'll tell you what," answered Dick, the individual described as tall, gaunt, and bony; "let's go and see old Mother Deb, the fortin-teller, to see whether we're going to be hanged or drowned."

"Hooray for Deb! she's a land-screamer, I've heerd," cried Fink; "and so here goes fur a trial."

Saying which, and without more ado, he sprang ashore, and followed by his two companions, at once set off for the residence of Deborah Mowrin, better known among the river men as old Mother Deb, the fortune-teller.

Turning to the left, the trio pursued their course along what is now called Front street, which could then boast but a few scattering houses, till they had passed Main street some two hundred yards, when, taking a narrow path that led into the open field, they continued to advance toward a small, miserable-looking hovel, which, standing solitary and alone, formed the extreme boundary of the village in that direction. On approaching the building in question, our worthies found the door and shutters closed, while every thing about the structure bespoke it uninhabited. However, this did not deter Mike and his companions from making several attempts to gain admittance, by trying the door and shutters, rapping hard, and hallooing lustily. For some time their efforts were without avail, and concluding the old woman was absent, they were about to give up and turn back, when Mike swore he would make one more trial with his fist on the door, and if no one answered to the summons, he would break it down on his own account.

This he said in a voice sufficiently loud to be heard by any one within; and as he concluded, he raised his brawny arm, and made the old house tremble to its center.

"Open, Deb," cried Fink, "or by all the fishes of the Dead Sea, I'll snag this old door in less time nor a Massassip alligator can chaw up a puppy!"

"G-g-go it, Mike," cried Jack Short, waddling to and fro, taking a rapid survey of the old edifice with his one eye, and giving his large quid a few extra turns. "G-g-go it, Mike, I say. G-g-give the old thing a few l-l-lugubrious salutations with y-y-your p-p-ponderosity."

At this moment one of the shutters slightly opened, and displayed a small portion of an old woman's head, and a red flannel skull-cap.

"Who are ye, and what d'ye want?" cried a shrill, tremulous voice.

"We want our fortins told, Mother Deb," answered Dick Weatherhead, striding forward toward the old woman.

"And d'ye thinks I can tell 'em?" rejoined the other, inquiringly.

"In course ye can," replied Dick; "'cause that's your trade.

Every body to thar business, from rowing a flat up to preachin'
the Scriptures, say I."

"T-t-that's right, Dick," cried Jack, enthusiastically. "I-I like
them q-q-qu-quadrangular t-t-touches, Dick; by G-G-Goliah, I
do"; and the speaker took occasion to empty and refill his
mouth.

"Well, hold on a minute, and I'll gin ye entrance," said the
old woman; and forthwith the head and skull-cap disappeared
from the window, and reappeared at the door.

Entering the residence of Deborah Mowrin, our river worthies
found themselves in a small, dark, noisome apartment, containing as furniture an old rickety table, a miserable pallet of straw
in one corner, two or three iron kettles, used for cooking, and a
few rough, three-legged stools. Bidding them be seated, the fortune-teller proceeded to throw open the shutters, thereby displaying her ungainly person in full light.

She was a small, inferior-looking being, with sharp, shrewd
features, so withered and wrinkled by age and covered with dirt
as to make their expression extremely repulsive. For lack of
teeth, her cheeks had fallen in, and her nose and chin seemed
bent on paying each other a long visit. Her eyes were small and
fiery, with which she now peered curiously at the boatmen, as if
to read their thoughts. In one long, skinny hand she held a
hickory staff, the handle of which was a horse-shoe, nailed on to
protect her from witches.[2] Her dress consisted of a dirty brown
wrapper, or loose gown, and the before-mentioned red flannel
cap, drawn tightly over the crown of her head, beneath which
her long flaxen hair fell down around her neck and shoulders in
sad disorder, and added a wildness to her otherwise hideous appearance.

"Well," said Mike, after surveying her a moment in silence,

2. Fifty years ago it was currently believed by many of the most respectable people in the country that a horse-shoe nailed on to a staff, or
over the doors and windows of a dwelling, was a sure safeguard against
witches; and the author is personally acquainted with an old woman who
follows the practice of so guarding herself and house even at the present day
[Bennett's note].

"ef you can't tell fortins, old woman, 'tain't because thar arn't no resemblance 'tween you and the critters what ride broomsticks through the air when honest folks sleep. Bile me fur a sea-horse, ef I wouldn't rather crawl into a nest o' wild-cats, heels foremost, than be cotched alone with you in the nighttime."

"Silence!" cried the old crone, angrily, producing a dirty pack of cards, "or I won't tell ye nothing."

"O, ef it comes to that, I'm dumb as a dead nigger in a mudhole," rejoined Mike, giving his companions the wink. "So push ahead, Deb, and don't run agin a sawyer, or you'll sink afore you can catch breath enough to make a rigular blow on't."

"Shall I begin with you?" inquired the fortune-teller, arranging her cards as she spoke.

"Yes, blaze away," answered Mike; "I can stand it, I reckon; for I've stood the fire of a dozen Injens afore now, without winking. Give us a quarter's worth, Deb, and don't stop to chaw your words."

"N-n-no, Mother Deb, g-g-give your l-l-language c-c-circumlocution and fluency, l-l-like I do," added Jack.

The old woman made no reply, but passing the cards to Fink, motioned him to draw from the pack; which done, she examined the selected ones, for a moment or two, very attentively, and then shuffling all together, presented the pack again. This was repeated some three or four times, when at length she said, abruptly:

"Ha' ye got a wife and child, stranger, or any one ye cares for?"

"What's that to you?" answered Mike. "I came here to git my fortin told, not to tell it myself."

"'Cause ef you have," continued Deborah, "let 'em pray for you!"

"Well, that's consoling," rejoined Mike, "I s'pose I'm to die, then."

"Every body's got to die sometime," replied the other, evasively.

"But me in particular, a little sooner, I reckon," responded Mike. "Well, blaze away, my broomstick rider, and tell us when it's to come off, and how."

"As to when, I'll give ye no answer; as to how, why, bloody," returned the old woman, impressively, "you needn't fear hanging nor drowning."

"J-j-jest t-tell me that s-s-satisfactory inwention," interposed Jack, moving his quid round with great rapidity, and making a spittoon of one of the old woman's kettles, that stood by his side. "T-t-tell me that I won't be h-hanged nor drowned, and you c-c-can jest t-take my surplus rev-revenue; by H-H-Helfenstein, you can!"

"Hold!" cried the old crone, turning fiercely to him, her small red eyes flashed angrily. "I'll tell ye your end now, for interrupting me. You shall die a dog's death!—by the spirits of Pluto's infernal regions, you shall!"

"G-g-good for you, Deb," retorted Jack, with a roar of laughter.

"Come, come, Mother She-wolf, row ahead, or you'll be aground afore you know it," cried Mike. "And, what's more, my angel, I hain't got a thousand years to spare; so blossom out, like a punched painter, and let us have the worst on't."

"I've a mind not to tell ye any more," returned the fortune-teller, "jest to pay ye for lettin' me be interrupted; for I sees by your eye, you're the head man of the three."

"O, well," returned Mike, evidently feeling himself complimented by the closing remarks of the other, "rush ahead, my beauty, and never mind such a snag as Jack here, who has to open his jaws once 'n a while, to blow like a porp'ise, else he'd choke to death like a cat-fish on a sand-bank. He didn't much, no how, though he was a right smart while a trying to. Jack," continued the speaker, addressing that individual more directly, "jest keep that ugly fly-trap o' yourn shut, till Deb here gits through, or I'll have to close it with something less easy to chawr nor torbacker."

"I-I'm dumb as a l-l-leviathan," replied Jack.

"All clear now, Deb," said Mike. "Take the chute[3] and run her through."

"First, then," rejoined Deborah, "let me caution you agin strangers, and to go guarded. Thar'll somebody cross your path afore long, that'll be mixed up with your fate, and for whom you'll run your life in danger, even ef you don't lose it. That somebody's a female."

"Bless her soul!" cried Fink, enthusiastically interrupting the other; "Run my life in danger, say you? Why, take the whole blessed race on 'em together, and each one's enough to run the d———(I beg pardon, Deb—didn't mean to be personal, no how); I say each one's enough to run—let me see—to run Dick Weatherhead's legs off; and they're long enough to pole a boat up the Massassip, in a high stage of water."

"Nothing like long under-pinins fur travel," rejoined Dick, satisfactorily, displaying, at the same time, an article of loco-motion, measuring a little less than four feet.

"I said ye must bewar' o' strangers," continued the old woman, unmindful of the interruptions; "and in particular o' a large, dark-visaged man, with heavy-black whiskers, who you'll also meet afore long, and who'll be dangerous to ye. Three times your life'll be in great peril; but ef you survive these ere three, you've many years afore ye; yit, as I said afore, your end'll be bloody!"

"Well, it's o' no use a whining for what's got to be," rejoined Mike. "As well might a stuck wild-cat think o' hollering for mercy. One thing's sartin, though; ef any one feller gits the bet-ter o' me, in a rough and tumble, or any way he pleases, I'll for-give him, though his roll o' sins be as long as Dick Weather-head's ugly carcass. But how do you know all this, Deb?"

"By the invincible spirits o' Pluto," answered the fortune-teller, solemnly.

"O, you deal in spirits, eh?" returned Mike, winking at his

3. A word in general use among the boatmen, signifying the channel, or main current of the river [Bennett's note].

companions. "Well, so do I, though I 'spect we differ in the article. Jest give me enough o' mine, though, and ef I don't beat you in this here business, I'll agree to swoller a bar, tail-eend foremost, and climb a peeled and greased saplin' heels up'ard. But crowd her through, my beauty, for I'm in a hurry."

"I'll tell ye no more," rejoined Deborah, her small eyes gleaming fiercely. "You've dared to make fun o' my powers, and ye shall hear no more from me."

"But arn't we agoing to pay you for't, my lovely?"

"Keep your base coins!" cried the old crone, more angry than ever. "Think ye I'm a begger, to be a slave to your wishes? You've insulted me," she continued, striding up and down the miserable apartment, and gesticulating wildly. "You've insulted me, I say; but that's nothing; I could forgive ye that; but you've insulted the powers I sarve; and that I never will forgive. Begone! Begone with ye, I say!—or woe betide ye!"

"Wh-why, you're gittin' s-s-sonorously diabolical, arn't ye?" queried Jack, working his immense jaws, and rolling his one eye from Mike to Deb, and from Deb to Mike, with great rapidity, as one who is looking to dodge a blow from either side.

"Well, ef it's all up, I 'spect we mought as well start our trotters, boys," said Mike; "for we'll catch the fever and ager, sure, ef we stay here much longer; and that'll shake the daylights out o' us."

In less than an hour from the foregoing events, the beautiful keel-boat, Light-foot, Mike Fink patron, was swimming gracefully down the smooth glassy surface of La Belle Riviere. The boat in question was a handsome specimen of its class, and seemingly rightly named; for great care had been bestowed on its construction; in making it of the lightest draught possible, so that it could be towed up stream without difficulty. In shape it was not unlike the canal-boats of the present day, with a cabin for passengers, very neatly and tastefully furnished. There was, besides, ample room for freight, which, on the present occasion, consisted of produce, destined for the lower country markets.

The day in question was a most delightful one, and on the deck of the Light-foot, as she swam slowly onward,

"Like a thing of life,"

with the tiny waves of silver rippling musically against her sides, stood, near the bow, a group of individuals, occupied in gazing upon the waters, the green and flowery banks of the river, and the village of Cincinnati,·now every moment growing more and more distant, with that quiet, pleased and satisfied look expressed on each of their faces which the day and the scene around them was calculated to inspire in breasts not otherwise occupied by important matters.

THE RAPIDS • THE MARKSMAN • THE INVISIBLE FOE

At the time of which we write, the Falls of the Ohio, at Louisville, were looked upon by the pioneer pilots of keel-boats and broad-horns with much the same sense of awe and fear as was, in the early settlement of New York, that dangerous passage connecting East River with Long Island Sound known to the mariner far and near by the ominous title of Hell-gate. These falls, however, present little that is attractive or alarming to one not familiar with river navigation. They are simply the rapids of an inclined plane, whose main channel is zig-zag and rocky, over which the water, in a low stage, boils and foams on its swift descent from the upper level. These falls, as we said before, were held in awe by the early boatmen of the river, who knew that a single mistake of the helmsman or pilot would result in their frail craft being dashed to pieces on the surrounding rocks, and their own lives, to say the least, being placed in great jeopardy; in consequence whereof, they were never approached without much anxiety and apprehension.

At this point it is we come once more upon the Light-foot, which, in the preceding chapter, we left slowly and gracefully gliding down the glassy surface of the beautiful Ohio. In due time she had arrived at Louisville—at this period, like Cincin-

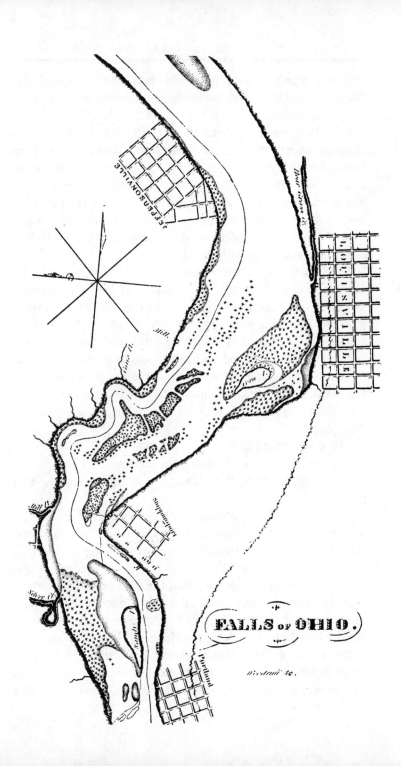

FALLS of OHIO.

nati, only a small village—where she had both discharged and taken on freight, and, at the moment presented, was preparing to pass the rapids.

Mike Fink on the present occasion stood at the helm; and along the deck of the vessel, with their poles and sweeps in their hands, were ranged the crew, ready to obey his slightest command; while the passengers previously described, together with others who had got aboard at Louisville, were in the cabin below, awaiting in much anxiety the moment which would place them in comparative safety, or dash them upon the rocks, and leave them struggling with the rushing waters.

"Bow to the right, thar—hard over!" shouted Mike, as the Light-foot now shot into the current and began to advance directly toward the first little whirlpool of the rapids, with a gradually increasing velocity.

"Stand ready now, boys—every one o' ye to your post!" continued Fink, as he noted with an experienced eye each slight bubble or commotion of the waters, indicating the narrow channel through which his boat must be guided, while he stood by the helm like a Hercules, with every nerve braced, ready for any emergency.

"All right ahead thar?"

"All right!" answered a voice from the bow.

"Give her the chute, then! Thar, thar, she goes!—steady, all—steady!"

As he spoke, the Light-foot touched the rapids, trembled for a moment in every timber, and then darted forward with the most frightful celerity through the many windings of that difficult channel. Now was the period of intense excitement and breathless suspense, as onward shot the light craft, with terrible velocity—now plunging, to all appearance, directly upon a rock, and, just as the more timid and inexperienced were about to utter a cry of fear and despair, yielding to the strong hand and unerring eye of the gallant steersman and darting away in another direction, apparently to produce the same sad catastrophe but ending in the same harmless manner. On, on she dashes, amid the roar and foam of the boiling waters, every plank and timber groaning, creaking, and trembling, like a frightened thing of life. On, on, she rushes, casting the sparkling spray from her beautiful sides and prow, while every tongue aboard her is mute, every eye fixed intently upon the roaring waters, and every heart beating wildly. On, on she plunges in fury, like to the wounded leviathan of the mighty deep, while at the helm stands one, calm and collected, whose steady eye and iron arms still guide her aright. On, on—still on—ha! that rock!—she strikes!—yet, no—no—she has passed it!—and now—now with a bound, as of joy, she leaps into the deep, calm waters once more, and glides smoothly forward, throwing the silvery particles from her prow, while a simultaneous shout from the excited boatmen announce that all is safe.

"Be the howly St. Pathrick!" cried Pat Flannegan, "It's meself that's niver going over that same spot, widout remimbering all me sins, and crossing meself a couple o' times or so, jist to keep the divil away, sure; and bad luck to't for a dirthy place, an' it is."

"Dirty!" echoed Dick Weatherhead; "why, Pat, what in thunderation would ye call clean, ef a place o' running water, like that is, arn't?"

"To the divil wid ye now," replied Pat, "for taking a feller up for mis-spaking a word of Inglish, jist."

"T-that's right; gi-give him the s-s-sententious settlers, Pat," put in Jack Short, winking his one eye, and stirring up the weed afresh.

"Well, boys, we're over now," said Mike, coming forward, "and who wants to bet me the whisky on thirty paces?"

"I'll do it," cried Dick, "jest to see ye shoot, Mike: for it acterly does a feller good to see that thar rifle o' yourn come up to your peepers, and then git so solid like, and blaze away."

Mike now gave orders to have the boat run in to the shore, during which operation most of the passengers came on deck, and learning that he was about to exhibit his skill as a marksman, became eager for the sight.

"Whar is Carpenter?" asked Mike.

"Here I am," replied a lad of fourteen, coming up from the cabin.

"Is your skull fit to butt a nigger's today, Bill?" continued Mike, addressing the boy.

"Why, I don't know's it's quite so thick as all that comes to," was the reply; "but ef you want to shoot, Mike, I'll venter it's bullet-proof, any how."

"That's the talk, my peacock," rejoined Fink; "so heave ahead, and let's have a pull, for I'm getting as dry as a salted herrin'."

By this time the boat had reached the right-hand bank of the river; and quitting her at once, the whole party, some eight or ten persons, headed by Fink himself, with his long rifle lying carelessly across his left arm, proceeded to select a convenient spot for deciding the wager.

In a few minutes a suitable place was found: thirty yards were paced off by Dick Weatherhead, when the boy advancing to the farther extremity placed a tin cup on his head, and looking Mike coolly in the eye, exclaimed:

"Blaze away, Mr. Fink, and be sure you elewate her low enough, or you'll have to pay, you know."

"That's true as gospel," replied Fink.

As he spoke, he threw back his right foot, deliberately raised his rifle to his eye, and glanced along the barrel. It was now a moment of painful suspense to all save the parties most directly interested, Fink and Carpenter, neither of whom manifested a single sign of doubt or hesitation. Among the rest, however, many of whom had previously seen this daring feat performed, there was not an unblanched face, while some of the passengers gave decided evidences of trepidation. Every eye now became fixed upon the boy, every lip was parted, and every breath so still that the dropping of a leaf might have been distinctly heard; while over each crept an indescribable thrill of awe, as that long rifle lay poised and pointed, motionless as a rock, ready to speed forth its leaden messenger, perchance on a mission of death. A moment there now was of painful, almost heart-sickening suspense.

"Pray God he may not miss his mark!" whispered Maurice to a fellow-passenger.

A nervous pressure of his arm was the only answer returned, as crack went the rifle of Mike, and away flew the tin cup from the head of the boy, some twenty or thirty paces, who, still cool and unmoved, stood eyeing the spectators, not having moved a single muscle, even when the ball struck within an inch of his skull. A tremendous shout now announced Mike the winner of the quart of whisky, for which trifling consideration the life of a fellow-being had been periled.[4]

The bet being now decided, the party began their return to the boat, some two hundred yards distant, when all were surprised and startled by the sharp report of another rifle, the ball of which grazed the cheek of Mike Fink, and passed through the hat of Maurice St. Vincent, who chanced to be a pace or two in front of him.

Mike started, and, wheeling suddenly around, bounded up from the earth, uttered an Indian yell, and tightly grasping his rifle, darted up the steep acclivity near by, from the brow of which the smoke of the discharged rifle could be seen, followed by Maurice and most of the crew, the rest flying to the boat in alarm.

When arrived at the summit of the hill, nothing could be discerned of the mysterious marksman; and, after a fruitless search of perhaps a quarter of an hour, the party returned to the Light-foot, which a few minutes after, was again floating down with the current.

CAVE-IN-ROCK • THE OUTLAWS • THE QUARREL • THE SUM-
MARY TRIAL AND SENTENCE • THE ESCAPE AND ALARM

Some twenty or twenty-five miles below old Shawneetown, in the State of Illinois, and perhaps an hundred rods from the

4. This was a celebrated feat of Mike Fink, and is strictly authentic [Bennett's note].

river's bank, which here, rocky and precipitous, rises to a goodly height, there stood, at the time of which we write, some three or four old cabins that had been erected by the French long prior to the date of our story, and the settlement of this part of the country by Americans. Even at the period here alluded to these buildings were rapidly going to decay, and presented little that would have been attractive to a stranger. But disagreeable as might be their outward appearance, they were comparatively

beautiful to the beings who inhabited them, with some of whom we must shortly make the reader acquainted.

At the time in question, Illinois was a wild territory, and that portion bordering on the river was thinly settled by various classes of beings of perhaps as many races, among which we may mention the Spanish, the French, the Dutch, and the Anglo-Saxon. As was then common in all territories, the inhabitants, if such they might be termed, looked upon themselves as beyond the pale of the law, and acted accordingly. With them, in most cases, might made right, and he who had not the will and power to protect his own property and person, stood but a poor chance of having either respected by his neighbors. In consequence of this but very few individuals whose intentions and pursuits were honest ventured to reside in a region so dangerous and possessing so few attractions; and, therefore, for those who did so reside, it would be hazarding much, perhaps, to even say of them that their characters were only equivocal.

Of all points on the Ohio, from Pittsburgh to Cairo, the one to which we have but now called the reader's attention was doubtless the worst; and legends of what there took place, narrated at the present day, are sufficient to excite in the breasts of the more timid feelings of awe and horror. At this point was congregated that band of outlaws whose deeds and depredations were the terror of the early boatmen and whose cave, in a steep ledge of rocks overhanging the river, is still pointed out to the traveler as he glides up and down the beautiful Ohio on some magnificent steamer. By whom or when the title was given we know not, but at this day the place referred to bears the name of Cave-in-Rock.

To Cave-in-Rock, then, reader, we pray you will accompany us, in imagination, at least, at a time when neither of us would have cared to venture there in *propria personae*.

It was a dark, gloomy night, some three or four days from the closing of the chapter immediately preceding, and the rain was descending in torrents upon the miserable roofs of the cabins previously mentioned. In one of these old structures, the most dilapidated of all, were collected some ten or twelve rough, ill-looking individuals. Some were seated on benches round a miserable table, whereon stood a pale light, whose gleams were just sufficient to relieve the apartment from total darkness and exhibit here and there grim, haggard, dirty, unshaved faces, with bloodshot eyes, that shot forth, from beneath low, villainous brows, expressions of the most wild, brutal ferocity, as from time to time their owners emptied the cans of liquor ranged before them. Some were standing upright and talking eagerly, mixing with their conversation oaths of the most diabolical and blasphemous character. Taken collectively, they seemed personifications of Hell's arch-fiends, let loose from their bonds to revel out a dismal night, and make earth hideous with their orgies.

Their costume was in keeping with their persons. On the heads of most were coarse red skull-caps, and the upper parts of their bodies and limbs, where not entirely bare, were covered by shirts striped with red and black, giving to them a wild singular appearance. Around their waists were broad belts, supporting pistols, knives and dirks, and their nether limbs were concealed under loose, linsey trowsers and heavy boots. They were a mixture of various races, and spoke different tongues— though all to some extent understood the English.

"It seems to me our cap'en is a ——— long while gittin' ready," said one, a large, fierce, cut-throat looking individual, with a red, bloated face, bushy hair, and matted whiskers, who was seated at the table, and who qualified a portion of his sentence with an oath.

"O, he al'ays takes his time, and be ——— to him!" replied another ruffian, of no better exterior than the first, who was seated alongside him, and who, as he concluded, struck the table with the tin can, the contents of which had just passed down his throat. "If I'd a had my way, I'd a had the hearts out on 'em afore this!"

"O, you'd do great things if you was cap'en, I 'spose—eh! Ned Groth?" rejoined a third, from across the table.

"I'd do one thing pretty ——— quick, Mr. Stoker," returned Ned, sullenly.

"What's that?" inquired the other.

"I'd hang you to the nearest sapling."

"O, you would, eh!—ha, ha, ha!—Why, you're gittin' merry over the bottle, Mr. Groth!"

"Don't mister me, you land-lubber, or I'll do it yit, by ———!" rejoined Ned, fiercely.

"Come, come," said the first speaker; "you're both on ye drunk, and it's no use for ye to quarrel now, when the cap'en's got work on hand for all on us."

"The cap'en be ———!" answered Ned, who felt in a humor

to quarrel with somebody. "I say the cap'en be ———! d'ye
hear?—and you, too, Andy Larkin—d'ye hear that?"

Andy, or Andrew, started to his feet, with an oath, and seizing the other by the throat, ere he could be prevented, threw
him violently on the ground; then placing his knee upon the
fallen man's breast, he drew a dirk from his belt, and cried:

"I'll teach ye to insult me, you villain!"

As he spoke, he raised the dirk aloft, and the next moment it
would have been buried in the breast of the other, but for the
interference of a huge, brawny, broadfaced Dutchman, who
now seized the arm of Andrew and held it fast, and exclaimed:

"Vat ish ye pe thinks, Andish? You wants to kill Neds, 'cause
he pe drunks, eh?"

By this time all had gathered round the trio, and some cried,
"Let 'em fight—take Dutch Hans off"; and other, "No, no!—
part 'em—part 'em!"

"Takes me off," echoed Hans, springing to his feet and looking fiercely round upon the crowd, at the same time exhibiting
a fist like an ordinary-sized mallet. "Who shays takes Hans off,
eh? By ———! somebody tells me, I shall knocks him next weeks
middlers to, putty quicks, eh!"

"Well, well, Hans," said Larkin, who had, meantime, released Ned and regained his feet; "never mind what's bin said.
You've saved Ned's life, and got me out o' a scrape—for I'd a
bin sorry arterwards for killing him drunk-like—and so now
don't go for to gittin' into a fight yourself, but give me your
fist, and we'll shake hands all round, drink, and be merry again."

"Yaw, dat ish rights—dat ish goots—dat ish as I likes 'em,
eh?" returned the Dutchman, giving the other a cordial grip.

"Come, Ned, your hand," said Larkin, presenting his own as
he spoke. "We's both rather hasty—but it's over now."

"No, by ———!" replied the other, using an oath; "I don't
make up this here quarrel quite so easy."

"Well, jest as ye like," replied Andy; "I know ye'r drunk, and
so I'll take it all coolly."

"Like a coward," sneered the other.

"Well, yes, like a coward, if that suits you better," answered Andy, now determined not to be again drawn into a quarrel.

"Then take that, and go where cowards belong," rejoined Groth, making a pass at the heart of the other with a dagger.

Larkin turned quickly round, and catching a glimpse of the steel, threw up his arm, and the next moment the weapon passed through it. With a howl of rage he now sprung back, and drawing forth the bloody blade, threw it upon the ground; then bounding forward, he seized the offender by the throat with one hand, and pistol in his belt with the other. At this moment a tall figure entered from without and a deep voice said:

"Hold!"

Instantly Andy released his opponent, and turned, with a crest-fallen look, toward the new-comer, on whom all eyes were now bent, while each seemed disposed to slink back from his searching gaze.

"What is this?—what means this disturbance?" continued the tall figure, in an authoritative and angry tone, as he glanced from one to the other, and strode directly to where stood Larkin and Groth, pale, and abashed.

"What means this disturbance, I say!" cried he again, more fiercely than before. "By the spirits of Hades! will no one answer me? Speak you, Andrew Larkin!"

"Why ye see, cap'en," answered the one addressed, hesitatingly, "Ned Groth, here, against my will—and—and—ye see, he drawed me into a quarrel with him, by stabbing me in the arm, as ye can see yerself, cap'en."

"Is this so, sir!" asked the captain, turning to Groth, with a dark determined frown on his brow, his lips compressed, and his teeth tightly set.

Groth hung down his head without reply.

"Is the statement of Larkin true?" continued the captain, addressing the bystanders.

"It is, Captain Camilla—it is!" answered some two or three voices.

"Gentlemen," said Camilla, "you all remember, I presume, the oath I swore not three months since, that in case of another quarrel on the eve of an adventure like the present, the life of the aggressor should be the forfeit."

"We do!—we do!" answered several voices.

"You hear, Groth!—you hear!" continued the captain, turning to the culprit, who, sobered by the excitement of the last few minutes, now stood trembling, with his eyes cast on the floor. "Your doom is sealed."

"Pardon! cap'en," said Groth. "I'd bin drinking too much."

"Ay, pardon!—pardon!" echoed several voices.

"No!" answered the captain, sternly: "Orlando Camilla breaks not his oath with the cry of pardon. There must be an example. Groth, your minutes are numbered. Here, Liston and Barker, take him to the cave, blow out his brains, and cast his body down the rocks into the Ohio!"

The two individuals called upon at once stepped forward and disarmed Groth, and then conducted him away to execute on him the bloody sentence of their brutal chief. As Groth quitted the apartment, he looked back, and shaking his fist at Camilla, he exclaimed with an oath:

"Monster of monsters! by my soul you shall repent o' this!"

Camilla stamped his foot fiercely on the rude floor of the cabin, placed his hand on a pistol in his belt, but made no answer. The next moment Groth had disappeared from his sight into the darkness and storm.

"Is every thing ready, Andrew?" inquired Camilla, turning to the person addressed.

"Every thing, I reckon, cap'en,—that is, as far as I know."

"It is now nearly time," continued Camilla, "and we must be speedy in the execution of our business, when we reach the river, and do it effectually. Remember our motto:

'Dead men tell no tales!'

Strike fast, my lads, and home—or we shall have our match—for such another crew you never saw. Most of them are large, powerful men; and their patron, Mike Fink, is decidedly what I have before heard him represented—the bully of the river—and if I do not greatly overrate him, is equal to any two of you, with the exception of Hans and Andrew, and more than a match for either of them alone. You smile, Hans; but I speak knowingly on the subject, having once felt the weight of his tremendous arm. Moreover, he seems to hold a charmed life; for twice have I shot at him at fair distance and missed my mark—and you know that seldom happens with me. But again, with regard to this affair of the boat: there is one aboard whose life must be spared—a dark-eyed, beautiful girl of sixteen or eighteen. Remember, now, her life must be spared, I say!—and if but a hair of her head be injured by one of ye, by the spirits of Hades, I swear to cleave the skull of him in twain who so offends! Remember, now, what I have said—bear it in mind— for you know me well, and know I make no idle threats.

"If we are as successful in this adventure," continued the captain of the outlaws, "and I know no reason why we should not be, it will, I believe, be one of the most fortunate things for us that has ever happened since the capture of Neil Renson's boat. Every thing thus far, too, seems propitious to our design. Had it not been for this storm, it is more than probable they had not landed—in which case we should have been obliged to follow them down the river, and perhaps even then have missed them altogether. But, come! I think we may as well prepare to sally forth. Look to your pistols, all—see that the priming of each is perfectly dry—and then secure them in such a manner as to prevent their getting damp."

At this moment some two or three reports of fire-arms were distinctly heard, followed immediately by loud shouts.

"Ha! what can that mean?" exclaimed Camilla, with a start. "Are we betrayed, men, think you?"

The ruffians grasped their weapons and looked from one to the other in amazement and alarm.

"Wasn't it the execution of Groth?" queried Larkin, in a suggestive manner.

"It could not be, I think," replied the captain; "the sounds were too near; unless, as is possible, they were borne hither by the blast. But then those shouts! Stand ready for a surprise, men! By heavens! I did not think of it before—but it now strikes me I have acted very imprudently, in having Groth shot by the cave; as the sounds may be heard by the boatmen, and alarm and put them on their guard."

At this moment the door was burst open, and one of the two individuals sent forth to execute Groth, entered, pale and breathless.

"Ha! what is it, Barker?—speak!" cried Camilla, springing forward and grasping the arm of the new-comer.

"Groth—" gasped Barker, nearly out of breath.

"Well?"

"Has escaped, cap'en—shot Liston—and has fled to alarm the boatmen!"

"And you here, alive, to tell me this!" almost shrieked Camilla. "By ———! you shall never repeat it."

As he spoke he cast Barker roughly from him, drew a pistol from his belt, and shot him through the heart. The poor fellow fell dead without a groan.

"Come!" shouted Camilla to the others, his face livid with passion, and his eyes glaring wildly. "Come, men! we are betrayed! Onward! Victory or death, by ———!"

He closed with an oath, and, springing over the lifeless form of Barker, rushed forth into the storm, followed by his band, all bent on a dark and terrible mission.

MIKE FINK AND THE BOATMEN • MAURICE AND AURELIA • THE ALARM

The night alluded to in the foregoing chapter was intensely dark. Clouds, low and heavy, concealed the heavens, and the wind came in fitful gusts, and the rain fell in torrents. Just before sunset, the Light-foot was rounding the last bend above Cave-in-Rock, when Mike, looking intently toward the west for a few moments, declared it would be unsafe to venture further with the boat before morning; and accordingly he soon after ran her into a small cove just under the rocks we have before spoken of as overhanging the river. Here, after having made all fast, and seen that his freight was all secure from damage by water, Mike sprang upon the barrel of whisky, and ordering his crew to form a circle round him, in his own peculiar and humorous way began as follows:

"Boys, this here's a night—well it is—as true nor deacon Pendleton's oath, when he swore his wife war the best-looking woman in creation. I say, boys, this here's a night; and ef I war poetically made, I'd describe it to you in a way to make your har stand like the tail o' a full blown peacock. How the wind rolls and tumbles about like a dying craw-fish, and sprinkles the water in your faces, my hearties; and all fur your good, too, ef you warn't so thunderation blind you couldn't see it, and the night warn't quite so dark. Why, ef it warn't for sech times like this, what in natur would become on ye, my angels?—fur ye never git water nearer to ye nor the river, and you're afearder o' that nor a dog that's got the hydrobothoby, or sum sech curious jaw-breaking name. Hurray fur a storm, then, say! Whoop! Hurray!

"Why in the name o' painters and catermounts don't ye holler, when it's all fur your own good?" continued Mike; "and not stand thar shivering and shaking the teeth out o' your heads, like a set o' grinning babboons?"

A tremendous shout from the crew was the answer returned.

"Well, now, that's suthing like doing business," resumed Fink; "them kind o' things tell on these here rocks, and makes 'em think we're about. Hurray for me, you scapegoats! I'm a land-screamer—I'm a water-dog—I'm a snapping-turkle—I can lick five times my own weight in wild-cats. I can use up Injens by the cord. I can swallow niggers whole, raw or cooked. I can out-run, out-dance, out-jump, out-dive, out-drink, out-holler, and out-lick, any white things in the shape o' human that's ever put foot within two thousand miles o' the big Massassip.

Whoop! holler, you varmints!—holler fur the Snapping Turkle![5]
or I'll jump right straight down yer throats, quicker nor a streak
o' greased chain-lightning can down a nigger's!"

Another shout followed, with a long life to Mike Fink, the
Snapping Turtle.

"Them's the kind as makes a feller feel good," roared Mike
again; "fur they stirs up his ambitionary faculties, and makes
him feel as ef he war walking tall into suthing.

"Oh, for a fight!" he continued, after a moment's pause, during which he turned his face toward the rocks, and strove in
vain to peer into the darkness: "O for a fight, boys, to stretch
these here limbs, and git the jints to working easy! But I 'spect
we needn't hope for nothing here, no how. What an orful
place! Rocks one side and river t'other—and not a varmint
about to light on, jest fur amusement even. Why, thunderation
to Halifax! I'd die here, sure—in less time nor a crippled cub
would in a pitfall. Thar'll have to be suthing done right quick,
or I'll ketch the blue fever and die off,—burnt brandy won't save
me. What'll we do, boys? what say ye? Shall we go below and
take an extra fillee,[6] and a game o' cards? or go ashore here and
try to hunt suthing kankariferous?"

"Below! below!—licker and cards!" cried several of the crew
at once, who were not so eager as Mike for pushing off in the
darkness and storm, merely for adventure.

"Be jabers, and I think so," said Pat Flannegan, shrugging
his shoulders, and chattering his teeth: "Don't you, Misther
Jack Short? To kape a decent feller out here in the storm, wid
the rheumathics may-be biting him like the divil, and all to hear
about going to fight wid somebody that's not iny body at all,
jist, ye see! Och! troth! it's not Pathrick Flanegan's mother's
son that'll iver be saan running afther the likes o' them wil-o-
the-wisps, in sich nights as this, I'm thinking."

"Y-y-your right, Pat," replied Jack, giving an extra movement

5. Mike Fink was known as the "Snapping Turtle" on the Ohio, and
"Snag" on the Mississippi rivers [Bennett's note].

6. Ration of liquor [Bennett's note].

to his jaws, as, in company with the worthy son of Erin, he waddled down into the cabin of the crew—a place somewhat roughly fitted up in the stern of the boat. "Y-y-your right, Pat, I s-say. N-n-never be o-o-ostentatious, n-n-nor o-oscilating, P-pat."

"Ah! troth! it's thim same big words that head me," replied the Irishman, with a laugh. "It's yer mother, Jack, that was afther swallering a dictionary afore ye was born, I' thinking, jist."

"T-t-that's a-am-ambiguous," replied Jack, quietly.

In a few minutes these two worthies, together with Mike Fink and the balance of the crew, were seated round a table on which were placed whisky and cards; and having by one round done justice to the former, they forthwith proceeded to amuse themselves with the latter. In the course of an hour or two all became very merry; and tales were told, jokes were cracked, and songs were sung, and still mirth prevailed, unmarred by an angry word.

Meantime, the passengers in the other cabin were endeavoring to relieve the night of its tediousness, as much as possible, by different topics of conversation. Some were telling humorous anecdotes, and striving to make themselves merry; others were conversing on matters of grave importance; while some were relating wild tales and legends of events that had from time to time come to their knowledge. One of their number, however, seemed to take no interest in any thing that was said; but sat apart, wrapt in the gloom of his own thoughts. This was Fontaine, who, for the few days since we last saw him, had said but little to any one—his mind evidently still occupied with the sad theme we then made known to the reader, during a conversation between himself and Maurice St. Vincent.

Maurice, on the present occasion, was seated by the side of Aurelia and striving to cheer her drooping spirits; for the place and the night had served to render her somewhat sad and abstracted.

At this moment every one was startled by hearing the reports of firearms, followed by cries of distress; and, starting up in alarm, each turned toward his neighbor a look of anxious inquiry. Aurelia, pale and trembling, grasped the arm of Maurice, timidly, and said:

"You see, Maurice—you see—my fears are not now without a foundation."

"Be calm," answered Maurice, as he drew his pistols. "Be not alarmed, Aurelia! I trust it is nothing of importance; but let it be what it may, no harm shall befall you while I have life and strength for your defense."

"Gentlemen," said Fontaine, drawing his pistols also, "those of you who have arms, prepare to use them—they will now be needed."

"By what do you know this?" asked one, in reply, a young man of twenty-five, while two or three ladies uttered exclamations of alarm.

"By an invisible monitor," answered Fontaine, solemnly.

"Perhaps you *knew* something of it before?" returned the other, pointedly, glancing at Fontaine suspiciously.

"I did, sir! I have known it for several days," answered Fontaine.

"Ha! are we entrapped—betrayed?" cried the young man springing forward and seizing hold of the other.

"I do not understand you," rejoined Fontaine.

"Release him, sir!" said Maurice, interposing. "I will answer for it, Mr. Hamilton—so I believe you are called—that his knowledge of what is about to happen, so far as any connection therewith is concerned, is as limited as your own, and that his intentions are as honest."

"Answer for yourself!" replied the other, with an angry look.

As he spoke and before Maurice could reply, a heavy shock was felt, as of some one springing on to the deck from the rocks above, and a voice shouted:

"Arm, here, and take care o' yourselves, or you'll be cut to pieces afore you know it!"

On hearing this the ladies screamed, while some of the opposite sex looked pale and frightened. Others compressed their lips, grasped their weapons, and, headed by Maurice and Hamilton, rushed up on deck.

"What's yer force here?" cried a figure, springing forward to Maurice at this moment.

"Who are you?" cried the latter, throttling the stranger, and by a dexterous movement throwing him upon his back, while the others gathered round to hear his answer.

"Easy, sir!—easy!" cried the fallen man; "I'm a traitor, but not to you. You'd better be taking care o' yourselves here, or it'll be too late; for Camilla and his band's already on his way here to murder ye all; and them's as true words as ever Ned Groth spoke."

"Camilla!" cried one of the by-standers. "Gracious heavens! then we are lost!—for he is one of the most ferocious cut-throats under heaven!"

"That's true, sir," rejoined Groth, springing to his feet, along with Maurice, who, on hearing the exclamation of the by-stander, released his hold on him at once.

"Then we must prepare to defend ourselves to the death!" exclaimed Maurice, with decision.

"There! there! They come! They come!" shrieked Groth, wildly. "I'll fight for ye, though out o' revenge; for my life's forfeit any how; and I don't 'spect to 'scape him. Oh! he's a terrible man!"

"Where's Fink and his crew?" cried Maurice. "Heaven grant they have not quitted the boat."

"In their cabin, I think," answered one; "for I heard loud laughter and singing, but a few minutes since, in that direction."

Maurice waited to hear no more, but darting along the deck of the Light-foot as fast as the darkness would permit, soon gained the door of the after cabin, burst it open, and beheld a scene which, under the circumstances, made his heart sink; while, to his consternation and despair, he heard at this moment at the other end of the boat loud shouts, and groans, and shrieks, and the rapid discharge of fire-arms, too truly announcing the awful fact that the attack of Camilla and his band, and the bloody work of death had already begun.

THE ATTACK • THE FIGHT • THE SANGUINARY STRUGGLE
THE ABDUCTION • THE VICTORY, ETC., ETC.

It has been said, and become a proverb, that "Nero fiddled while Rome was burning"; and though there is not much similarity between the character and positions, as they existed, of Nero and Mike Fink, yet in one thing perhaps we may be allowed to make a comparison; both, in their respective spheres, were making merry at a moment when the life of each was in the most imminent danger.

In the preceding chapter, we left Mike and his companions round a table with cards and whisky before them; and it was very natural that men like themselves, under such circumstances, should occasionally take a drink of the latter, if for nothing else than to remove the chilliness felt from having breasted the storm so long to listen to the harangue of their worthy commander. Moreover, it was very natural also, that in so drinking, if they drank a little too much at once, and a little too often, they would in the course of time become somewhat tipsy; and this was the exact result which had been produced prior to the entrance of Maurice to give the alarm. At the moment when he burst into the apartment, pale and breathless, Mike Fink, with a bottle in his hand, was singing, in a coarse, drunken voice, the chorus to a song which had in it some allusion to himself; while his comrades, with the exception of the Irishman, too drunk to comprehend it, were beating time with their fists on the table, and endeavoring to look very wise and dignified, though neither had the power to support his body in an upright position without the assistance of his hands, or some artificial means.

"Go it right,
Loose or tight,
The Snapping Turkle's out to-night—
Fal la diddle de da,"

[175]

roared Mike, smashing the bottle on the table as he concluded, and then throwing the neck thereof at the head of Jack Short, missing him by barely an inch.

"C-c-close-o-over-l-linctum," muttered Jack, too far gone to understand what he was saying himself.

"Up and arm—or you are all dead men!" shouted Maurice, as at this juncture his ear caught the sounds of the attack from without.

"Be howly jabers! what's that?" cried Pat, bounding up from his seat and looking wildly at Maurice.

"It means that the boat is attacked by Camilla and his band, and that in five minutes or less time you will all be murdered!" replied the latter; and turning abruptly round, he again rushed to the deck and darted forward to the assistance of his friends.

"Howly murther! Mike," shouted the Irishman, "Camilla, the dirthy blaggard, and all his black divils is afther us, and we'll all be dead, sure, afore we can spake the saints to defend us! Ochone! blatheration to it! that I, Patrick Flanegan, should live to be kilt this way, jist."

"What's that?" said Mike, starting to his feet with a stagger. "Ef ye're talking about a fight, my angel, I'm in—whoop!—hur-ray! I—I can lick my—"

"Act wid ye, thin, and not be there blarnying!" interrupted the Irishman; and as he spoke, he caught up a bucket of water that was standing by his side, and dashed it upon the other's head. "Act wid ye, I say, or the divils will be afther roasting our hearts for us, to breakfast on."

"Corn-cobs and catermounts!" roared Mike, now somewhat sobered by the water, grasping Pat by the throat; "what's the meaning of all this here catarumpus, eh?"

"Camilla, ye blaggard ye, has attacked the boat! Don't ye hear him now, shouting and shooting away yonder?—and ye a standing here dhrunk as a baste, and be ———— to ye!"

At this moment a wild shriek arose from the other cabin, and Mike for the first time seemed to comprehend what was taking place. Glancing round upon his comrades, and perceiving their sad condition, he uttered an oath, and grasping a brace of pistols that were hanging against the wall, and a heavy bar of iron lying on the floor, he bade the Irishman follow him; and springing up the ladder leading to the deck, he rushed forward with a wild yell that sounded above the roar of the storm and the confusion of the fight like something more than earthly, and made many a bold but superstitious heart of the outlaws tremble with very fear. And well they might; for if not a demon incarnate, Mike Fink was a being to be feared by his enemies; and he now rushed among the already retreating freebooters, like some giant madman endowed with supernatural strength laying about him right and left, every blow bringing its man to the ground, while each was accompanied with a terrible yell of fury that would have done credit to the best-trained warrior of the savage race.

Had the design of Camilla not been betrayed, it is more than probable that not a single soul aboard the Light-foot at the time of the attack, owing to the drunken condition of the crew of Mike, had escaped to tell the tale. As it was, even, the contest for a time seemed likely to be decided for the robbers. Led by Camilla and knowing that success in the present case would much depend upon a desperate and sanguinary assault, they made a simultaneous rush upon the boat, and with loud cries discharged several of their pieces at their opponents on deck, and then drawing their knives, rushed in among them, cutting about fearfully and doing much execution, though not without meeting a severe repulse from the determined few there assembled, and losing two of their party, who were shot dead at the onset. Overpowered by numbers, our gallant little band gave way before the freebooters, and had begun to retreat toward the stern of the boat as Maurice joined them.

"Below all!" shouted Camilla, at this moment, thinking, probably, that all on deck were vanquished; and, obedient to his orders, the robbers turned and followed him down into the forward cabin.

"Onward!—press on!—and give no quarter to the inhuman wretches!" cried Maurice to the disheartened few. "Now is our time! Head them at the gang-way—kill and spare not!" and encouraged by his words and the retreat of the others, the party in question rushed back to the stairs leading to the cabin, and placed themselves in readiness to take the robbers at an advantage so soon as they should come up from below.

Meantime Camilla reached the cabin, amid the screams of the ladies, and found himself opposed by some four or five individuals among whom, and foremost, stood Fontaine, with a pistol in either hand.

"Ha! Hardick—it is then as I believed, thou art the villain!" shouted Fontaine; and as he spoke, he discharged both his pistols at Camilla, which, unfortunately, missed him, but wounded two of his followers close behind. His example was imitated by the others, and another of the ruffians fell mortally wounded.

"By ——!" cried Camilla, uttering an oath and gnashing his teeth, "it is my turn now!" and as he spoke, he leveled his pistol and shot Fontaine through the heart. Then, as he fell, Camilla bent over him, and tore from his vestments a package, which he concealed in the bosom of his shirt, and sprang to his feet just as Aurelia, with a scream of terror, rushed forward to throw herself upon the dead body of his victim.

"Ha!" cried Camilla, with an oath, "the spirits favor me tonight!" And suddenly clasping Aurelia in his arms, and shouting to his band: "Remember your oaths—strike fast and home!" he turned to rush up on deck; but perceiving by a gleam of light from the cabin the small force with Maurice at their head there drawn up to oppose him, he wheeled suddenly around again, and, darting through the cabin, found himself amidships of the boat among the freight. At this moment Aurelia uttered that piercing and prolonged shriek which had so startled Mike Fink, and swooned away in the robber's arms. Nothing daunted, Camilla still bore her forward to the hatchway, the door of which he threw open, and then, by the aid of a barrel, placed his victim on deck, and sprang up after her.

The storm was still raging fiercely, and the darkness so intense that nothing could be discerned six inches from the eye.

For a moment the bold robber-chief paused, undecided what course to take, when the sound of Mike's voice, as he sallied forth from his cabin, startled him; and turning on the impulse of the moment, he made a sudden bound into the dark turbid waters of the Ohio, bearing Aurelia with him.

The pause of Maurice and his companions at the head of the staircase was of short duration; for shouts, groans, and curses, the discharge of fire-arms, and clashing of knives, resounding from below, together with the thought of Aurelia, urged him on to immediate action; and darting down the steps, pistols in hand, he called upon his companions to follow him. Here an awful scene presented itself. Some two or three bloody and mangled corses, lying on the floor at his feet, were dimly seen through the sulphurous smoke of the discharged weapons; while several dark figures were struggling in the grasp of others for that victory which could be won only by the death of their opponents. Just before him was a tall ruffian, dragging forward a female, who was piteously crying for help; and placing his pistol to the breast of the former, Maurice shot him dead; then clasping the lady in his arms, he attempted to pass through the cabin to a spot where she would be comparatively safe. For a short time this attempt was in vain; as the passage from the cabin to what was called the midships, was blocked up by the combatants—some few of the passengers having here placed themselves in such positions as would bar all further advance of the assailants save over their dead bodies. This was done to protect the ladies, each of whom, with the exception of Aurelia and the one rescued by Maurice, having fled in this direction.

Maurice still had one undischarged pistol, and placing this against the head of one of the assailants, he fired, and the bandit sunk down with a groan. The rest of the passengers had by this time commenced an attack on the rear of the ruffians, who now finding themselves in rather too close quarters and having no commander to urge them to continue, turned in desperation and commenced their retreat, shooting and stabbing as they went, and being shot and stabbed in turn by their opponents.

Now it was that the terrible yell of Mike Fink, as he rushed forward to join in the affray, sounded in their ears like a supernatural omen of evil, and not a little accelerated their speed. By the time they gained the deck, Mike himself had reached the bow; and rushing in among them, as we before stated, he laid about him in such a frightful manner that the outlaws became alarmed in earnest; and the Irishman at this moment coming up also with one of his peculiar yells decided the day; and such as could fled in precipitation, leaping over the sides of the boat upon the rocks and into the stream in the utmost consternation and confusion, leaving the boatmen and passengers victors of the bloody fight. The whole affray occupied far less time than we have in describing it.

"I'm an arthquake!" roared Mike, as the last outlaw disappeared, giving another yell, which we can liken to nothing but a yell of Mike Fink. "Sea sarpents and sea sharks! that I should ha' bin drunk, like a fool, and missed all this here sport, which mebby won't happen agin in a feller's lifetime. The infernal cowards, to run afore I'd got half o' my jints in a playing order! O, but ef they'd come back, wouldn't I walk tall into 'em, eh?— and make 'em see stars ef it is cloudy! Only four knocked down, and three o' them got away—the varmints! the infernal possums! But this here feller," continued Mike, placing his foot upon a fallen man, "I reckon he's snagged in arnest, and gone down with all his freight o' sin aboard, which is enough, mebby, to sink fifty o' him."

"Be all the powers of Sathan, Mike Fink, but this has bin one of thim owld fights, sure!" cried Pat, coming up from the cabin, whither he had been during the soliloquy of Mike. "Will ye jist be afther stipping down below, Misther Mike, to see if your mother's child iver saw the likes on't afore, jist?"

As Mike turned to descend, a loud and prolonged shriek and a single heart-piercing cry of "Help," evidently proceeding from a female, resounded from the shore some fifty yards down the river—on hearing which, some two or three individuals rushed up on deck.

"What's that?" cried one.

"A woman, by heavens!" answered another. "The villains have borne off a female from the boat, and we are too few in number to rescue her."

"A curse on liquor!" rejoined Mike. "Ef I and my crew'd bin sober, this wouldn't a happened."

"Give way—make room—give way!" shouted a voice; and swift as lightning, Maurice came bounding up the stairs. "I know these tones," he continued, wildly. "I go to rescue or to die!" and ere he could be prevented, he sprang from the boat upon the rocks, and was quickly lost to sight in the surrounding darkness. Immediately on the retreat of the bandits, he had quitted the lady under his protection, and commenced a search for Aurelia. Not finding her among the living, he had sought her among the dead, and in his search had found the body of Fontaine.

"Alas! thy predictions have been sadly fulfilled!" he sighed, as he bent over the pale, ghastly face of the dead. "But Aurelia! Aurelia!" he added, starting up and looking wildly around. "Oh! where art thou?"

As he spoke, he heard her shriek. He listened, and heard her cry for help. He knew those silvery and to him now dearly loved tones—for now Maurice loved—and pausing but an instant longer, he flew up the staircase and vanished in the darkness, as we have just related.

"Shall we pursue and give him aid?" asked one of the party on the boat.

" 'Twon't do," answered Mike; "as we're fixed now, we must take care o' ourselves."

"Be saint Pathrick, I think so!" rejoined the Irishman. "And our hands full we've got on't, sure; the living, the dead, and the dead dhrunk—a beauthiful night's business, be my sowl!"

"First, then," said Mike, "to rouse up the sleepers."

As he spoke, he strode across the deck to the cabin of the

crew, where, by the aid of cold water, a few oaths, and not altogether the mildest personal treatment possible, he at length succeeded in bringing them to a state of consciousness.

The boat was then unfastened and pushed across the river, to avoid another surprise from the robbers; after which, a consultation was held among the passengers and crew, whereby it was decided to await the morning and be guided by circumstances regarding their further proceedings. The dead were then collected together, and each body wrapped in a separate cloth, and the wounded on both sides cared for as well as circumstances would permit.

It was a terrible night to all, but more particularly to those who had lost some of their dearest friends in the affray; and heart-rending cries of anguish, and sobs, and groans, from the disconsolate, mingled sadly with the howlings of the storm.

MIKE FINK'S SPEECH TO HIS CREW • THE CONSULTATION
THE DEAD • THE BURIAL

The morning succeeding the attack on the Light-foot was fair and beautiful. Before daybreak the storm had subsided; and the few broken clouds, which for a time floated through the heavens, were all dispersed, as the god of day resumed his wonted place, to smile again upon the late-sleeping earth, and gladden the dewy blade and flower and leaf with his presence. It was a lovely morning—surpassingly lovely; for the storm had served to render the atmosphere clear, and the drops of rain, as they hung glistening in the sun, spangled the green earth like so many brilliant diamonds. Spring was just sufficiently advanced to make every thing look enchanting; and the very birds, as they turned off their morning roundelays, seemed to sing sweeter and more lively than ever.

What a contrast did the day present to the night which preceded it—to that night of storm and blood and death which we but imperfectly described in a former chapter! How rapturously did it make the light unalloyed heart bound! and how the generous blood leaped through the veins of youth, who had as yet felt no care and seen no sorrow! But alas! it could not so move those whose souls were racked with the loss of some dearly beloved friend, snatched from them without a moment's warning, and sent into the presence of his Maker! To such it was only a morning of gloom, making them the more sad and depressed that it contrasted so forcibly with the melancholy thoughts rife within them; and of such there were a few aboard the Light-foot, to which we must again call the reader's attention.

It will be remembered by those who have closely followed the thread of our story, that we left the Light-foot on the Kentucky side, opposite to Cave-in-Rock, where she lay moored for the night. Early in the morning, all aboard her were astir; and a consultation was held among the passengers and crew as to their next proceedings with regard to the wounded and dead, and the propriety of attacking the outlaws in their own stronghold.

Previously to this, however, Mike Fink called together his crew in his own cabin, and, mounting upon a chair, thus addressed them:

"You're a purty set o' beauties now—you are—arn't ye?—you landlubberly ragmuffins, what gits drunk jest when you're wanted fur a fight. What in the name o' possums and catermounts would ha' become on ye', ef it hadn't bin fur me and Pat Flanegan here, (Mike patted the Irishman, who was standing by his side, on the shoulder,) who's a hoss, out and out, and no mistake, and who I'll set aginst the best among ye any day, fur a gallon o' the rale corn-cob? What 'ud become on ye, I say, ef it hadn't bin fur us? Why, you'd a had you're double-soaked whisky-pipes—I can't call 'em wine-pipes, fur a bit o' wine niver gits down 'em—you'd a had 'em cut, I say—slit up in every direction—and your beastly carcasses sent to color the water, what you hates, and feed fishes on. How'd ye a liked that, my culiflowers, eh? how'd ye a like that?"

Here Mike, with a mischievous smile, took a general survey of his audience, not one of whom ventured a reply.

"Mr. Weatherhead," added he at length, "as you're putty

long fur this here world, I'll jest trouble you to reach me that thar bottle, (pointing to one on a high shelf in an adjoining pantry), fur my throat's a gitting a little rough like."

This request being complied with, Mike took a long pull at the bottle, and then smacking his lips, with an air of satisfaction, resumed:

"Say what you please, thar's nuthing like whisky for taking the cobwebs out o' a feller's throat, arter all. But whar was I? O, I remimber: I's jest lashing it to you, my cupids. Well, now, to change the subject—fur you know thar's nothing like variety— I've heerd from somebody, furget who, that this Camilla, as they calls him, war no body else but the feller what got aboard with us at Cincinnati, and the chap that Jack and myself sort o' hustled ashore. Now, my trumps, all I've got to say about the matter is, that we've got to scuttle him and send him to Davy Jones' Locker, with all his bloody ripscallions, and no mistake. I say, boys, it's jest got to be done, in right good arnest. Who-ever heerd o' sech imperdence afore? Jest walking right straight aboard o' us, and slashing away, and killing and capturing like they had a right to do it. I tell ye, boys, it's more nor human nater can stand, without biling clean over. Now the fact is, to come to the pint, I'm jest agoing to walk tall into them fellers, and I'd jest like to be informed which o' you suckers is agoing to sneak out and stay behind? That thar gal as war taken off has got to be brought back agin, or else Mike Fink'll be split on the sawyer, and sent down over timbers, afore the world is a great deal older. And that young hot-headed feller too—unless he's dead, and I 'spect he is—must be got out o' thar clutches. I say it's got to be done; and I wants to know who's agoing to sneak out on't—who?"

"Not I—not I," cried each and all.

"Dick," said Mike, complacently, "I'll kind o' trouble you fur that thar bottle agin. I feel drier nor a sun-baked mud-turkle, that han't seen water sence the last flood."

Taking another drink, Mike turned suddenly to Jack Short and said:

"Well, my one-eyed beauty, what's your opinion about this here afair o' pitching into them thar land pirates, eh?"

Jack started, and peering curiously around upon his comrades, while his huge jaws started the juice of the weed afresh, answered:

"W-w-why, M-Mike, I-I think the effort ph-phi-philanthropic, to-to say the l-least on't. I-I think we'd b-b-best to excavate 'em entirely."

A roar of laughter followed, during which Jack modestly took occasion to remove his old quid of tobacco, and replace it with a new one of double size.

At this moment the boy Carpenter, who had not been among the party during the remarks of Mike, hastily entered the cabin.

"Well, what's up now?" asked the latter, turning to the newcomer.

"They wants to see you on deck," was the answer, "to consult about them thar dead bodies, and other things."

"Jest tell 'em I'll be thar quicker nor a monkey can turn a somerset," replied Mike.

The boy disappeared, and Fink soon ascended to the deck, followed by the others in silence. Here they found the passengers, with the exception of the ladies and one or two who were wounded in the last night's affray, all assembled, awaiting their appearance with troubled faces. There were five of them altogether; among whom was the young man before introduced as Hamilton, and another who took a prominent part in the fight, by the name of Summers. Both were young, well-dressed, good-looking men, to whom—or perhaps more particularly to Hamilton alone—the others seemed to look with that deference generally accorded to a superior.

As Fink approached the party, Hamilton advanced a pace, and said:

"We have sent for you, to hold a consultation concerning the burial of the dead, and whether it will be safe to venture an attack upon the robbers or not."

"Why that thar last is what we've jest bin debating on," answered Mike; "and we've decided to go and snag every ———— one of 'em, or sink ourselves in trying to. But you mention the dead. Poor fellers! they must be buried as well as circumstances'll allow. 'Spect we'd better sink thar bodies in the Ohio, eh?"

"I presume that to be the better way," answered Hamilton.

"Well, d'ye think 'ud be a right decent trick, to give them thar infernal cut-throats Christen burial 'long side?"

"I should spend but little time with their carcasses," replied Hamilton, bitterly.

"Well, that's my opinion on the matter. Here you, Jack and Dick, jest go and snake 'em out here, and pitch 'em overboard!"

"But had you not better push into the stream first?" queried Hamilton.

"Per'aps I had. Well, then, hold on, boys! But let me see— thar's one o' the scoundrels that's not dead yit, I reckon."

"The one you probably allude to, died this morning, a little before day-break."

"So much the better," answered Mike, compressing his lips; "fur I don't much like to string a feller up in cold blood, and that's what I'd had to done, I 'spect, ef he hadn't slipped his bow-line. So then, that makes four, don't it?"

"Ay, four of the robbers, and three of our own party."

"A putty tough fight, and no mistake; but what I grieves most about is, that I didn't git to it a little sooner. O, it's bin so long sence I fou't, you can't think. Why, my very bones aches for the want o' one. And here was one close to me, and I, like a fool, drunk as a nigger on a holiday night. And these here angels," added Mike, pointing to his crew, "all drunk too, 'cept Pat, and he's a hoss."

"Don't be afther complimenting a man to his face, sure," rejoined the Irishman.

"See thar now," pursued Mike, winking; "he's modest—Pat is."

"Well," said Summers, addressing Fink, "how about this business of attacking the freebooters, and rescuing that young lady! I for one am ready to risk my life for her, and to revenge myself on them for one of my dearest friends, who now lies below, cold in his winding sheet."

His lips quivered, his voice was tremulous, and many a sad face turned toward him a sympathizing look.

"We are all ready to do our best to aid you," said another of the party; and with his eye he appealed to the rest.

"All! all!" was the response.

"Then for our plan at once," rejoined Hamilton, looking toward Fink.

"Isn't thar a chap aboard here, what gin us the alarm!" inquired Mike, in reply.

"There is; one Ned Groth, so he calls himself," answered Summers. "He is now below."

"Tell him he's wanted on deck," said Mike to the Irishman.

The latter disappeared, and presently returned with the personage in question. Groth came up to the group rather shyly, as one who is not exactly certain of his reception, and fearful of something wrong. He now carried one arm in a sling, which had been wounded by a pistol-ball during the affray.

"See here," said Mike, confronting him rather sternly, "you belong to that —— infernal band of robbers, don't you?"

"I-I *did* belong to 'em once," stammered the traitor, emphasizing the word "did," and turning pale.

"So I'd judge, ef you never told me," responded Mike, "jest from one look at that thar ugly face o' yourn. But don't be looking skeered now! We arn't agoing to hurt you—that is, unless you get tricky—in which case it might be a leetle, jest a leetle, dangerous fur you. You understand?"

"O, I'll swear to be true to you forever."

"I don't think as how it makes it any stronger, 'cause you swear it; but never mind. What we want o' you now is, to tell us what you know about this here Camilla and his band."

"We wish to know their force, and whether it will be prudent for us to attack them?" put in Hamilton.

"Well," said Groth, evidently relieved of his apprehensions

for his own safety, "as to numbers, I don't think there's more nor ten of 'em there now, the rest being down the river; and I shouldn't, for my part, be afeard to venter what force there is here agin 'em."

"But what do you think will be our best plan to pursue?" asked Hamilton.

"I knows it; it's jest the easiest thing in the world."

"But who will guide us?"

"I will, if you want me to."

"But you might betray us?"

"And who'll I betray ye to, d'ye s'pose?" rejoined Groth, in an offended tone.

"Why to Camilla, to be sure."

"D'ye think as how I don't want to live as well nor the rest on ye?"

"I presume you have no desire to die immediately."

"Then you may calculate I'll not trouble Camilla agin in a hurry."

"But if you betray us into his hands, he may forgive you all past offenses."

"Umph! not he. You don't know much about him, to say that. *He* never forgives nobody that he once quarrels with. Besides, I'm under sentence o' death, for having broke one o' his orders; and so the first time we meet, the one that can kill t'other first's the best feller."

"I'll take care he don't play us false," said Mike to Hamilton.

"Enough, then," answered the latter; "I will trust him in your hands, and I doubt not this will be satisfactory to the others. Is it so?" he added, appealing to them.

Each replied in the affirmative.

"It's decided, is it," said Fink, "that we're all agoing to walk tall into 'em?"

"That I believe is the decision," answered Hamilton.

"Whoop!—hurray! I've got suthing to live for yit. Only wish the time war at hand. But come, here, you vagabones, stir your trotters now, fur thar's work on hand! Cast off the bow-line, and push her into the stream."

The orders of Mike to his men were speedily obeyed, and in a few minutes the Light-foot was swung from her moorings, and floating down with the current. As she gained the center of the stream, several figures were discerned on the rocky ridge of the Illinois shore, apparently watching her motions.

"They're on the look-out for us, the infernal possums!" observed Mike to the Irishman.

"Be me sowl! an' I jist think it'll be afther doing 'em good to look out, till they git tired on't; and thin we'll jist be looking out for thim, sure, and see how they'll like that, the blaggards!"

In a short time the Light-foot turned a bend in the river, which completely hid her from Cave-in-Rock, when Mike Fink gave orders to have the dead brought on deck, preparatory to consigning them to their watery graves. In a few minutes his orders were obeyed, when followed a solemn and affecting scene.

There were three females on board, two of whom had lost their husbands in the affray, and were nearly distracted in consequence. It had been found impossible to persuade them to remain below, and they now came on deck, weeping and moaning piteously, and wringing their hands in an agony of mind indescribable, and calling upon the names of their departed friends, in tones that went to the hearts of all who heard them, and caused many an eye, unused to the weeping mood, to fill with tears.

"Alas! Henry," exclaimed one, a good-looking female of thirty years, as she came and stood over the bloody corse of her late husband, "I can not, can not part with thee! Oh! return to me, return—for pity's sake, return! You must not, can not, shall not be dead! Dead? No, no!—not dead—not dead! Henry, speak!—'tis I, thy wife, thy dearly-loved wife, that is calling thee! Oh God! why does he look so pale and ghastly?" continued she, wildly, turning to those around her. "He used not so to look"; and she would have thrown herself upon the body, had not some of the bystanders restrained her.

"Be calm, lady—be calm!" said one, soothingly.

"Calm!" cried the other, almost fiercely; "who talks to me of being calm, and he lying there, motionless and cold and dead!" And she sobbed aloud.

"Alas! poor lady," said one, aside, "well may you weep!"

The other female, mentioned as her companion in grief, was not less affected; and the tears, and sighs, and sobs, and lamentations of both were enough to make the sternest heart soft with pity.

"They shall be revenged!" observed Mike sternly, as he gazed upon these two poor bereaved unprotected beings, with a heart swelling with emotion. "They shall be revenged!" and he compressed his lips, and clenched his brawny hands, as one whose resolve is not to be shaken.

"My life shall be freely exposed, to rescue the living and avenge the dead," said the voice of Hamilton.

"And mine," rejoined Summers.

"And mine, and mine," cried several voices.

"Thar's no cowards here, I'm thinking," rejoined Mike, glancing around upon the stern faces of the group. "And so now's all's settled, let's bury the dead."

There were in all seven bodies, four of which were of Camilla's band. Stripping these latter of whatever was valuable, they attached to them weights, and not very ceremoniously cast them into the river. The three remaining bodies, one being that of Fontaine, were treated with some ceremony. They were sewed up in sacks, and lowered into the water with ropes; while all save the bereaved ones, who made great lamentations—stood in silence, with uncovered heads and solemn faces, till the waters of the Ohio had closed over the mortal remains of those who had so lately been their companions and friends.

INCIDENTS • THE PREPARATIONS TO ATTACK THE OUTLAWS

For several hours the Light-foot continued to glide gracefully down the now somewhat swollen and turbid Ohio, keeping near the center of the stream, and avoiding either shore; for at this period there were many roving bands of savages in the dark forests lining the banks, who ever made war upon the whites, and stopped at no crimes short of the extreme barbarisms of their nature and education.

On the present occasion, Dick Weatherhead was master of the helm; and as the boat in its progress now required but little other aid to keep her in the channel, the remainder of the crew took occasion to lounge upon the deck, and speculate on the dark events which had so lately taken place, and anticipate the probable result of their forthcoming assault upon the freebooters.

"Be the howly St. Pathrick!" exclaimed the Irishman, at length, in reply to previous observations, "it's meself that's afther thinking we'll be the boys to walk into thim sons of Sathan, and taach thim a few things sich as their mothers niver taught 'em afore, at all, at all."

"T-t-that's a fact," replied Jack; " 't-'t-wont do t-to be c-c-circumlocutory in this here m-matter—not-not a bit of it. W-we'll have to-to take 'em diagonally, P-Pat."

"Well, Misther Short, all I've got to say about it is, jist let 'em give Michael Flanegan's son Pathrick a fair shake, and if he don't walk clean through 'em, like wather through—a—a—"

"What in the name o' the great white-bar o' the polar seas, is ye a making comparison with water fur?" interrupted Mike, at this moment joining the circle, which consisted of some half a dozen individuals. "Why don't ye talk about suthing ye know's about?—whisky, fur instance."

"Be jabers!" returned the Irishman, shrugging his shoulders, "and is it whiskey ye're afther spaaking about? Och, honey, I didn't sae ye before, or whisky'd bin the ounly thing I could ha' thinked on, jist."

"Do you mean to say, Pat," asked another, "that Mike particularly reminds you of suthing strong?"

"Faith an' I do—strong and spiritual," answered the other.

"You're a hoss," rejoined Fink, "you are. What'll ye take for your body, Pat, when the hangman's done with it?"

"Who wants to buy?" asked the Irishman.

"I do," answered Mike.

"Faith, thin, I'll not bargain it to ye."

"Why not, Patrick?"

"Jist for the very rason that it 'ud be chating ye."

"How so? I think it'd be a grand speculation, ef you don't ask too much for it, 'cause arter stilling out the whisky, ye see, my trump, I could sell it to the doctors for full valuation."

"Could ye?" queried the Irishman, winking to the others. "Oho, blatheration to ye! and do ye think ye'd be wanting it thin, Misther Fink?"

"And why not, Pat?"

"For the same rason that Jimmy Stady wasn't at his brother's wake in the oulden time—'cause he was hung himself afore his brother."

"Come, I'll licker, and call it quits, Pat," rejoined Fink, amid a roar of laughter from the bystanders; and forthwith the bottle was produced and passed among the group.

At this moment Hamilton approached and addressed himself to Mike.

"What are your calculations concerning our proposed attack on the outlaws?" he inquired.

"Why," replied Fink, "we must run the Light-foot down a piece further, to a certain creek I knows on, and then conceal her thar, and take it afoot back through the country, so as we can reach 'em about dark, and watch our chance. I 'spect it'll be hot work, Mr. Hamilton."

"There is no doubt of that at least," was the answer; "and unless we take them at great advantage, we shall be likely, I fear, to come out second best."

"They may kill me, per'aps," rejoined Mike; "but ef they lick me alive, in fair fight, I'll agree to gin in that I'm nobody. Any how it'll be a fight, and that's suthing I've bin aching for this three months. But come, boys," he added, addressing the others.

"Bring out your shooting irons, and have 'em cleaned, ready to go ahead when the time comes for to fight, when, my angels, I'll 'spect to see you doing suthing that'll reflect credit on ye fur a long while to come, ef not longer."

In a few minutes the crew of the Light-foot, such of them as could be spared from their other duties, together with most of the passengers, were engaged in cleaning their arms, and new-flinting and repairing such locks as were out of order, preparatory to the coming dangerous expedition against the freebooters of Cave-in-Rock.

"Whar's Groth?" inquired Fink.

"I've not seen him this two hours," answered one.

"Nor I," replied another.

"Per'aps he's down below," suggested a third.

"Bill, go down and see," said Mike, addressing the boy; "and ef you find him, tell him he's wanted up here instanter."

The youth departed, and in a few minutes returned and reported that nothing could be found of him.

"By ——!" cried Mike, making use of an oath, "ef he's turned traitor to us and got off, then it's all up, sartin; fur we can't do any thing unless we take 'em by surprise."

"I do not think he has left the boat," replied Hamilton; "and so supose we commence a search for him at once."

A search was accordingly set on foot, but was for some fifteen minutes unsuccessful, when the missing man was discovered amidships, beside a barrel of whiskey, in a state of insensibility. At first he was thought to be dead; but a slight examination, aided by the sight of a straw protruding from a gimblet hole in the barrel, explained the mystery, and convinced all that he was only dead drunk.

"Thar's a great propensity fur licker on this here boat, somehow," observed Mike; "and ef a man's wanted to do any thin, he's jest sure to have his upper story the heaviest; consequently, tharfore, I 'spect I'll have to make an example o' somebody soon, in order to stop it; and so I reckon I mought as well begin on this here chap, fur fear I won't git a better subject soon.

Here boys, (addressing two or three of his crew) up with him to the deck, and don't spill him on the passage."

As soon as his order had been obeyed, Mike, who had kept close to the body, said:

"Now some o' ye fetch me a long rope, and we'll teach this here chap how to imitate the fishes."

"Howly mother! is't drowning him ye're agoing to be afther doing, Misther Fink?"

"No; ducking," replied Mike, laconically.

"Ah, troth, then ye've not forgot the pail of wather ye swollered yerself, I'm thinking," returned Pat, alluding to the means by which the other had been sobered the night before.

"C-c-call it a h-h-hogshead, n-n-not a pail, observed Jack; "f-for I know s-s-something how it felt, I c-c-calculate"; and the speaker glanced his one eye mischievously round upon the group, and gave his tongue pull play upon the weed within his capacious jaws.

Fastening a rope securely around the waist of the deserter, Mike gave orders to have him thrown overboard; and in less than a minute the body of Groth fell with a splash into the stream, and floated alongside of the Light-foot, care being taken to keep it on the surface of the water. The effect of this bath at first was not apparent; but ere long the drunken man began to show signs of consciousness; and in a short time he was drawn aboard, nearly sober.

"You're a putty sucker now, arn't ye?" said Mike, addressing him. "You're a putty sucker, I say, to git drunk at this here perticular time, and lay belly up'ards, like a dead sun-fish."

"Why-why the fact is, ye see, cap-cap-'en," stammered Groth, "I saw the barrel, and the straw, and feeling a little dry, the temptation was so strong, ye see—"

"O, I see, in course," interrupted Mike. "But look here: I've got a word to say to you in private"; and he took Groth aside. "Now we've bin making our calculations on walking tall into them Camilla chaps tonight, and I'd like to know what you think about it."

"I'm in favor on't, of course," answered the other.

"Well, do you think as how you can guide us right straight among 'em, without making any mistake?"

"That's what I think."

"Are you ready to stake your life on't?"

Groth looked closely at Fink, as if to divine his motive for asking.

"I'm in arnest about this," pursued Mike; "and ef you arn't willing to stake your life on the 'venter, don't say so."

"I am," replied Groth; "for I'd do any thing to git revenge on Camilla."

"Then look here: d'ye see that?" and Fink pointed a pistol toward the deserter.

Groth turned pale.

"D'ye see that?" continued Mike.

"Yes-yes—I-I sees it."

"Now what in thunderation are ye gitting so skeered about? 'Twont hurt ye, because it arn't loaded."

"O yes—ha, ha!—a good joke," said Groth, with a grin, as he found that his life was not menaced.

"Thar's no joke about it," replied Mike. "I war only jest showing you that thar pistol, in order to say, that I'm about to put two balls into it; and ef you conduct us right, well and good; but ef you don't—why I'll let you guess the rest"; and Mike turned away, leaving Groth standing alone.

As he crossed the deck, Mike espied a negro sitting on the Kentucky bank of the river, about a hundred yards distant, with one of his legs extending down the bank, so that his feet just touched the water.

"Who sees a nigger any whar?" shouted Mike.

This drew the attention of each, first to the speaker, and then to the object of his remarks.

"Bring me my rifle, some o' ye," continued Fink.

"Good heavens! you are not going to shoot the negro, are you?" queried Hamilton, in alarm.

There was something rather mischievous in the look of Fink, as he replied coolly:

"Why you don't think niggers o' any 'count, do ye?"

"Kill him at your peril then!" rejoined Hamilton, as Jack reached to Mike his long, unerring weapon.

Mike measured with the ramrod the charge in his gun, and then deliberately cocked it, raised it to his eye, and pointed it toward the negro.

"For heaven's sake, don't shoot," spoke up Summers.

Mike lowered his rifle and laughed heartily, and some of his crew, suspecting there was more mischief in his design than malice, joined him in his merriment.

"Who ever seed a nigger with a short heel?" inquired Mike, playfully, as again he brought his long rifle to his shoulder.

There was a momentary suspense, during which every eye was fixed upon the African, who, all unconscious that he was an object of particular regard, sat quietly upon the bank, in turn watching the progress of the boat, as smoothly it glided along before him. Suddenly there came a flash and a crack, and the negro bounded up from the earth with a yell of pain, and catching his heel, which had been partly shot away, with his hand, stood for a moment irresolute. Then shaking his fist at the spectators on the boat, he turned and disappeared. Mike and his crew laughed heartily at the occurrence, considering it decidedly a good joke; but the others looked upon it far more gravely, and joined them not in their levity.

For an hour or two longer the Light-foot continued her course without interruption when she suddenly ran upon a sawyer, with such force as to cause her to tremble in every timber, and create no little consternation among all aboard. On examination it was found no damage had been done, and the fears of all were soon quieted.

A mile farther on, the Light-foot gained the creek spoken of by Mike, when he at once gave orders to have her run into it.

This creek, or inlet, set back from the river some two hundred yards, between steep hills, and was rendered dark by the dense foliage of the trees overhead. For a place of secrecy, none better could have been found; and having entered it, the boat was rowed up, by the crew, to a spot where the thick branches completely concealed her from the view of any one standing five paces distant, and there made fast. It was then agreed to here leave the females and the two who had been wounded in the affray in charge of two other passengers and the boy, while the rest set forward on their expedition against the freebooters.

Of those now preparing to depart, there were in all, including Groth, ten individuals, namely, Fink, Weatherhead, Flanegan, Short, and two others of the crew, and Hamilton, Summers, and another young man by the name of Clinton, of the passengers.

Having seen all well equipped with rifles, pistols, and ammunition, Mike glanced around him with a proud smile, and said:

"Boys, I 'spect, by your looks, you've all on ye made up your minds what you've got to do, and that it arn't no sneak o' a business nether. The short on't is, we're agoing to lick somebody or die—that's the way to say it; and ef thar's one here as 'spects to be troubled with a leak, I'd like him to mention the fact now, so as we can overhaul and have him calked, or left in the dry dock altogether. We're agoing to run on to some snags, boys—thar's no doubt 'bout it; and it can't be 'sposed we'll git off with whole timbers; 'tan't in the nater o' things; and what's agin nater's agin law; and what's agin law won't stand; and so I tell ye on't at the start. Now who's agoing to spring a leak, I say—who?"

"I guess we're all putty considerable kind o' tolerable sound," observed Dick Weatherhead, in reply.

"Dick, you're an ace," resumed Mike, complacently; "and the feller what turns you up's got a good hand, provided he's got a Jack o' the same suit to back it"; and he winked at Short.

Jack smiled, winked his one eye in return, and, screwing up his mouth, was preparing to reply, when Mike interposed.

"Never mind," he said, "nater never calculated you to say much, no how, or else she'd put a fixin into your face to let it out smoother and quicker. It don't matter ef you don't say it, Jack, 'cause we can guess the gist on't, and know it's suthing complimentary. Don't Jack," continued Mike, motioning with his hand, "don't try it now, 'cause it gives me the ager to see you twist your handsome phiz that way, and makes me so infernal dry—you can't think. By the way, Dick, 'spose you pass me that thar bottle; it'll relieve me so to take a parting salute."

Having drank, Mike passed the bottle to the next, and so it went to each of the party.

"Now," he pursued, "let us start, fur we han't got any too much time on hand, ef we do any thing to-night. It's not like we'll all come back agin, any how, and so I 'spose we'd better say good bye to them as stays behind. By the way, Dick, you remember, I reckon, what old Mother Deb said 'bout us gitting into difficulties?"

"I han't forgot it," answered the one addressed. "I b'lieve you and Jack, though war the ones in for't."

"That's a fact, Mr. Weatherhead; I think she did say suthing 'bout my gitting into a scrape, for some gal or other—per'aps this here's the one. She said, too, I'd die a bloody death, the old sarpent—wonder ef it's near? Never mind, though, ef she thinks to skeer me from a fight, she'll git mistaken; fur unless I'm jumping into suthing, I won't be able to live six months no how; and so I mought as well die one way as t'other; tharfore, boys, jest allow me to conclude by saying, I'm in for a fight, I'll go my death on a fight, and a fight I must have, one that'll tar up the arth all round and look kankarifferous, or else I'll have to be salted down to save me from spiling, as sure nor Massassip alligators make fly traps o' thar infernal ugly jawrs. Whoop!—hurray!" and Mike concluded by jumping up and striking his feet together, and declaring that he was an "out-and-out seahoss."

In a few minutes from the close of his harrangue, Fink, at the head of the party described, set out on his dangerous expedition against the freebooters of Cave-in-Rock.

THE ONSET • THE CONFLICT • THE CONFLAGRATION • THE
DEAD AND THE DYING • DEATH OF THE OUTLAW AND HIS
DAUGHTER • MEETING OF THE LOVERS • CONCLUSION

Guided by Groth, who knew the ground well, our river friends
pushed forward at a fast gait, and reached their destination
about an hour from the setting in of night. The first sounds
which greeted them on their arrival, were those made by the
revelers; and stealing up carefully to the old building wherein
the outlaws were congregated, Mike Fink and his companions
were enabled to get a partial view of them and overhear a portion of their conversation.

For half an hour longer, all remained quiet without, during
which the sounds within showed that the outlaws were gradually progressing to a state of intoxication. At length the mention of Maurice St. Vincent by Camilla, together with his foul
design of having him put to death, arrested the attention of the
boatmen, and, grasping their weapons, each stood ready to take
advantage of the first opportunity to fall upon the freebooters.
The order addressed to Anthon to call the negro was also distinctly heard by the boatmen and whispering a few words to
Short, Mike and his crew drew aside to let him pass.

Anthon, all unconscious of the proximity of enemies, had advanced but a few steps from the threshold, when Jack, who, like
some dark spirit, had noiselessly glided up to his side unnoticed,
threw all his strength into the blow, and buried his knife in the
doomed man's heart, who sunk down without even a groan.
Then wrenching out the bloody weapon, Jack as noiselessly
glided back to the others.

As the reader is aware, nothing of this was known to any
within and as Camilla reached the door, he found himself con-
fronted by Mike, who, shouting the words recorded,[7] discharged
a pistol at the outlaw's body. The force of the charge staggered
Camilla back, but the ball striking against the blade of a knife
in his belt, he was left unharmed.

7. The words, recorded in a previous chapter, were "Hell seize the fiend!"

For a moment, but a moment only, Camilla seemed thunder-struck and confused; and then perceiving who was the daring intruder, and that he was backed by a considerable force—for the heads of the boatmen could just be dimly seen over the shoulders of their leader—he gnashed his teeth in fury, and leaping into the midst of his astonished companions, shouted in a voice of thunder:

"We are surprised! Out with the lights, and follow me! We must do or die, or—!" and grasping a pistol and knife, he rushed to the rear door of the building, followed by his band in wild disorder.

"Arter 'em," cried Mike, with a yell of delight. "Arter the hellians, and don't give 'em no quarter. Chawr 'em up like a Varginna nigger does cabbage."

Whooping and yelling, the boatmen now rushed after their leader, upsetting the table as they went and discharging their pistols at the retreating outlaws, one or two of which took effect, as could be told by their cries of pain and curses.

"They come," said Hamilton, to his companions. "Let every shot tell upon them!" And as the robbers gained the open air, they were greeted by some five or six bullets in front, and two of their number fell badly wounded.

"Surrounded, by ——!" shouted Camilla, hoarse with passion, uttering a terrible oath. "Hell's curses and mine upon them! Turn, men, and rend them asunder! Down with the wretches—down!"

Obedient to his orders, the outlaws drew their weapons, and each singling out his antagonist, rushed upon him, uttering yells and curses, and for a few minutes the conflict was fierce and bloody. Every man there, on both sides, was resolved to conquer or die; and the report of fire-arms, the clashing of knives, the oaths, the yells, the groans, and the stamping of feet made a din and a scene worthy a regular battle field.

Rushing into the building so lately occupied by the revelers, Mike snatched up a lamp, and, after pitching the silver plate out

of the window, set fire to the tablecloth, and some other very
ignitable matter, and then darted out the way he entered. In a
few minutes the building was in flames; and the fire, with its
many tongues, roared, and crackled, and twined itself around
the table, the benches, and the floor, and gradually crept up the
logs to the thatching of the roof, and burst out above and on all
sides, seeming like some terrible spirit sent to do vengeance.

The conflict had been short and bloody, and was now over.
Here and there, by the light of the burning building, could be
seen a dark form stretched upon the green earth, pale and
ghastly, besmeared with blood, and motionless. On one side of
the burning pile lay the body of Anthon; on the other, the
bodies of Selman and Groth, locked in each other's arms; and,
scattered around them, the mortal remains of Larkin, Hans, and
two others of the outlaws; and Clinton, Short, and another of
our river friends. Dick Weatherhead, too, had been mortally
wounded; and he now came staggering toward Mike and the
Irishman, his face covered with blood, and his eyes glaring
wildly.

Fink and Flanegan rushed to him.

"It's all over, Mike, my friend," said the dying man, in a
feeble voice, grasping the hand of his old patron.

Mike was not used to the weeping mood; but he had seen, by
the light of the crackling flames, a scene which softened his
heart, and he now brushed a tear from his eye. Flanegan did the
same for himself.

"It's all over, my friends," pursued Dick. "There he lays, the
foul fiend! what gin me my death blow"; and Dick pointed to
the body of one of the outlaws, a few paces distant.

"But Dick, don't die yit," said Fink, "jest as we've got the
victory!"

"Got to do it," said Dick, laconically. "It's here—it's coming";
and he placed his hand upon a deep gash in his abdomen.
"Farewell, Mike. Farewell, Pat. Going! God forgive me!" and as
he spoke, he sunk down and expired.

"Expensive victory, this here!" observed Mike, gazing upon the dead man a moment, with an expression of grief on his rough features.

"Och! troth! and it's all that same," returned Pat, walking to and fro uneasily. "Och! the divils—the hathen! Is there iny more to kill, Misther Fink, to revinge thim as is dead now, jist?"

"Don't seem as ef thar war," replied Fink, looking round him. "All that arn't dead have traveled, I reckon—fled—gone—bin k·ered away like pigeons in hunting time."

Such was the fact. Save those who had fallen in the skirmish, not one of the robbers could now be seen.

"Whoop!" shouted Mike, his old habits getting the better of him, even here in the presence of his dead comrades. "Whoop! I say. Hooray for a fight! Whar's Camilla—the bloody coward?"

"I seed him running, and two fellers arter him," answered a voice close behind Mike.

Fink turned round, and recognized in the speaker one of his crew, the only one, save the Irishman, that had escaped.

"Whar'd you turn up, Lewis?" questioned Mike.

"O, I fou't one o' the chaps clean out here, for a quarter o' a mile, and he got away from me at last, and run for life."

"Hurt any, Lewis?"

"Only a few scratches."

"Then keep with me, ready for business. Did ye see whar Camilla went to?"

"Thought he run into one o' the houses?"

"Got to burn him out then, sartin."

"Howly murther!" exclaimed the Irishman, suddenly; "may be it's his captives ye'd be afther burning along wid him?"

Mike started back in dismay, and exclaimed, with an oath:

"Right, Pat; I'd forgot. Let's follow. Ef 'tan't too late, we must save 'em or die. Push ahead, Lewis, and show us the chute."

As Mike said this, all three darted away in the direction of Camilla's house.

"Be howly St. Patrick! somebody's ahead o' us, in the burning line, I'm thinking," cried Pat as they neared the residence of the bandit-chief, distant from the place of the skirmish some two hundred yards.

"What d'ye see, Pat?"

"Sae, is it, ye're asking? Look yonder! Now ask what is that, may be ye will!"

"Fire, by ———!" cried Mike, making use of an oath, as he perceived, at the moment, a lurid flame light up the windows of the outlaw's dwelling, at the door of which Hamilton and Summers were striving with all their might to gain an entrance.

"What are ye doing here?" cried Mike, as he came up to them, panting.

"Camilla fled hither, and within his prisoners are confined," answered Hamilton.

"Why 'dye fire the building then, till ye'd got 'em out?"

"We did not. Camilla fired it himself. He swore he would have revenge with his dying breath, and this is the way he takes it."

"Hell seize him!" rejoined Fink. "But we must down with the door, and save 'em."

"Too late—too late!" cried Summers. "See!—see! The flames are already bursting from yon window, and lapping the roof. No one could live five minutes within."

"Ha, ha, ha!" laughed a voice at this moment, so unearthly as to make every one involuntarily shrink back and shudder.

Looking upward, each saw Camilla standing on the roof of the burning building, his form displayed by the light of the fire in bold relief against the dark background of the distant sky, and seeming, from his position, the light by which he was seen, and the imaginations of those who saw him, like some hideous phantom of twice his ordinary size.

"Ha, ha, ha!" laughed he again. "Fools!—fools all! I defy you! I spit at you! Thus, thus I take my revenge!—and thus my prisoners and your friends die with me! Fools!—ha, ha, ha!— fools!" and he pointed his finger at the spectators with a gesture of derision; then, ere any one was aware how, he suddenly disappeared.

For a few minutes, in speechless wonder, our friends kept their eyes riveted on the spot where they last saw the outlaw. Every moment the greedy flames seemed to become more and more greedy; and they writhed and rolled, and ran out their devouring tongues, and snapped, and crackled, and seemed to hiss, while out rushed volumes of smoke, and the walls fairly trembled, and the heat grew so intense as to make it uncomfortable for any one to stand near.

While occupied thus, in silently gazing upon the devouring elements and thinking of the fate of those supposed to be within, our friends were startled by hearing a voice shout:

"Save her! save her!—for the love of heaven, save her!—save them both!"

On looking round, what was their surprise, to behold Maurice St. Vincent, accompanied by the negro, rushing to them from the direction of the river!

"Heavens!" exclaimed Hamilton—"we thought you lost!"

"I might as well be; for she—she—is—oh God!—lost!" and he pointed to the burning structure. "But I must save her!" and, before any one could interfere, he had reached the door.

It was already on fire; and pushing hard against it, it flew open, and the flames rushing out, drove him back several paces. Recovering himself in a moment, and without pausing to think on the rash step he was taking, Maurice again darted forward, and would have jumped into the building, had not Hamilton and Summers together sprang to and restrained him by force. Maurice in vain struggled to free himself. At length, when he saw that all hope of saving his beloved was indeed over, he threw himself upon the earth, and groaned like one in pain.

Suddenly all were again startled by the voice of a female shrieking for help, proceeding from the river. Maurice bounded to his feet.

"God of mercy!" he cried, "it is her voice! I know it! I would know it among a million! Follow, in the name of heaven!" and he bounded away himself like the startled roe.

"Dat's she—dis chile knows um too," said the negro, setting off at full speed after Maurice.

" 'Spect it's a race for all on us," rejoined Mike; and the next moment every one was striving as if for life to be first at the river's bank.

The light of the surrounding buildings made all around, for a considerable distance, like to day; and when our friends gained the river's bank, to their unbounded astonishment, they beheld the tall form of Camilla far below them, rapidly moving over the rocks, bearing a female in his arms, who was still screaming for aid. By the outlaw's side was another female arrayed in white, who seemed by her gestures entreating him to forbear. As they gazed down, the superstitious boatmen felt their blood run cold; for having seen Camilla so lately on the roof of his own dwelling, they could not conceive how he had got here unseen by any. Maurice, however, had not stopped to consider the point; for to him there was no mystery; and he was now fast leaping over the rocks, and nearing Camilla at every moment. There was a boat near, floating on the water, but fastened by a line to the shore. Reaching this in advance of his pursuers, the outlaw, with Aurelia in his arms, sprang into it, followed by Celia, and, cutting the rope with his knife, pushed into the stream, uttering a laugh of derision.

"He's more devil than human!" exclaimed Mike, who with the others had watched Camilla from the brow of the cliff. "Give me a rifle, somebody; and ef he's mortal, I'll soon make him immortal."

"Here is one," said Summers.

Mike caught and cocked the piece, and brought it to his eye.

"For heaven's sake, don't miss your mark!" exclaimed Hamilton.

There was now a moment of breathless suspense, when the silence was broken by a sharp report, and Camilla, who had been standing erect, was seen to stagger and reel, and finally fall over the side of the boat, upsetting it as he did so, and plunging all within it into the watery element.

"Onward to save them!" cried Hamilton; and with lightning speed, every one plunged forward, down the rocks to the river.

Maurice was far in advance; and with a piercing cry of hope and despair, he now leaped into the dark waters. Being an expert swimmer, he reached Aurelia just as she was sinking, and, by great exertions, brought her to shore, at the moment when the others joined him.

"Save her!" he said, breathlessly, pointing toward the water.

Without a moment's pause Fink, Hamilton, and Summers, dashed into the stream, and struck out in various directions. For some time nothing was seen of either Camilla or his daughter. Then a white and dark object—Camilla and Celia—locked in each other's arms—rose to the surface, and, before either of the swimmers could reach them, disappeared. Again they rose, and sank again. Sank, to rise no more in life. Slept, to wake no more till the great day of judgment. All was over. Their spirits were with their Maker. Father and daughter—vice and virtue—crime and innocence—hand in hand, had together passed the threshold of eternity.

The bodies of the drowned, after repeated trials, were at last recovered, brought to the shore, and laid upon the rocks. It was an impressive sight, then and there, to behold, by the glare of the conflagration, the living and the dead, side by side on the rocks, with the dark river rolling by—its gentle ripples, together with the roaring of the distant flames, the only sounds that broke the otherwise awful silence. It was a striking scene. There, upon the ground, lay the bold outlaw-chief, a deep wound in his breast, his dress spotted with blood, and his dark, sinister features contorted with the last agonies of death. By his side, robed in white, emblematical of her innocence and purity, her pale features still calm and sweet in expression, lay his lovely daughter. By her side, upon the ground, her long, wet tresses fairly sweeping the face of the dead, knelt Aurelia, weeping bitterly. Near her, with his arms folded, and a solemn expression on his countenance, stood Maurice. In front of him, one hand resting upon a rock, his hard weatherbeaten features relaxed into a softened expression as he gazed downward, stood Mike Fink. Grouped around, in various postures, their faces all wearing saddened expressions, stood the rest. All seen by the light of the conflagration! What a scene for the pencil!

The sun was just rising above the eastern hills, when Mike and his party, after having buried their companions, as well as circumstances would permit, and fired the other two old buildings, quitted Cave-in-Rock, on their return to the Light-foot, which they reached in the course of the day, nearly exhausted, and found all aboard safe, but in a state of alarm at their long absence. Ere the sun had passed the western ridge, the Light-foot was again floating down the beautiful Ohio, as smoothly and quietly as if nothing had occurred to interrupt her passage.

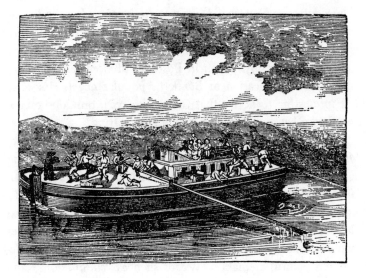

Crockett Almanac Stories
(1850-53)

ISSUES OF THE "CROCKETT ALMANACS" in 1850, 1851, 1852, and 1853 contained several passages about Fink. The first three of these booklets were published by Fisher & Brother, so the title pages said, in Philadelphia, New York, and Boston. The fourth was published in New York by Philip J. Cozans. All, therefore, were eastern publications. The origin and the nature of these anecdotes make it highly unlikely that they were anything more than fillers written to formula by hacks. The flurry of anecdotes suggests that Mike was at the time famous in the East, possibly because of the story about him printed in the pamphlet descriptive of "Banvard's Panorama" (see p. 281)—a huge picture recently shown in Boston and elsewhere—and because of the publication of Bennett's popular novel. However, it is interesting to notice that the stories, with only one exception, had a backwoods rather than a river setting.

In one of the stories, Davy Crockett's wife figures; in one, Mike's wife (name unspecified); and in two, Mike's charming daughter Sal. Davy and Mike were both being endowed with kinfolk worthy of such mighty men. In the story about Sal we are rather fond of the "Injuns," who "determined to skin Sal alive, sprinkle a leetle salt over her, an' devour her before her own eyes"; so we are saddened somewhat to read of their wholesale and painful cremation. Words such as "somniferous" and "suddenachous," strangely enough, were long thought by easterners to be characteristic of western dialogue.

MIKE FINK TRYING TO SCARE MRS. CROCKETT (1850)

You've all on you, heered of Mike Fink, the celebrated, an self-created, an never to be mated, Mississippi roarer, snag-lifter, an flatboat skuller. Well, I knowed the critter all round, an upside down; he war purty fair amongst squaws, cat-fish, an big niggers, but when it come to walkin into wild cats, bars, or alligators, he couldn't hold a taller candle to my young son, Hardstone Crockett. I'll never forget the time he tried to scare my wife Mrs. Davy Crockett. You see, the critter had tried all sorts of ways to scare her, but he had no more effect on her than droppen feathers on a barn floor; so he at last bet me a dozen wild cats that he would appear to her, an scare her teeth loose, an her toe nails out of joint; so the varmint one night arter a big freshet took an crept into an old alligator's skin, an met Mrs. Crockett jist as she was taken an evening's walk. He spread open the mouth of the critter, an made sich a holler howl that he nearly scared himself out of the skin, but Mrs. Crockett didn't care any more for that, nor the alligator skin than she would for a snuff of lightnin, but when Mike got a leetle too close, and put out his paws with the idea of an embrace, then I tell you what, her indignation rose a little bit higher than a Mississippi flood, an she throwed a flash of eye-lightnen upon him that made it clear daylight for half an hour, but Mike thinkin of the bet an his fame for courage, still wagged his tail an walked out, when Mrs. Crocket out with a little teeth pick, and with a single swing of it sent the hull head and neck flyin fifty feet off, the blade jist shavin the top of Mike's head, and then seeing what it war, she trowed down her teeth pick, rolled up her sleeves, an battered poor Fink so that he fainted away in his alligator skin, an he war so all scaren mad, when he come too, that he swore he had been chawed up, and swallered by an alligator.

MIKE FINK'S TREAT TO THE INDIANS (1851)

The celebrated Mike Fink once observed some Indians stealing into a widow's milk-cave, from which they had frequently
stolen quantities of cream, meat, cheese, &c. He watched them
until they got in, fastened the door outside, and then bored
holes through the bank above. He and his son then commenced
pouring hot water down on them, until they yelled, kicked, and
fainted; while those who could broke out, and ran off to the
woods, half scalded, telling their people that the milk-cave
rained hot water.

THE BRAVERY OF MIKE FINK'S WIFE (1851)

One day a Snake Indian walked into Mike Fink's cabin,
when he was out hunting, picked up a venison ham, and ran
off with it. Mike's wife hearing a noise, looked out, and saw
the robber making off with his booty. She picked up a gun and
a hunting-knife, and started in pursuit. Finding that he could
outstrip her in running, she fired a ball into his right thigh,
which disabled him. She then came up to him, secured the
ham, tied the villain's hands together, dragged him back to the
cabin, and kept him prisoner until her husband returned; who,
thinking that the poor devil had already suffered enough, let
him go. He went limping off, saying he would never steal anything more from Mrs. Fink.

MIKE FINK HUNTING A MOOSE (1851)

The celebrated Mike Fink, the great admiral of flat-boatmen
on the Western rivers, the William Tell of marksmen on land,
and the most daring of all wild-forest adventurers, was the
Prince of moose-catchers. A moose reader, is a very large species
of deer, with a body like a fat horse, without the tail, and a
head something like that of a jackass, to which is appended a
large pair of horns, weighing sometimes as much as ninety
pounds. They are higher than an ordinary horse, and frequently
weigh more. A mammoth specimen of one of these brutes had

long baffled the skill of the best of marksmen and hunters, principally from his furious character, his peculiar ability to ford the most rapid streams, and his practice, on observing a single hunter on his track, of darting from an ambush, and, with the force of his horns and hoofs, dashing him to pieces. Mike Fink in a late moose hunt, had gone far ahead of his companions, and remained so long away that they became alarmed. They lit the hunters' signal fires all along the ravine, but could discern neither sign nor sound to respond to their hopes. A short and awful time elapsed, when, amid the roar of a torrent, they heard a wild cry of a human being, accompanied by a tremendous snorting. They sprang upon a cliff, from the top of which they beheld Fink clinging to the horns of a huge moose, which was swimming rapidly towards an island, and at the same time endeavouring with all his fury to shake the intruder off. On reaching the shore the animal was somewhat weakened by his journey and heavy burthen, yet he darted back, disengaged himself, and prepared for a last, death-like effort. Fink's gun and pistols being wet, were of course incapable of being discharged; yet he up with the butt of his rifle, which, at the second blow, was shivered to pieces by the heavy horns and head of the animal. He made a third, yet fainter dart, but Fink dodged him, and he fell upon his knees; upon which Fink, turning quickly, plunged his long knife into his throat—a second blow, and Mike Fink stood in triumph over the conquered moose.

THE CELEBRATED MIKE FINK ATTACKED BY A WOLF
WHILE FISHING IN THE MISSISSIPPI (1852)

Mike Fink, having turned his attentions and adventures from the forest to the water, was one day pursuing his famed fishing skill on the Mississippi, without the slightest notion of any interruption from his old antagonists, the wild beasts of the wood: when suddenly, he found himself attacked, while in his very boat, by a monster wolf—who, it was evident, thought to surprise and overcome him without much resistance or danger. A most terrible struggle ensued, and in a most dangerous place for the brave Fink. But our indomitable hero was not to be daunted by anything that threatened him—and he wrestled and tugged with his sturdy antagonist, till the beast foamed at the mouth, and howled—as if more under the effects of pain than rage. Fink next contrived to secure the fore paws of the wolf within the powerful gripe of his two hands—and by a quick and most herculean effort, he flung him from the side of the boat, into the water. The animal slipped from his gripe only to come at him with renewed fury. Fink kicked and pelted him with the oar; but still he managed to bound back at him, as if determined to overcome his intended prey, or die in the effort; at last, Fink, taking advantage of his approach at him, seized his fore paws again, and pressing them up against his head, plunged him back into the torrent, and held him fast there, till he was completely drowned.

SAL FINK'S VICTORY OVER AN OLD BEAR AND CUBS (1852)

Sal Fink went out one morning to gather acorns for her pet pigs, and upon approaching a huge hollow oak tree, and taking a characteristic peep into the opening, she was instantly startled by a loud growl, which was followed by the sudden egress, from the aperture, of a huge she bear, followed by her cubs, who instantly arrayed themselves for an attack upon her. The old bear made a grab at her fair and inviting shoulders, while the young ones sprang and snapped at her exposed extremities, with the fury of wild cats, while Sal greeted their repeated approaches with a furious kick, worthy of a two-year old colt, which sent them rolling over each other, and causing them to bite the ground. But how was the girl managing the mother bear all this time? Springing upright before her, the old one most zealously endeavored to lock her in one of those close embraces or *hugs* for which Bruin is so famous. With her naked fists, (for she scorned the use of her side arms on the occasion) did the intrepid Sal Fink send the creature such a succession of ponderous thumps in the chest, and under the wind, that the old bear became too weak to rise erect before her, although in the last effort, she so far succeeded as to get her forepaws and teeth entangled in Sal's hair, which she held on to with terrible tenacity—and the brave girl struck and kicked to effect her release, like an enraged wild cat—and, darting back to the full length of her hair, she seized on a piece of loose rock, with which she dealth Bruin a death-blow—and dragged her home to her father, Mike Fink.

MIKE FINK KILLING A WOLF WITH HIS FISTS (1852)

During the life of Mike Fink, the great roarer of the Mississippi, large and ferocious wolves were the terror of those regions to both the natives and settlers: and although the government offered high rewards for their extirpation, yet few persons were found with sufficient daring and courage to go far in their pursuit, or even venture in the vicinity of their known haunts. One of these monsters, belonging to a pack, and become a particular terror—and this one, the celebrated Mike Fink determined to seek out, and, as he said, "spiflicate him hull." But it happened that Mike fell in with the object of his adventure when he did not expect him: for, being out one morning strolling, for an appetite, he suddenly encountered the identical monster wolf in a spot well known ever since as "Wolf's den," and the furious beast, being urged by hunger, sprang upon the defenceless intruder with a howl and a bound, that made the spot fairly groan. The daring Fink received his antagonist with nothing but his huge fists. At almost every blow, the animal was disengaged, and thrown upon his haunches. Finally, the wolf succeeded in getting Fink down upon the earth, where the struggle, if possible, became more desperate—while the hideous howls of the beast would have terrified any human being out of all consciousness, but the indomitable Fink. Just as the wolf, with distended tongue and jaws, was making a death bite at him, Mike gave one terrible blow under the pit of the stomach, which rolled him over harmless and defeated.

MIKE FINK'S FIRST VIEW OF A STEAMBOAT (1853)

Mike Fink, on seeing the first steamboat on the Mississippi river, said that he thought that *Noah's ark* was passing by, and that the breath of all the creatures in creation was smoken through the *stove pipe*.

HOW TO ESCAPE A BEAR (1853)

Mike Fink says if you don't like the fun of a fight with bruin, spring up a saplin' that's too small in the trunk for him to hug, and he can't follow; and while he is pawing at the root, drop tabacco juice into his eyes, and he'll walk off as quietly as a Quaker!

MIKE FINK'S IDEE OF A GYMNASTIC SCHOOL (1853)

Mike Fink on being shown the apparatus of a gymnastic school in Cincinnatti, said that the best machinery for making the muscles of youth come up, was to put a pitchfork in his hands, and place him naked in a nest of wild cats.

SAL FINK, THE MISSISSIPPI SCREAMER

HOW SHE COOKED INJUNS (1853)

I dar say you've all on you, if not more, frequently heerd this great she human crittur boasted of, an' pointed out as "one o' the gals"—but I tell you what, stranger, you have never really set your eyes on "one of the gals," till you have seen Sal Fink, the Mississippi screamer, whose miniature pictur I here give, about as nat'ral as life, but not half as handsome—an' if thar ever was a gal that desarved to be christened "one o' the gals," then this gal was that gal—and no mistake.

She fought a duel once with a thunderbolt, an' came off without a single, while at the fust fire she split the thunderbolt all to flinders, an' gave the pieces to Uncle Sam's artillerymen, to touch off their canon with. When a gal about six years old, she used to play see-saw on the Mississippi snags, and arter she war done she would snap 'em off, an' so cleared a large district of the river. She used to ride down the river on an alligator's back, standen upright, an' dancing *Yankee Doodle*, and could leave all the steamers behind. But the greatest feat she ever did, positively outdid anything that ever was did.

One day when she war out in the forest, making a collection o' wild cat skins for her family's winter beddin, she war captered in the most all-sneaken manner by about fifty Injuns, an' carried by 'em to Roast flesh Hollow, whar the blood drinkin wild varmits detarmined to skin her alive, sprinkle a leetle salt over her, an' devour her before her own eyes; so they took an' tied her to a tree, to keep till mornin' should bring the rest o' thar ring-nosed sarpints to enjoy the fun. Arter that, they lit a large fire in the Holler, turned the bottom o' thar feet towards the blaze, Injun fashion, and went to sleep to dream o' thar mornin's feast; well, after the critturs got into a somniferous snore, Sal got into an all-lightnin' of a temper, and burst all the ropes about her like an apron-string! She then found a pile o' ropes, too, and tied all the Injun's heels together all round the fire,—then fixin a cord to the shins of every two couple, she, with a suddenachous jerk, that made the intire woods tremble, pulled the intire lot o' sleepin' red-skins into that ar great fire, fast together, an' then sloped like a panther out of her pen, in the midst o' the tallest yellin, howlin, scramblin and singin', that war ever seen or heerd on, since the great burnin' o' Buffalo prairie!

Rev. Peter Cartwright, Jocose Preacher
(1850)

I N 1850, SOME ANONYMOUS WRITER included in an anecdotal
article about Peter Cartwright a story about Cartwright's lick-
ing Mike Fink. The article, printed in the Columbus, Georgia,
Southern Sentinel in 1850, was probably reprinted in other
newspapers; but the likelihood is that the story gained its widest
circulation in the popular autobiography of James B. Finley,
an old-time Methodist circuit-rider, published in 1854. Finley
uses it in a chapter, "Backwoods Preachers," introducing readers
to some of these stalwart men of God.

Cartwright was a mighty man, famous in his own right. In
1790, at the age of five, he went with his family over the Wilderness Trail to Kentucky. At eighteen, he became an itinerant
preacher. Thereafter for years, in every kind of weather, he went
traveling through forests and valleys, preaching his sermons.
He was physically well equipped for the hard life—nearly six
feet tall and stocky and well-muscled to boot. Stories about
the giant show that at times he did deal with frontier rowdies
in the fashion set forth in the anecdote.

But it is doubtful that he dealt with Fink in this fashion.
Since Fink died in 1822 or 1823, the date set down in the story,
1833, seems a bit late. Moreover, Cartwright twice denied that
he had fought Fink. In his Autobiography, he wrote: "Somewhere about this time, in 1829–30, the celebrated camp-meet-
ing took place in Sangamon County and Circuit; and, as I suppose, out of incidents that then occurred was concocted that
wonderful story about my fight with Mike Fink, which had no
foundation in fact." And William Epler tells about a talk he
had with Cartwright in 1870. "Tradition," he told the preacher,

*"says Mike Fink was the terror and fistic autocrat in early days
from Ohio to New Orleans among flatboat men. His custom
was, before forming new acquaintances with strangers, to challenge them for a combat, a real combat, no pretentious affair.
His object was to ascertain how worthy they would be as companions. On first meeting you, the usual challenge followed.
You promptly accepted, sailed into him, giving a good thrash-
ing. Ever after you were friends." "At this,"* says Epler, *"he
laughed. I think his reply was, he never saw Mr. Fink, but had
heard of him."*

Then, says Epler, *"My father who had been on the rivers as
a flatboat man corroborated that part of the story, as to Mike's
personality and his domineering tendencies."* Beginning in 1850
most of those who told stories about Mike's fights admitted
that he was domineering but refused to let him domineer. Following that date, he was almost always defeated in whatever
accounts appeared. Was it the American sympathy for the un-
derdog? Or was it a sign that Mike's fame had begun to tarnish?
Whatever the reason, the new fashion was very hard on Mike.

At a camp meeting held at Alton in the autumn of 1833,
the worshippers were annoyed by a set of desperadoes from St.
Louis, under the control of Mike Fink, a notorious bully, the
triumphant hero of the countless fights, in none of which he
had ever met an equal, or even second. The coarse, drunken
ruffians carried it with a high hand, outraged the men and insulted the women, so as to threaten the dissolution of all pious
exercises; and such was the terror the name of their leader,
Fink, inspired, that no one individual could be found brave
enough to face his prowess.

At last, one day, when Cartwright ascended the pulpit to
hold forth, the desperadoes, on the outskirts of the encamp-
ment, raised a yell so deafening as to drown utterly every other
sound. Cartwright's dark eyes shot lightning. He deposited his

Bible, drew off his coat, and remarked aloud—"Wait for a few minutes, my brethren, while I go and make the devil pray."

He then proceeded with a smile on his lips to the focus of the tumult, and addressed the chief bully—"Mr. Fink, I have come to make you pray."

The desperado rubbed back the tangled festoons of his blood-red hair, arched his huge brows with a comical expression, and replied—"By golly, I'd like to see you do it, old snorter!"

"Very well," said Cartwright. "Will these gentlemen, your courteous friends, agree not to show foul play?"

In course they will. They're rale grit, and won't do nothin' but the clear thing, so they won't," rejoined Fink, indignantly.

"Are you ready?" asked Cartwright.

"Ready as a race-hoss with a light rider," answered Fink, squaring his ponderous person for the combat.

But the bully spoke too soon; for scarcely had the words left his lips when Cartwright made a prodigious bound toward his antagonist, and accompanied it with a quick, shooting punch of his herculean fist, which fell, crashing the other's chin, and hurled him to the earth like lead. Then even his intoxicated comrades, filled with involuntary admiration at the feat, gave a cheer.

But Fink was up in a moment, and rushed upon his enemy, exclaiming—"That wasn't done fair, so it warn't." He aimed a ferocious stroke, which Cartwright parried with his left hand, and grasped his throat with the right, crushed him down as if he had been an infant. Fink struggled, squirmed, and writhed in the dust; but all to no purpose; for the strong, muscular fingers held his windpipe, as in the jaws of an iron vice. When he began to turn purple in the face, and ceased to resist, Cartwright slackened his hold, and inquired, "Will you pray now?"

"I doesn't know a word how," gasped Fink.

"Repeat after me," commanded Cartwright.

"Well, if I must, I must," answered Fink, "because you're the devil himself."

The preacher then said over the Lord's prayer line by line,

and the conquered bully responded in the same way, when the victor permitted him to rise. At the consummation the rowdies roared three boisterous cheers. Fink shook Cartwright's hand, declaring—"By golly, you're some beans in a bar-fight. I'd rather *set to* with an old *he* bar in the dog-days. You can pass in this 'ere crowd of nose-smashers, blast your pictur'!"

Afterward Fink's party behaved with extreme decorum, and Cartwright resumed his Bible and pulpit.

A thousand other incidents, equally material and ludicrous, are related as to Cartwright's adventures in Kentucky and Illinois. Many of them are probably fictitious; but those genuine alone, if collected, would be sufficient to stock at least two volumes of romantic reality.

Deacon Smith's Bull, or Mike Fink in a Tight Place (1851)

SCROGGINS

T HE AUTHOR of this story has not been identified, and the
purported first appearance of the story in a Pennsylvania
newspaper, the Milton Miltonian, has not been run down. We
came upon it in the Spirit of the Times for March 22, 1851,
and assume that editor Porter had clipped it from a recent
exchange. (He credits the Pennsylvania paper.) The author's
claim that he knew Fink is pretty well discredited when he calls
him "a notorious Buckeye [i.e., Ohio] hunter" and claims that
Mike told the story at the age of seventy. His coupling of Fink
with Crockett as a "contemporary" is somewhat more accurate.
However, his story of the animals' fear of Mike is pilfered from
a Crockett legend which, in turn, had probably been stolen
from one Captain Scott. Scroggins' story is unrelated to the general run of lore about the riverman, and it is quite possible that
he gave Mike's name to the protagonist because of his current
fame.

Whether it was previously told about Mike or not, and
whether this was the first telling or not, the tale seems to have
had fairly wide currency (probably oral as well as written) in
the nineteenth century. It was retold in its essence by George
W. Harris' character, Sut Lovingood, about Old Burns of the
Knobs in Tennessee in 1858; by "Shepard Tom" Hazard about
Timothy Crumb of Rhode Island in 1880. Mark Twain switched
the scene to England and wrote it up for The Prince and the
Pauper in about 1880. Not having used it in that book, he wrote
it up for Personal Recollections of Joan of Arc, where, rather in-

congruously, it appeared in chapter xxvi in 1896. The story also had affiliations with Twain's "Jim Wolfe and the Cats," a yarn which he told twice. Twain may have seen the story in the Hannibal Missouri Courier, which reprinted it in 1851. For the story's history, see Richard M. Dorson, "The Jonny-Cake Papers," Journal of American Folklore, LVIII (April–June, 1945), 107; and D. M. McKeithan, "Mark Twain's Story of the Bull and the Bees," Tennessee Historical Quarterly, XI (September, 1952), 246–53; and "Bull Rides Described by 'Scroggins,' G. W. Harris and Mark Twain," Southern Folklore Quarterly, XVII (December, 1953), 241–43.

Mike Fink, a notorious Buckeye hunter, was contemporary with the celebrated Davy Crockett, and his equal in all things appertaining to human prowess. It was even said that the animals in his neighborhood knew the crack of his rifle, and would take to their secret hiding places on the first intimation that Mike was about. Yet strange, though true, he was but little known beyond his immediate "settlement."

When we knew him, he was an old man—the blasts of seventy winters had silvered o'er his head and taken the elasticity from his limbs; yet in the whole of his life was Mike never worsted, except upon one occasion. To use his own language, he never "gin in, used up, to anything that travelled on two legs or four," but once.

"That once, we want," said Bill Slasher, as some dozen of us sat in the bar-room of the only tavern in the "settlement."

"Gin it to us now, Mike—you've promised long enough, and you're old now, and needn't care," continued Bill.

"Right, right! Bill," said Mike, "but we'll open with a licker all round fust, it'll kind o' save my feelin's, I reckon—"

"Thar, that's good. Better than t'other barrel, if anything!"

"Well, boys," commenced Mike, "you may talk of your scrimmages, tight places and sich like, and subtract 'em altogether in one all-mighty big 'un, and they hain't no more to be compared to the one I war in, than a dead kitten to an old she b'ar! I've fout all kinds o' varmints, from an Ingin down to a rattlesnake, and never was willin' to quit fust, but this once—and 'twas with a bull!

"You see, boys, it was an awful hot day in August, and I war nigh runnin' off into pure *ile*, when I war thinkin' that a *dip* in the creek mout save me. Well, thar was a mighty nice place in ole deacon Smith's medder for that partic'lar bizziness. So I went down amondst the bushes to unharness. I jist hauled the old red shirt over my head, and war thinkin' how scrumptious a feller of my size would feel a wallerin' round in that ar water, and was jest 'bout goin' in, when I seed the old Deacon's Bull a makin' a B-line to whar I stood.

"I know'd the old cuss, for he'd skar'd more people than all the parsons o' the 'settlement,' and cum mighty near kill'n a few. Thinks I, Mike you're in rather a tight place—get your fixins' on, for he'll be a drivin' them big horns o' his in yer bowels afore that time! Well, you'll hev to try the old varmint naked, I reck'n.

"The Bull war on one side o' the creek and I on t'other, and the way he made the 'sile' fly for a while, as if he war a diggin my grave, war distressin!

"Come on ye bellerin, old heathin, said I, and don't be a standin thar; for, as the old Deacon says o' the devil, 'yer not comely to look on.'

"This kind o' reach'd his understandin', and made him more wishious; for he hoofed a little like, and made a drive. And as I don't like to stand in anybody's way, I gin him plenty sea-room! So he kind o' passed by me and come out on t'other side; and, as the Captain o' the Mud-Swamp Rangers would say, ''bout face for 'nother charge.'

"Though I war ready for 'im this time, he come mighty nigh runnin' foul o' me! So I made up my mind the next time he went out he wouldn't be alone. So when he passed, I grappled his tail, and he pulled me out on the 'sile,' and as soon as we war both a' top of the bank old brindle stopp'd and war about comin' round agin when I begin pull'n t'other way.

"Well, I reck'n this kind o' *riled* him, for he fust stood stock still and look'd at me for a spell, and then commenc'd pawin and bellerin, and the way he made his hind gearin play in the air, war beautiful!

"But it warn't no use, he couldn't *tech* me, so he kind o' stopped to get wind for suthin devilish, as I *jedged* by the way he stared! By this time I had made up my mind to stick to his tail as long as it stuck to his backbone! I didn't like to holler for help, nuther, kase it war agin my principle, and then the deacon had preached at his house, and it wan't far off nuther.

"I knowed if he *hern* the noise, the hull congregation would come down; and as I warn't a married man, and had a kind o' hankerin arter a gal that war thar, I didn't feel as if I would like to be seed in that ar predicament.

"So, says I, you old sarpent, do yer cussedest! And so he did; for he drug me over every briar and stump in the field, until I war sweatin and bleedin like a fat bear with a pack o' hounds at his heels. And my name ain't Mike Fink, if the old critter's tail and I didn't blow out sometimes at a dead level with the varmint's back!

"So you may kalkelate we made good time. Bimeby he slackened a little, and then I had 'im for a spell, for I jist drapped behind a stump and thar snubbed the critter! Now, says I, you'll pull up this 'ere white oak—break yer *tail!* or jest hold on a bit till I blow!

"Well, while I war settin thar, an idea struck me that I had better be a gettin out o' this in some way. But *how*, adzackly, was the *pint!* If I let go and run he'd be a foul o' me sure!

"So lookin at the matter in all its bearins, I cum to the conclusion that I'd better let somebody *know* whar I was! So I gin a *yell* louder than a locomotive whistle, and it wan't long afore I seed the Deacon's two dogs a comin down like as if they war seein which could get thar fust.

"I know'd who they war arter—they'd jine the Bull agin me, I war sartain, for they war orful wenemous and had a spite agin me.

"So, says I, old brindle, as ridin is as cheap as walkin, on this rout, if you've no objections, I'll jist take a deck passage on that ar back o' yourn! So I wasn't long gettin astride of him, and then if you'd bin thar, you'd 'ave sworn thar warn't nothin human in that ar mix! the sile flew so orfully as the critter and I rolled round the field—one dog on one side and one on t'other, tryin to clinch my feet!

"I pray'd and cuss'd, and cuss'd and pray'd, until I couldn't tell which I did last—and neither warn't of any use, they war so orfully mixed up.

"Well, I reckon I rid about an hour this way, when old brindle thought it war time to stop to take in a supply of wind and cool off a little! So when we got around to a tree that stood thar, he nat'rally halted!

"Now, says I, old boy, you'll lose one passenger sartain! So I jist clum upon a branch kalkelatin to roost thar till I starved, afore I'd be rid round in that ar way any longer.

"I war a makin tracks for the top of the tree, when I heard suthin a makin an orful buzzin overhead. I kinder looked up and if that war'nt—well ther's no use a swearin now, but it war the biggest hornet's nest ever built!

"You'll 'gin in' now, I reckon, Mike, case thar's no help for you! But an idea struck me then that I'd stand heap better chance a ridin' the old Bull than where I war. Says I, 'old feller, if you'll hold on, I'll ride to the next station! any how, let that be whar it will!'

"So I jist drapped aboard him agin, and looked aloft to see what I'd gained in changin quarters; and, gentleman, I'm a liar if thar war'nt nigh a half a bushel of the stingin varmints ready to pitch into me when the word 'go' was gin!

"Well, I reckon they got it, for 'all hands' started for our company! Some on 'em hit the dogs—about a quart stuck me, and the rest charged on old brindle.

"This time, the dogs led off fust, 'dead' bent for the old deacon's, and as soon as old brindle and I could get under way, we followed! And as I war only a deck passinger, and had nothin' to do with steerin the craft, I swore if I had we should-n't have run that channel, any how!

"But, as I said afore, the dogs took the lead—brindle and I next, and the hornets dre'kly arter. The dogs yellin—brindle bellerin, and the hornets buzzin and stingin! I didn't say nothin, for it warn't no use.

"Well, we'd got about two hundred yards from the house, and the deacon hern us and cum out. I seed him hold up his hand and turn *white!* I reckoned he was prayin, then, for he didn't expect to be called for so soon, and it wan't long, nither, afore the hull congregation, men, women and children, cum out, and then all hands went to yellin!

"None of 'em had the fust notion that brindle and I belonged to this world. I jist turned my head and passed the *hull* con-gregation! I seed the run would be up soon, for brindle couldn't turn an inch from a fence that stood dead ahead!

"Well, we reached that fence, and I went *ashore,* over the old critter's head, landing on t'other side, and lay thar stunned. It warn't long afore some of 'em as war not so scared, come round to see what I war! For all hands kalkelated that the Bull and I belonged *together!* But when brindle walked off by him-self, they seed how it war, and one of 'em said, 'Mike Fink has got the *wust of the scrimmage once in his life!*

"Gentlemen, from that day I drapped the *courtin* bizziness, and never spoke to a gal since! And when my hunt is up on this yearth, thar won't be any more FINKS! and it's all owin to Deacon Smith's Brindle Bull!"

Mike's Practical Jokes (1852)

BEN CASSEDY

B EN CASSEDY WAS, so his townsfolk say, a poet of parts, a journalist, and a historian. As a delver into history, he wrote at least two violently contrasting books, a Life of Petrarch and The History of Louisville, from Its Earliest Settlement to the Year 1852, the latter a very valuable local history published in 1852. In a section about the boatmen of early days, Cassedy told three anecdotes about the king of the keelboatmen. One was the account of Mike's trimming the Negro's heel from the Western Monthly Review of 1829, which he credits as a source. (This is left out of the passage which follows.) The other two, so far as we know, he published for the first time.

The tale of Mike and the sheep, as Cassedy suggests, may well have been transferred to him from a James River bargeman, William Creasy, whose fame was fading: frequently stories are so transferred. (Mike, it will be recalled, had been assigned a Crockett exploit in Scroggins' story a year before. In Paulding's novel, Westward Ho! (New York, 1832), I, 119, one of Mike's most famous feats, the shooting of the cup, had been assigned to Daniel Boone.) Yet it, like the other yarn about Fink's trip to and from the Louisville courthouse in a yawl, is in keeping with the boatman's pranksomeness and his comic disregard for the law. The second story is highly reminiscent in portions of John S. Robb's "Trimming a Darky's Heel" of 1847. Stith Thompson lists a motif similar to that of the first story as prevalent among the North Pacific Coast Indians, concerning a recurrent character, "the Trickster": ". . . sometimes, in one way or another, he frightens people from their food and eats it himself" (The Folktale [New York, 1946], p. 326). See also the Uncle

Remus stories, "*How Mr. Rabbit Saved His Meat*" and "*Brother Rabbit Breaks up a Party*," for variants among the Georgia Negroes. Other references are cited under K335 in Thompson's Motif-Index of Folk-Literature (*Bloomington, Ind., 1932–36*).

Among the most celebrated of these [the boatmen], every reader of history will at once remember MIKE FINK, the hero of his class. So many and so marvellous are the stories told of this man that numbers of persons are inclined altogether to disbelieve his existence. That he did live however does not admit of a doubt. Many are yet living who knew him personally. As it is to him that all the more remarkable stories of western river adventure are attributed, his history will form the only example here given to illustrate the character of the western bargemen. It is however necessary to observe, that while Mike possessed all the characteristics of his class, a history of the various adventures attributed to him would present these characteristics in an exaggerated degree. Even the slight sketch here drawn cannot pretend to authenticity; for, aside from the fact that, like other heroes, Mike has suffered from the exuberant fancy of his historians, he has also had in his own person to atone to posterity for many acts which never came from under his hand and seal. As the representative, however, of an extinct class of men, his ashes will not rise in indignation even if he is again made the "hero of fields his valor never won."

His practical jokes, for so he and his associates called their predations on the inhabitants of the shores along which they passed, were always characterized by a boldness of design and a sagacity of execution that showed no mean talent on Mike's part. One of the most ingenious of these tricks, and one which affords a fair idea of the spirit of them all, is told as follows: Passing slowly down the river, Mike observed a very large and beautiful flock of sheep grazing on the shore, and being in want of fresh provisions, but scorning to buy them, Mike hit upon the following expedient. He noticed that there was an eddy near to the shore, and, as it was about dusk, he landed his boat in the eddy and tied her fast. In his cargo there were some bladders of scotch-snuff. Mike opened one of these and taking out a handful of the contents, he went ashore and catching five or six of the sheep, rubbed their faces very thoroughly with the snuff. He then returned to his boat and sent one of his men in a great hurry to the sheep-owner's house to tell him that he "had better come down and see what was the matter with his sheep." Upon coming down hastily in answer to Mike's summons, the gentleman saw a portion of his flock very singularly affected; leaping, bleating, rubbing their noses against the ground and against each other, and performing all manner of undignified and unsheeplike antics. The gentleman was sorely puzzled and demanded of Mike "if he knew what was the matter with the sheep."

"You don't know?" answered Mike very gravely.

"I do not," replied the gentleman.

"Did you ever hear of the black murrain?" asked Mike in a confidential whisper.

"Yes," said the sheep owner in a terrified reply.

"Well, that's it!" said Mike. "All the sheep up river's got it dreadful. Dyin' like rotten dogs—hundreds a day."

"You don't say so," answered the victim, "and is there no cure for it?"

"Only one as I knows on," was the reply. "You see the murrain's dreadful catchin', and ef you don't git them away as is got it, they'll kill the whole flock. Better shoot 'em right-off; they've got to die any way."

"But no man could single out the infected sheep and shoot them from among the flock," said the gentleman.

"My name's Mike Fink!" was the curt reply.

And it was answer enough. The gentleman begged Mike to shoot the infected sheep and throw them into the river. This was exactly what Mike wanted, but he pretended to resist. "It mought be a mistake," he said; "They'll may be git well. He

didn't like to shoot manny's sheep on his own say so. He'd
better go an' ask some of the neighbors ef it was the murrain
sure 'nuf." The gentleman insisted, and Mike modestly resisted,
until finally he was promised a couple of gallons of old Peach
Brandy if he would comply. His scruples thus finally overcome,
Mike shot the sheep, threw them into the eddy and got the
brandy. After dark, the men jumped into the water, hauled the
sheep aboard, and by daylight had them neatly packed away
and were gliding merrily down the stream.[1]

In all his little tricks, as Mike called them, he never displayed
any very accurate respect to the laws either of propriety or
property, but he was so ingenious in his predations that it is
impossible not to laugh at his crimes. The stern rigor of Justice,
however, did not feel disposed to laugh at Mike, but on the
contrary offered a reward for his capture. For a long time Mike
fought shy and could not be taken, until an old friend of his,
who happened to be a constable, came to his boat when she was
moored at Louisville and represented to Mike the poverty of
his family; and, presuming on Mike's known kindness of disposition, urged him to allow himself to be taken, and so procure
for his friend the promised reward. He showed Mike the many
chances of escape from conviction, and withal plead so strongly
that Mike's kind heart at last overcame him and he consented—
but upon one condition! He felt at home nowhere but in his
boat and among his men: let them take him and his men in the
yawl and they would go. It was the only hope of procuring his
appearance at court and the constable consented. Accordingly a
long-coupled wagon was procured, and with oxen attached it
went down the hill, at Third Street for Mike's yawl. The road,
for it was not then a street, was very steep and very muddy at
this point. Regardless of this, however, the boat was set upon
the wagon, and Mike and his men, with their long poles ready,
as if for an aquatic excursion, were put aboard, Mike in the
stern. By dint of laborious dragging the wagon had attained half

1. This incident is by some accredited to William Creasy, a bargeman
of the James River [Cassedy's note].

the height of the hill, when out shouted the stentorian voice of Mike calling to his men—SET POLES!—and the end of every long pole was set firmly in the thick mud—BACK HER!— roared Mike, and down the hill again went wagon, yawl, men and oxen. Mike had been revolving the matter in his mind and had concluded that it was best not to go; and well knowing that each of his men was equal to a moderately strong ox, he had at once conceived and executed this retrograde movement. Once at the bottom, another parley was held and Mike was again overpowered. This time they had almost reached the top of the hill, when *Set Poles!—Back her!* was again ordered and again executed. A third attempt, however, was successful and Mike reached the court house in safety; and, as his friend, the constable, had endeavored to induce him to believe, he was acquitted for lack of sufficient evidence. Other indictments, however, were found against him, but Mike preferred not to wait to hear them tried; so, at a given signal he and his men boarded their craft again and stood ready to weigh anchor. The dread of the long poles in the hands of Mike's men prevented the *posse* from urging any serious remonstrance against his departure. And off they started with poles "tossed." As they left the court house yard Mike waved his red bandanna, which he had fixed on one of the poles, and promising to *"call again"* was borne back to his element and launched once more upon the waters.

Jack Pierce's Victory (1874?)

MENRA HOPEWELL, M.D.

I N 1874 OR THEREABOUTS a new subliterary type of writing—the
Sunday School tale—influenced the quality of one of the
Fink stories. Jack Pierce, the hero, showed a strong resemblance
to the lads portrayed in pious narratives of this sort by promising
his mother that he would stop drinking and fighting. Then
along comes Mike and the boy, though sorely tempted, keeps
his promise. Later, when he backslides, he fights and licks Mike,
probably aided by a residue of the strength which virtue has
stored up in him. The story appeared just two years before Mark
Twain, who had made a similar promise to his mother—and
who had later broken it—had a go at this type of fiction and its
Good Boy heroes in The Adventures of Tom Sawyer.

Reference books have neglected to indicate who Menra Hopewell, M.D., the chronicler of Jack's triumph, was. In 1860, he
had made another contribution to belles-lettres by collaborating
with a more prolific antiquarian, Richard Edwards, on a history
of St. Louis. Jack Pierce had been celebrated in this history in
the role of one of the best of butters, and Mike had appeared,
too, as a river boatman as well as a treacherous murderer and as
a murderee (see p. 274). But the two did not get together for
their wrestling match and their fight until Edwards collected
and published a book of legends some fourteen years later. The
circumstances give rise to an uneasy suspicion that Dr. Hopewell may have invented this particular legend himself. It follows
the current fashion of having Mike get licked.

Despite his great performance here, Pierce soon after, we are
told, had a butting match with a ram which had a harder head
than his, and got himself killed.

[231]

After this interview with his mother [during which he promised to stop drinking and fighting], Jack Pierce went and engaged himself to take command of a flat-boat laden with wheat, and destined for the Orleans market. It was necessary for him to engage two or three others to navigate the boat, and for that purpose he went to one of the litle groggeries where the flat-boatmen were accustomed to congregate, for the purpose of engaging those he wished. As was usual, he saw many of his companions, was welcomed on all sides, and invited to drink; but true to the promise that he had made his mother he had determined to avoid all intoxicating fluids, and refused the invitation. Some of his comrades were surprised, and some piqued by the refusal, and at length one of them said:

"Come, Jack, and drink with Mike Fink; you have never met him before, though he has often been in St. Louis, but at the very time you were not here. There ain't a better man than Mike Fink ever stood in a flat-boat on the Mississippi."

The individual alluded to as Mike Fink was a heap of flesh and blood, nerve and muscle, so firm, hard, and coarse in his general make-up, that he looked of the consistence of iron. He had the reputation of being the strongest man that boated on the Mississippi, except Jack Pierce, and, between the two, who was the strongest and best fighter, opinion was equally divided.

Mike Fink glared upon Jack Pierce with his small grey eye that had all the brilliancy and fierceness of that of the adder. He had heard of his immense strength, his fame as a fighter, and of his last triumph over the renowned Negro Jim. He was envious of his growing fame, which had commenced to overshadow his, and he determined on the first opportunity to provoke a quarrel with him that might lead to a collision.

Jack Pierce guessed by the expression of Mike Fink's countenance what was passing within, and determined to avoid any difficulty with him, having promised his mother to leave off all vicious habits, went over to Mike Fink, and took his hand in token of friendship.

Mike Fink then brought all his iron nerve to bear upon the

hand of Jack Pierce, but the bones and sinews were unyielding. The grip was then returned by Jack Pierce, and though the countenance of Mike Fink changed not, he felt a pain from the grasp that he never felt before, and it increased the prejudice and the hate to the man whose deeds were already eclipsing the fame which he had won in many a hard-contested fight. Envy touched his heart with her poisoned fang, and he determined to force him into a fight, relying on his experience and muscular strength. Should he prove the victor, of which he felt confident, he would then stand alone as the champion of the Mississippi.

Jack Pierce then drank and touched his glass with Mike Fink, and the conversation turned upon Negro Jim of New Orleans. Mike Fink took it upon himself particularly to eulogize the negro, declaring with an oath that with fair play the negro, with the exception of him, Mike Fink, could whop any man that lived between St. Louis and New Orleans.

This was a direct insult to Jack Pierce and was intended as such, and there was a look of surprise among the rough spirits there congregated to see Jack Pierce pocket the insult. Mike Fink then said that he could throw down any man that boated on the Mississippi, looking significantly at the same time towards Jack Pierce, and then to show that the challenge was expressly meant for him, he advanced towards him, and laying his heavy hand upon his shoulder, said, "Jack Pierce, you are a strapping young fellow, have you got pluck enough to take a wrestle with me?"

The blood of Jack Pierce boiled in his veins at this second insult, and the fire of battle was in his eye when he recollected his promise to his mother. In an instant he calmed his fury, rose to his feet, and, throwing off a sort of round jacket worn by people of his class at that day, said, "I'll try you, Mike Fink."

It was in the afternoon in the month of September, and the party then went on the "Hill," as it was then called, to the square now occupied by the Gaol and Court-house, and which then had not been built upon. After some preliminaries, the combatants took their holds. They were nearly equally matched, but Mike Fink was broader across the shoulders, and his muscles appeared firm and knotted as a gnarled oak. Jack Pierce had less brawn, was more youthful and active, and though his brute force was not as great, he had more activity and intelligence than his adversary, and possessed a skill which the other could never acquire.

They both stood a few seconds with their arms locked and legs as far out as possible, in a colossal position. Then the feints commenced, succeeded by tugs and twists of their bodies, and then, as if desiring to bring the contest to an issue, each drew his adversary's body towards him, and each tried to raise his antagonist, and neither was successful. At length Mike Fink made a desperate effort, and Jack Pierce suddenly yielded to it a moment, and, as he was rising, got his right leg between his opponent's, brought Mike Fink to the ground with a fall that made the earth shake, falling heavily upon him.

It was the first time that Mike Fink ever was thrown, and when he arose his small grey eyes flashed like meteors, and he foamed at the mouth like an enraged bull.

"Now, Jack Pierce, you have got to fight," said he. "There is no cheating in fighting—the best man takes the day, each one doing his best, and in his own way."

"I won't fight you, Mike Fink," replied Jack Pierce. "If you want to know why, I tell you I promised the old woman, my mother, to be quiet for some time, and I want to keep my promise."

"By God, I'll make you," replied this desperado of the Mississippi, advancing in a threatening attitude towards Jack Pierce.

"I'll fight you some other day, Mike Fink, but not now," said the latter. "Don't strike."

"Wait, Mike," cried several of his friends, interfering—"another time. He has promised to fight you another time—that is all you can ask. He ain't ready now."

"I guess he will ask the old woman to give him leave," said Mike Fink, with a coarse laugh, "and I will whip her baby so that he will never leave her side again."

Jack Pierce replied not, but took his jacket, that was held by one of the bystanders, and putting it on, and accompanied by some of his friends, went back to the village, determining to keep the pledge he had given his mother.

He had scarcely arrived at the cabin of his mother when he found one of the neighbours relating to her an accident that had occurred to a young man that morning from an attack made upon him by a vicious ram as he was crossing the common, and the owner of the ram, having heard of it, came to the cabin at that moment to solicit Jack Pierce's assistance to capture the vicious animal. They went to the common, and on approaching the ram, the animal, by his movements, showed that he was ready to give battle.

"Fight him his own way, Jack," said one of his companions, laughing; "your head is as hard as his horns."

"I'll do it," replied Jack Pierce, feeling in one of his daredevil moods, and immediately approached the ram, which, giving an angry bleat, made towards him.

To the astonishment of his companions, who thought he had been jesting, Jack Pierce dropped on all fours, and stooping his head to avoid the direct blow of the ram, raised it just in time to strike him under the lower jaw; and so sudden was the shock that the animal's neck was broken.

This novel feat in twenty-four hours became the topic of conversation of the whole village, and such was the curiosity to witness a similar one, that quite a sum of money was made up to induce Jack Pierce to give battle to another ram. The feat came off in presence of a large multitude of persons, Jack Pierce breaking the neck of the ram as he did in the battle with the first.

Whatever may be said of the strong will—of the power of resisting temptation—of the option between good and evil—man, after all, is much the creature of surrounding influences. They will trammel him as a network, nor can he break loose from them at will.

Jack Pierce found it impossible to resist the temptations by which he was surrounded. Though he was successful in many instances, in some unguarded moments he would yield to them, and becoming discouraged in his efforts at reformation, he no more tried to avert the moral ruin to which he was fast approaching. He again caroused at the drinking-shops and indulged in all the vices incident to a flat-boatman's life, yet strove to keep continually employed so that his mother should have every comfort during her helplessness. His happiest moments were when he laid the money he had received for his wages upon her pillow, and whatever might have been his frailties, no unkind look or word added to the sufferings of his parent.

Mike Fink left St. Louis for some months after his wrestling-match with Jack Pierce, and returned to New Orleans with his flat-boat. During the whole time, the mortification of his defeat by Jack Pierce was rankling at his heart and goading him to revenge. He determined to force him to a fight, and felt a demon-like joy as he anticipated the bloody horrors of the fight.

Again business required him to ascend the Mississippi to St. Louis, and, acting on his premeditated design, directly he met with Jack Pierce, before he gave him any greeting and in the presence of a number of flat-boatmen, he walked to him whilst he was sitting, and with the back of his hand struck him a powerful blow in the face, saying "How does mamma's baby now?"

Jack Pierce rose to his feet, retreated a few steps, and pulled off his coat, remarking, "I am in for a big fight," and advanced toward Mike Fink, who, in a fighting attitude, was awaiting him.

"Go out of the house," cried several voices, and the combatants silently acquiescing walked out of the door, and both cautiously as belligerent tigers approached each other.

The first blow was attempted to be given by Mike Fink, which was successfully parried by his opponent, who planted his large fist between his peepers with such effect that he staggered backwards, and stars of every hue danced before his reeling vision. He recovered himself in a moment, and with his face flushed and glowing like the full round orb of the sun when he looks with fiery redness protending storms and tempest, rushed at his opponent. Another tremendous blow on the temple for a moment staggered him, but with his face bathed in blood he grappled with Jack Pierce, and throwing his whole strength into an effort, heaved him upon the ground. With the chuckle of a demon he sprang upon his prostrate foe and tried to fix his knee upon his breast, but Jack Pierce struggled so manfully that he could not accomplish his design.

It was evident, however, to all that the brute strength of Mike Fink was superior to that of Jack Pierce, and he was gradually getting his antagonist more and more at his mercy. Jack Pierce, however, managed to get the forefinger of Mike Fink's hand in his mouth, to which he held on with the tenacity of a bull-dog. This neutralized in a great measure the advantage of his antagonist, and he managed to clutch him by the throat; but with a desperate effort Mike Fink drew his lacerated finger from the mouth of Jack Pierce, and, breathing a deep curse, again hurled him to the ground. Another powerful blow from Jack Pierce before Mike Fink had time to fetter his arms again brought the stars before his eyes, and produced a confusion of ideas, and then with a herculean effort he succeeded in overturning him and regaining his feet, but not quicker than Mike Fink regained his; and again the combatants closed, and again Jack Pierce would have been thrown, but he thought of turning the hardness of his head to some account, overmatched as he was in the combat. With both hands he caught Mike Fink by the ears, and brought his forehead against his three times in quick succession, the blows sounding like a maul upon timber. The knees of Mike Fink trembled, his head drooped, his hands relinquished their hold, and when his adversary released his grasp he fell senseless upon the ground, sputtering white froth and blood from his mouth. He, however, did not die. He recovered, but Jack Pierce had gained the victory.

Mike Fink—Last of the Flatboatmen (1883)

COLONEL FRANK TRIPLETT

COLONEL FRANK TRIPLETT published The Life, Times and Treacherous Death of Jesse James in 1882, The Authorized Pictorial Lives of Stephen Grover Cleveland and Thomas Andrews Hendricks in 1884, and History, Romance and Philosophy of Great American Crimes and Criminals in the same year. The story of Mike, with its somewhat hackneyed (and somewhat inaccurate) title appeared in chapter xxxv of his book, Conquering the Wilderness . . . published in 1883. His research carried him back to the 1829 story about Fink, and he repeated several anecdotes from it (deleted from the passage). Somehow, too, he picked up the story of the kicking sheriff of Westport, which had previously eluded print. As was customary at the time, the newly found legend told of Mike's being defeated.

The era of steam swept out of existence much that was picturesque, some things that were good, and many that could lay claim to neither of these merits. From our highways it drove the romantic stage coach, with its multiferous traditions, and the clumsy wagon, with its lazy team and obstinate driver; from our water-ways it banished the batteau and the barge, the keelboat and the flat, with their amphibious crews, "half horse, half alligator." Along our western waters those men in their day, filled the proud position occupied at a later date by the overland coach driver on the broad stretches of our western plains, and excited a universal admiration in the breasts of small boys, hostlers and rural damsels.

These men were the models from which the stage borrows its "Roaring Ralph Stackpoles, chock full of fight and fond of the women." They were extravagant boasters, whose desperate bravery was ever ready to redeem their roystering challenges. The man who, braggart-like, would boast of his ability to out-run, out-jump, knock down and drag out more men "than any other cuss from the roarin' Salt to the mighty Massasip," would brave untold dangers in defense of a comrade, and would fight to the death against any odds, no matter how desperate, if only duty, friendship or affection called him into the breach.

Their courage was the God-given quality of the hero; their quaint, bizarre ways and expressions, the overflowing of too exhuberant animal spirits. They were the western Gascons, whose strength and vitality must find expression in words, lest, like the overcharged boiler, without a safety valve, their very light-heartedness might endanger them. Their life was hard and full of excesses, but like other necessary evils, they filled what would otherwise have been a void in the economy of their day and generation, and when the wizard motor, steam, arose to take their place, they vanished as completely as the frozen tracery of the frost-work beneath the ardent glances of the golden sun.

It is to be regretted that but few, if any, of their exploits have survived the lapse of even this short time, and we are forced to turn to the records of those of Mike Fink, the last, and by no means the best, of the fraternity. This man was born in Pittsburg, and like most of the rising generation of his day, his sole ambition was to become a keelboatman. This ambition he took the earliest opportunity to gratify, and soon became noted along the Ohio and Mississippi rivers as one of the most dexterous of his class.

It was the custom, when two or more boats met on the river or tied up in port, for the rival crews to adjourn to some convenient spot and pair off at fisticuffs, until all hands were satisfied, or the proper grade of a fighter's powers established. In these combats Mike's gigantic strength made him a formidable competitor, weighing as he did one hundred and eighty pounds, without an ounce of superfluous flesh. His talk was that of the regular "Salt River Roarer," and was seasoned with a rough sort of humor that gained for its possessor the reputation of a wit, and of this he was very proud.

It was his custom, when he had given utterance to what he considered a joke, to lead the laugh at his own wit, and woe to the man who was so dull of comprehension that he could not see the point or join in the cachinnation. His jokes, said Fink, were made to laugh at, and he did'nt intend that they should be slighted, and forthwith he would proceed to belabor the unlucky wight. On one occasion, while his boat was tied up at Westport, on the Ohio River, Mike was as usual cracking his jokes to an admiring audience. In one corner sat a small, quiet-looking man, evidently very much abstracted, and deeply bent on attending to his own business. Joke after joke of Mike's passed unheeded until at last the "roarer" could stand it no longer, so going over to the quiet man, he touched him and told him that it would pay him to give a little heed to the first-class jokes that he was getting off, for if he did'nt, somebody would get hurt. "Ah," said the quiet man, "is that so," and he immediately lapsed into his reverie.

The next joke was told and duly enjoyed, but no laugh came from the corner of the quiet man, and Mike, now thoroughly indignant, went over to him, and told him he intended to whip him. "Ah, indeed," said the man, "is that so?" and hardly were the words out of his mouth, than with a tremendous blow under the ear he struck the giant, felling him to the ground. Rising quickly, Fink made for the stranger, who slipped down upon his back and began that fight with the feet for which so many of the borderers were noted, and in a few minutes a worse whipped man than the jolly flatboatman was never seen.

When Fink called for quarter, or, as he expressed it, "hollered calf rope," the quiet man said to him: "I am Ned Taylor, sheriff of this county; if you don't board your boat and push off in five minutes, I'll arrest you and your crew." To this Fink did not demur, and was soon floating down the Ohio.

Some Recently Published Stories about Mike Fink (1950–56)

COLONEL HENRY SHOEMAKER

COLONEL HENRY W. SHOEMAKER, born in 1882 in New York City but long a resident of Pennsylvania, has had a varied career as a railroad man, a member of the diplomatic service, a soldier, a newspaper publisher, a writer, and a historian. He is a member of the Pennsylvania Historical Society, the Waldensian Historical Society of Pennsylvania, the Pennsylvania Folklore Society, the Sojourners, the Loyal Legion, the Boone and Crockett Club, the Ends of the Earth Club, and other organizations. He has written several biographies, several books of verse, and a number of books, brochures, and articles on Pennsylvania history, folklore, folksongs, proverbs, and wild life.

From his office in the Pennsylvania State Museum in Harrisburg, Colonel Shoemaker issues at intervals articles on Mike Fink which are made available by the Capitol News, a clip sheet, for publication in newspapers. His chief informant was John Rathfon of Millersburg. "Ever since I met him about 1925," Shoemaker wrote on December 1, 1955, "I have been endeavoring to set Mike Fink's ancestry right as a Pennsylvania German and in no sense a Scotch Irishman." In subsequent letters, he wrote: "Rathfon was born in Lykens Valley about 1830. He went to St. Louis about 1848, and for the next twenty years he plied up and down the Mississippi and Missouri Rivers as a voyageur and trader, etc. Every place he stopped he said there were people who gave him some fresh adventure of Fink. He visited Fink's last resting place and I think met his widow and best friends. He was a tall powerful man, his memory at ninety prodigious. He died about 1923. I only saw him a few times, but he could have given me enough to fill a book." Shoemaker writes that he also heard about Fink "from old people around the water front in Pittsburg and some of Rathfon's friends."

One interesting point about the stories is that they have come to light in such numbers. Another is that they contain so much that is new and so little which has appeared elsewhere. We print all for which we have room.

REMOVAL OF MIKE FINK GRAVE TO FORT
PITT IS URGED (1950)

"The remains of Mike Fink, widely known in the 19th century on the Allegheny, Ohio, Monongahela and Mississippi Rivers as king of keelboatmen, raftman, expert rifleman, Indian-fighter, hunter and explorer, may be reinterred at his birth-place in Pennsylvania," Henry W. Shoemaker, President of the Pennsylvania Folklore Society, State Museum, said today.

"With the rehabilitation of Fort Pitt Park under way," Shoemaker said, "the Society of Old Boatmen is urging that the body of the intrepid riverman and pioneer hunter be transferred from its lonely western resting place at the mouth of the Yellowstone River to the Point in Fort Pitt Park.

"In all of western Pennsylvania on the Allegheny, Ohio, and Monongahela Rivers and on the Mississippi River from New Orleans to the Yellowstone, the name and fame of Mike Fink are still remembered in every port and dock in this wide area," Shoemaker said.

"He takes his place alongside such famous legendary Pennsylvanians as 'Cherry Tree' Joe McCreery, 'Roaring Joe' Campbell, 'Lost' Connors, and 'Giant' Gable. Gable was the son of a diminutive father and mother who wanted a tall son. But, when Gable's height reached seven feet and further growth was indicated because of his youth, his mother became alarmed and placed iron weights on his head.

"Mike Fink was born in the latter part of the 18th century but his Pennsylvania German parents left him with his aunt and uncle, Mr. and Mrs. Adam Taub, when they moved to the west. Adam Taub was appointed by Col. Henry Bouquet in 1763, as official custodian of the Redoubt.

"Mike Fink's first occupation was as a market hunter and like Annie Oakley he supplied the early Pittsburgh markets with fresh game, even at the age of 10 years being able to outshoot mature men in marksmanship contests. At nineteen he had become a trapper and fur trader.

"His first claim as a local hero came when he tracked and killed two Indians who had ambushed and slain Arthur Graham and Alexander Campbell, his fishing companions on July 1, 1789. When Fink was told of their death he said he would kill their slayers and bring back their scalps within 24 hours. True to his word, when the town building opened the next morning, Mike Fink was waiting with two Indian scalps. Offered a reward, he haughtily turned down the money and sold the two scalps to a hair-buyer.

"After that the Indians seemed to fear that Fink had a charmed life and gave him a wide berth. Then as the Indians disappeared from the Pittsburgh area, he turned to the river and became a raftman, starting from the Allegheny river headwaters with choice white pine timber for New Orleans.

"But danger still beset his path. Once a pit was dug for him and as he clambered out rifle balls whistled past his head. At other times, along the long trek down the Mississippi he was fired on, either by lurking Indians or jealous rivermen, but none touched him.

"His next venture was keel boating, the freight barges used on rivers before the advent of the steam boat.

"One day he was challenged to a seven mile race upstream from Coraopolis to Logstown (now Legionville). His challenger was a Mike Frink (cq), whose similarity in name made him eager to establish Frink as a greater hero than Fink.

"The Pittsburg newspapers put up a prize of $50, and great crowds lined the banks. Mike Fink was an easy winner, but as he walked away with his prize, Frink slipped up and hit him behind the ear. The crowd drew back, making a ring, and the two stalwart young men fought for an hour. The fight ended with Frink asleep on the grass, clearly knocked out by Mike Fink's powerful right jab in the solar plexus.

"Once at Natchez-under-the-Hill, Davy Crockett was waiting for a boat, and was introduced to Fink. There were several hours to wait so Crockett offered to shoot Fink for a Kentucky thoroughbred Crockett was taking down the river. At every distance, Fink was the victor, until Crockett shook him by the hand, saying, 'If you and I had been together there would have been no Indians' and 'no Crockett,' Fink said in Dutch, but Crockett probably understood as he smiled broadly at Mike's bitter humor. Before he left, Fink bowing low, boarded his flat, returned the steed to Crockett, saying, 'I'm a water man, I have no use for horses.'

"In later days when steamboats had superseded keelboats, broadhorns and batteaux, and southern longleaf had replaced the need for Pennsylvania white pine, Mike Fink reverted to his earlier career as a professional hunter and fur trader, and around 1825 was at Fort William, at the mouth of the Yellowstone River, where occurred his famous exploit with the buffaloes, which was referred to in later years with admiration by such famous shots as Buffalo Bill, Captain Carver, and Annie Oakley. Fink went to the commissary who sold ammunition and purchased 100 bullets saying, 'I will bring in 100 choice hides and meat for all the post tonight.' With a prodigy of marksmanship and skill in skinning and butchering he killed 100 bison with the 100 shots, where as many hunters would fill a single animal full of shots before it went down. There was feasting at the post for days, and he sold the 100 Buffalo hides for 50 cents apiece, cash."

MIKE FINK'S RACE WITH RAFT STIRRING
TALE OF ALLEGHENY (1952)

Henry W. Shoemaker, President of the Pennsylvania Folklore Society, State Museum, Harrisburg, today told the tale of

Mike Fink's race with a raft on the Allegheny River to nab four bank bandits and recover the stolen bank safe.

"Mike Fink, the Pennsylvania German Paul Bunyan, raced the raft from Trunkeyville to Pittsburgh, a reputed distance of 160 miles by water, but Fink took overland short cuts," Shoemaker said.

"Some shrewd lumbermen had started a small bank at Trunkeyville in Warren County, and at the time of the robbery all of the bank's $15,000 was stored in a small safe.

"Rafts were being 'readied' one April to start for Pittsburgh when what looked like a raft crew walked into the bank and held up the cashier and a 17-year-old girl clerk. Two of the robbers, in raftsmen's garb, picked up the safe, loaded it aboard the platform and cut loose, steering into the middle of the current. The other two, having tied up the cashier and his helper, reached the waterside in time to climb aboard and make off with the others.

"Mike Fink was rolling logs on a side hill and, seeing the men running away from the bank, dropped his axe and peavy, and 'hotfooted' to the bank where he found the staff bound and gagged.

"He cut the girl loose and told her to unbind the cashier while he ran to the river bank, only to see the raft with its golden spoils swirling down the Allegheny.

"Mike Fink did not hesitate an instant, but started in pursuit of the escaping raft. He was a swift and fearless runner, but was unable to catch up and get abreast of the raft. He felt it might tie up to get provisions or water, hence felt that his pursuit would be rewarded. Yet the sun set, night fell, and the raft was still running on ahead of him, travelling fast in the 'live water.' He shouted, but the winds and the roar of the waters drowned out even his stentorian voice. As the raft showed no signs of snubbing, there was nothing to do but follow, hoping that it might be caught in a jam and slow up, that he could run abreast of it and obtain help in stopping it.

"He had a pair of derringers at his belt and at first he did not wish to kill the men, as the raft, unmanned, might run afoul and upset and the safe go to the bottom and be lost forever like the brass French cannon in the Cannon Hole. Pittsburgh was reported to be 160 miles on water from Trunkeyville.

"He was not the man to falter and went on and on.

"Past Tionesta, Baum, Oil City the raft swept along, always tantalizing ahead, unbeatable. Franklin 'where French Creek' refreshes the Allegheny, Foxburg, Kittanaing, Freeport. At Garver's Ferry where the ropes hung low, he hoped the robber band would break their necks, but the head pilot called out, 'Low bridge' in plenty of time, and they ducked and flashed by.

"Then Mike took a short cut through Sharpsburg to Pittsburgh, as he knew the basin where all river craft found mooring and turned up at the Penn Avenue Police Headquarters, and re-enforced with the strong-arm squad, hurried to the place of debarkation at the Point. There, coming across the landing dock, were the four marauders, two carrying the safe, and the other two with hands on their holstered derringers. Caught off their guard, Mike Fink held them up while the officers covered his aim. The gang, caught 'red-handed,' surrendered.

"Mike, who was well-known to every law officer in Allegheny County, took over the safe, while the officers led the robber band to the county jail. There were no telegraphs in those days, but four days later, Mike, carrying the safe, crawled off the stagewagon at Trunkeyville. The first to kiss his bronzed cheeks was the girl bank clerk he had rescued and again he became an acclaimed hero for his part in a courageous act which will long be a part of the saga of Pennsylvania folklore and history."

MIKE FINK WAS REAL LIFE PAUL BUNYON
OF PENNA. (1953)

Henry W. Shoemaker, President of the Pennsylvania Folklore Society, State Museum, Harrisburg, today said the late Robert Rathfon, of Millersburg, Dauphin County, probably knew more of the real life of Mike Fink, the famous Paul Bunyon of Pennsylvania, than anyone who survived past the first quarter of the twentieth century.

"He lived among a sparsely settled region on the upper Missouri river where memories of Fink were actively retained by reliable friends and neighbors of the remarkable Pennsylvania German heroic character. He pictured the real man to one, and one saw him as an actual personality always performing matchless deeds with a vein of fun, and amusement, even going to his death in a whimsical mood. He was a unique figure, an outstanding personality, hence his memory has lived.

"Probably his greatest adventure, according to Mr. Rathfon, was on his first voyage down the Missouri by boat, when the Sioux, realizing a rich cargo, killed the bison crossing the river and made a seriously impassable wall, to check the progress of the steamer named the Penn-Excelsior. The bison clogged the course so massed together it seemed impossible a ship could pass through. With his field glasses, the captain sensed the danger, 'what will we do,' he said to Fink, 'by the time we are freed our boat will be stripped of everything by those angry redskins, and we have not enough ammunition to fight them off indefinitely.' 'I will get us through,' said the dark-eyed, sphinx-like Fink, who stood at his side, 'I am heading the relief party immediately.'

"On the deck were a dozen husky young fellows who admired Fink as the first out door man of his time, and were eager to serve under him in any kind of breath-taking expedition.

"First of all Mike gave the would be followers a fire ax, others he armed with cross-cut saws and meat-axes, and the war-like gang leaped ashore, and hurried down the bank, guarded from the rear by Fink himself, and a few furloughed regular army soldiers armed with rifles. When they reached, what the old timers called the 'great buffalo bridge' Fink set them to chopping a channel, wide enough for the boat to pass. It was a carnival of butchery, and soon a bloody channel was opened and Fink took his red handkerchief from around his neck, and waved it upstream where it was seen by the captain of the river boat. He started the vessel moving and it bore down on the opening. A spy for the Indians noticed the doings and semaphored to the tribe hiding in the river hills, and they swept down to the river just in time to meet the ship passing through. Fink and his crew got on board in plenty of time, and from their positions on the high deck poured down bullets on the dismayed Indians, still riding their horses. Mr. Rathfon related that not a single member of the crew was hit yet a dozen Indians fell off their ponies, dead or dying, and flopped over the bank into the reddened water. As the boat moved through the opening, the Indians who survived, pursued firing endlessly into the vessel. The ship with its fabulous load of skins and ores reached St. Louis in safety, and the various contractors put together, and presented their deliverer with a pot of gold.

OLD BOATMEN SEEK RETURN OF FINK'S
BODY TO PENNSYLVANIA (1956)

Henry W. Shoemaker, Pennsylvania Folklore Chief, today said that the recent appearance of two books treating on the life and career of Mike Fink, known as the "Pennsylvania Paul Bunyan," has revived the efforts of the Old Boatmen's Association to have his body brought back to Pennsylvania. His body is at the mouth of the Yellowstone River and the boatmen's group want his body reinterred on the grounds of Col. Henry Bouquet's Redoubt at the forks at Pittsburgh, where he grew up at the home of his Uncle Captain Adam Taub, who was the honorary custodian of the fort.

"Fink was born in the Lykens Valley in Dauphin County, the son of a respected miller, had a yearning for vast open spaces which led him to spend considerable time in his early youth at his uncle's home in Pittsburgh where he heard tales of Indian warfare, not only in his uncle's home but from old soldiers who were daily visitors there," Shoemaker said.

"His personal brushes were equally memorable. He shot and killed six Shoshone Indians who attempted to hold him up on the prairie, getting his Pennsylvania rifle made by Henninger into action while the redskins were trying to surround and capture him.

"Exploits like these gave notoriety to Fink, but built up his numerous enemies. Yet in private life he was a gentle character playing games with the Indian and trappers' children and courting many young girls with a manner which favored old-time chivalry. A drunken boy at the Military Canteen 'pot shotted him' through his coonskin cap, and later Talbott, a bar keeper, fired at him and killed him. It is said that his funeral was attended by a thousand horsemen, redskins, and whites, who 'came mostly out of curiosity,' a St. Louis trapper stated. But despite the great tumult of friends or curiosity seekers, no one put a stone on his grave.

"He stood about five feet ten inches, slender, yet muscular form, dark complexioned, black Dutch eyes, curly black hair and like Davy Crockett, affected wavy black sideburns.

"Crockett's was a revival of popularity, Mike Fink is famous for the first time, since he was killed, over a century ago."

A Missouri Superstition (1951)

VANCE RANDOLPH

VANCE RANDOLPH, born in Pittsburg, Kansas, in 1892, won his A.B. in Kansas State Teachers College and did graduate work at Clark University and the University of Kansas. Between 1941 and 1943, he was a field worker, Archive of American Folksong, Library of Congress. Long a resident of Eureka Springs, Arkansas, he has published a number of books about the people of the Ozarks and their folklore.

The paragraph following is from We Always Lie to Strangers (1951). In a letter of November 7, 1955, Randolph told of his source, Price Paine, "a guide at the O-Joe Club House, Noel, Mo., in 1900 . . . he was still there in 1930 or thereabouts, but died shortly after 1930 as I recall. He told several Davy Crockett stories, and Mike Fink appeared in some of them, but I have no details. One was about shooting a comb off a woman's head, and one about shooting a Negro's heel off. . . . The story in my book . . . was not told as a tale, but as a superstition, which Paine had heard near Noel."

The story involving the comb probably was the almanac story of 1839 (p. 65), and the story about shooting the Negro's heel was first printed (sans Crockett) in 1823 (p. 281). In 1932 Meigs O. Frost, New Orleans newspaper reporter, testified that Mike had achieved immortality of a sort along the river: "Back in the sandy bottoms and the thick brush, there are barefooted children in little cabins who kind of believe Mike is on the river yet. Their Mammies scared them into good behavior, when they were very little, by tales of Mike Fink." Here he was a sort of bogey man to frighten children. When youngsters were obstreperous, they still were told in 1932, "Mike Fink'll get you!"

Randolph's informant, however, is the only one on record to have heard of the superstition which made Mike a monster of the river.

Another historical character who became a kind of Ozark superman was Mike Fink, king of the keelboatmen. He was never famous like Colonel Crockett, and the younger generation of hillfolk knew little about him. Price Paine, a guide who lived on Cowskin River, near Noel, Missouri, used to tell several good Mike Fink stories. According to one of these big tales Mike did not die at all, but disguised himself as a big catfish which stirs up storms by lashing the water with its tail. As late as 1920, according to Paine, there were still old-timers who said that floods which destroy lives and property are really caused by Mike Fink, the immortal water demon who hates all humanity.

Two Stories about Mike Fink
(1956)

JULIAN LEE RAYFORD

JULIAN LEE RAYFORD *is a free-lance writer, who lives in Mobile, Alabama. He has written a number of articles on American folklore and folk heroes, a novel,* Cottonmouth, *and another novel,* Child of the Snapping Turtle: Mike Fink, *published in 1951. In preparing to write the latter book, he traveled along the river and found the two stories which follow. These were published in fictional form in the novel about the boatman. In a letter of January 1, 1956, he told them as he heard them.*

THE FIGHT WITH NINE EYES (1956)

A professor of history at Louisiana State University told me there used to be a river pirate named Nine Eyes, who was a confederate of Col. Plug, in a pirates' den on the Ohio, near Fort Massac. Col. Plug banished Nine Eyes when he began making passes at Plug's wife. So, one day Nine Eyes appeared at Natchez-under-the-Hill, telling everyone he was an honest boatman—and he issued a challenge to all the boatmen. He was willing to sit at a table with any man who would accept his challenge. They would join hands under the table—with a knife sticking in the top of the table—and the first man to get loose was free to grab the knife and use it.

Mike accepted the challenge. They fought according to Nine Eyes' conditions, and Mike killed him. This is almost exactly as the story was told me.

[252]

CAPERS IN NATCHEZ (1956)

In Natchez, the editor of the Natchez paper told me an old forgotten story about Mike. One night Mike went up into the Spanish residential section of Natchez and stripped off his clothes and, stark naked, ran through the streets pulling a buggy loaded with keelboatmen until the Spanish soldiers chased them all back down Silver street.

Accounts of Mike Fink's Death

Accounts of Mike Fink's Death

IN 1844, J. M. FIELD wrote in the St. Louis Reveille, a famous
newspaper of the old southwest which published several
items about Mike Fink during the 1840's:

> As regards Mike, it has not yet become that favourite question
> of doubt—"Did such a being really live?" Nor have we heard the
> skeptic inquiry—"Did such a being really die?" But his death
> in half a dozen different ways and places has been asserted, and this,
> we take it, is the first gathering of the mythic haze—that shadowy
> and indistinct enlargement of outline, which, deepening through
> long ages, invests distinguished mortality with the sublimer at-
> tributes of the hero and the demi-god.

If Field counted correctly, he had encountered one more account of Mike's death previous to 1844 than we have: we have
only five. Regardless, his point is a good one, and it can be
documented even better now than when he wrote. We have,
first of all, a newspaper account of 1823 (see p. 14) which says
that Fink was engaged in shooting the cup "when aiming too
low or for some other cause" he shot and killed his companion.
A bystander protested, Fink threatened to kill him, and he
"drew a pistol and shot Fink dead upon the spot." These questions are unanswered: Where? Why did Mike miss? What does
"or from some other cause" imply? Why did the bystander protest? Why did Mike threaten him? And was the bystander justified in shooting Mike?

We have an "official" account in a Record Book of 1832
which gives a few more details (see p. 13): The man Mike shot
was one Carpenter; Mike's killer was one Talbot. Talbot "soon
after was himself drowned at the Tetons."

These are two of more than a hundred accounts of Fink's

death which appeared in print between 1823 and 1955. The tangle of fact and folk invention in them is fascinating: they have infinite variety. For instance:

Where did it happen? Place unspecified, 1823, 1848, 1855, 1856, 1860; on the Missouri in 1828, 1845, 1882 (the story of 1882 was the one by White [p. 275], published in 1939); mouth of the Yellowstone, 1829, 1844, 1847; at Smithland behind the Cumberland bar, 1837; on the Mississippi, 1842, another story of 1847; in the Rockies, 1848.

Whom did Mike shoot? "Another man," 1823; his companion, 1828; Carpenter, 1829, 1832, 1844, 1847, 1860, 1882; "a fellow" 1837; nobody, 1842, 1855 (the bullet grazed the man's skull); "an unarmed youth," 1845; his brother, 1847; a desperado, 1848; his friend, 1848; Joe Stevens, 1856.

Why did he shoot him? Accident, 1823, 1837, 1848; he was drunk, 1828, 1845, 1847, 1882; a quarrel about a woman, 1829, 1845, 1856, 1860; no specified reason, 1832; man moved his head, 1842.

Who killed Mike? "Another man in the expedition," 1823; "a friend of the deceased," 1828; Talbot, 1829, 1832, 1882; a man "who had an old grudge," 1837; the brother of Mike's victim, 1842, 1855, 1856; Talbott, 1844, 1847; one of his comrades, 1845; a hunter who was a passenger on Mike's keelboat, 1847; a spectator, 1848; a boon companion of Carpenter, 1860.

These represent only a few of the variations. Mike shot at unspecified distances as a rule, but he shot at sixty yards in 1829, at fifty in 1842, at forty in 1844 and 1847, and at eighty in 1860. He usually shot at a tin cup, but in 1847 a German writer gave him a tin mug—three tin mugs, come to think of it—and in 1855 and 1860 the cup was swapped for an apple. (William Tell influence? Or temperance?) The 1860 victim held the apple in his hand, and still Mike missed. (It may have been the distance —eighty yards.) And so on.

Which is most accurate, one wonders? Neville's story of 1828, it may be, since it is very close to the newspaper account. But of course, it is almost as skimpy, and it fails to answer some questions. It says that Mike missed because he had "corned too heavy," and then "a friend of the deceased . . . suspecting foul play" shot Mike. But is it not said again and again that Mike always corned heavy before shooting the cup? And if he was drunk, why did the friend suspect foul play?

Of the more detailed stories, the 1829 version seems the best. It is based upon the account of an "intelligent and respected fur-trader" and relayed by "a valued correspondent in St. Louis." Furthermore, it mentions for the first time in print, we believe, both Carpenter and Talbot; places the event correctly; and tells of Talbot's drowning afterward in the Titan River (which is pretty close, in sound at least, to the Tetons). The cause of the quarrel, it suggests plausibly enough, is a squaw. But it says that Carpenter "was sure Mike would kill him," and he therefore bequeathed his pistol and other items to Talbot, then stood there and let Mike shoot him. This behavior is a little puzzling. And when Talbot later shoots Mike with Carpenter's own pistol, it seems a bit too neat.

A competing story is Field's of 1844. It is based upon an account of Keemle, who was on the spot shortly after the shooting. Field locates the events correctly and correctly names Mike's companions, though he has Talbott drown in the Missouri. His motivation for Mike's miss—unintentional, he says— is better than that of the 1829 story, and that for Talbott is equally good. But there is evidence that Field had powers of invention and could stray from the strict truth: witness his complicated account of 1847—the most complicated of all the narratives about Fink.

However, as Field says, the mythic mists have gathered, and the truth is probably irrevocably lost in them. The tales offer a fascinating puzzle and a beautiful example of folk and literary invention. And they prove that print does not necessarily "freeze" the details of a widely told story.

[259]

The Last of the Boatmen (1828)[1]
MORGAN NEVILLE

Some years after the period at which I have dated my visit to Cincinnati, business called me to New Orleans. On board of the steam boat, on which I had embarked at Louisville, I recognised in the person of the pilot one of those men who had formerly been a patroon or keel boat captain. I entered into conversation with him on the subject of his former associates.

"They are scattered in all directions," said he. "A few, who had capacity, have become pilots of steam boats. Many have joined the trading parties that cross the Rocky mountains; and a few have settled down as farmers."

"What has become," I asked, "of my old acquaintance, Mike Fink?"

"Mike was killed in a skrimmage," replied the pilot. "He had refused several good offers on the steam boats. He said he could not bear the hissing of steam and he wanted room to throw his pole. He went to the Missouri, and about a year since was shooting the tin cup when he had corned too heavy. He elevated too low, and shot his companion through the head. A friend of the deceased who was present, suspecting foul play, shot Mike through the heart before he had time to re-load his rifle."

With Mike Fink expired the spirit of the Boatmen.

Mike Fink: The Last of the Boatmen (1829)

In 1822, Mike and his two friends, Carpenter and Talbot, engaged in St. Louis with Henry and Ashley to go up the Missouri with them in the threefold capacity of boatmen, trappers and hunters. The first year a company of about sixty ascended as high as the mouth of the Yellow Stone river, where they built a fort for the purposes of trade and security. From this place, small detachments of men, ten or twelve in a company, were sent out to hunt and trap on the tributary streams of the Mis-

1. For details about the publication of this and other accounts see the Bibliography, pp. 282–86.

souri and Yellow Stone. Mike and his two friends, and nine others were sent to the Muscle Shell river, a tributary of the Yellow Stone, when the winter set in. Mike and company returned to a place near the mouth of the Yellow Stone; and preferring to remain out of the fort, they dug a hole or cave in the bluff bank of the river for a winter house, in which they resided during the winter. This proved a warm and commodious habitation, protecting the inmates from winds and snow. Here Mike and his friend Carpenter quarrelled a deadly quarrel, the cause of which is not certainly known, but was thought to have been caused by a rivalry in the good graces of a squaw. The quarrel was smothered for the time by the interposition of mutual friends. On the return of spring, the party revisited the fort, where Mike and Carpenter, over a cup of whiskey, revived the recollection of their past quarrel; but made a treaty of peace which was to be solemnized by their usual trial of shooting the cup of whiskey from off each other's head, as their custom was. This was at once the test of mutual reconciliation and renewed confidence. A question remained to be settled; who should have the first shot? To determine this, Mike proposed to "sky a copper" with Carpenter; that is, to throw up a copper. This was done, and Mike won the first shot. Carpenter seemed to be fully aware of Mike's unforgiving temper and treacherous intent, for he declared that he was sure Mike would kill him. But Carpenter scorned life too much to purchase it by a breach of his solemn compact in refusing to stand the test. Accordingly, he prepared to die. He bequeathed his gun, shot pouch, and powder horn, his belt, pistols and wages to Talbot, in case he should be killed. They went to the fatal plain, and whilst Mike loaded his rifle and picked his flint, Carpenter filled his tin cup with whiskey to the brim, and without changing his features, he placed it on his devoted head as a target for Mike to shoot at. Mike levelled his rifle at the head of Carpenter, at the distance of sixty yards. After drawing a bead, he took down his rifle from his face, and smilingly said, "Hold your noddle steady, Carpenter, and don't spill the whiskey, as I shall want some presently!"

He again raised, cocked his piece, and in an instant Carpenter fell, and expired without a groan.—Mike's ball had penetrated the forehead of Carpenter in the center, about an inch and a half above the eyes. He coolly set down his rifle, and applying the muzzle to his mouth blew the smoke out of the touch hole without saying a word—keeping his eye steadily on the fallen body of Carpenter. His first words were, "Carpenter! have you spilt the whiskey!" He was then told that he had killed Carpenter. "It is all an accident," said Mike, "for I took as fair a bead on the black spot on the cup as I ever took on a squirrel's eye. How did it happen!" He then cursed the gun, the powder, the bullet, and finally himself.

This catastrophe, (in a country where the strong arm of the law cannot reach) passed off for an accident; and Mike was permitted to go at large under the belief that Carpenter's death was the result of contingency. But Carpenter had a fast friend in Talbot, who only waited a fair opportunity to revenge his death. No opportunity offered for some months after, until one day, Mike in a fit of gasconading, declared to Talbot that he did kill Carpenter on purpose, and that he was glad of it. Talbot instantly drew from his belt a pistol (the same which had belonged to Carpenter), and shot Mike through the heart. Mike fell to the ground and expired without a word. Talbot, also, went unpunished, as no body had authority, or inclination to call him to account. Truth was, Talbot was as ferocious and dangerous as the grizly bear of the prairies. About three months after, Talbot was present in the battle with the Aurickarees in which Col. Leavenworth commanded, where he displayed a coolness which would have done honor to a better man. He came out of the battle unharmed. About ten days after, he was drowned in the Titan river, in attempting to swim it. Thus ended "the last of the boatmen."

Mike, the Ohio Boatman (1837)

"Down there at Smithland, behind the Cumberland bar," continued Jo [Chunk], "used to be Mike's headquarters; and one day when he had made a bet that he'd shoot the tin cup off from a fellow's head, he happened to fire a little too quick, and lodged the ball in his brains. A man who stood a little way off, and had an old grudge against Mike, leveled his rifle and shot him dead on the spot; and this was the end of Mike Fink, the first boatman who dared to navigate a broad horn down the falls of the Ohio."

To Correspondents (1842)
WILLIAM T. PORTER

The author of "Tom Owen the Bee Hunter" has sent us another of those graphic illustrations of Western Life which have been so eagerly read on both sides of the Atlantic. The title of the present communication is "The Disgraced Scalp Lock," the hero of the story being no other than the celebrated "Mike Fink, the last of the Mississippi Flat-boat Men." This Mike Fink was an extraordinary and real character. He was shot somewhere on the Mississippi, and the thrilling incident of his death will make a chapter for our columns in due time. As we have heard the story, Mike engaged, for a wager, to knock a gill cup of whiskey off a man's head at fifty yards with a rifle ball—a feat he had performed a hundred times! On this occasion, owing to the man's moving his head, Mike's ball grazed his skull, and stunned him for a moment; a brother of his being present, thinking Mike had killed him, and intentionally, shot Mike dead on the spot.

The Death of Mike Fink (1844)[2]
JOSEPH M. FIELD

"The Last of the Boatmen" has not become altogether a mythic personage. There be around us those who still remember him as one of flesh and blood, as well of proportions simply human, albeit he lacked not somewhat of the heroic in stature, as well as in being a "perfect terror" to people!

As regards Mike, it has not yet become that favourite question

2. Compare Field's more elaborate fictional account of 1847, pp. 93–142.

of doubt—"Did such a being really live?" Nor have we heard the skeptic inquiry—"Did such a being really die?" But his death in half a dozen different ways and places has been asserted, and this, we take it, is the first gathering of the mythic haze—that shadowy and indistinct enlargement of outline, which, deepening through long ages, invests distinguished mortality with the sublimer attributes of the hero and the demi-god. Had Mike lived in "early Greece," his flat-boat feats would, doubtless, in poetry, have rivalled those of Jason in his ship; while in Scandinavian legends he would have been a river-god, to a certainty! The Sea-Kings would have sacrificed to him every time they "crossed the bar" on their return; and as for Odin himself, he would be duly advised, as far as any interference went, to "lay low and keep dark, or pre-haps," &c.

The story of Mike Fink, including a death, has been beautifully told by the late Morgan Neville of Cincinnati, a gentleman of the highest literary taste as well as of the most amiable and polished manners. "The Last of the Boatmen," as his sketch is entitled, is unexceptionable in style and, we believe, in fact, with one exception, and that is the statement as to the manner and place of Fink's death. He did not die on the Arkansas, but at Fort Henry, near the mouth of the Yellow Stone. Our informant is Mr. Chas. Keemle of this paper [St. Louis Reveille], who held a command in the neighbourhood at the time, and to whom every circumstance connected with the affair is most familiar. We give the story as it is told by himself.

In the year 1822, steamboats having left the "keels" and "broad-horns" entirely "out of sight," and Mike having, in consequence, fallen from his high estate—that of being "a little bit the almightiest man on the river, any how"—after a term of idleness, frolic and desperate rowdyism along the different towns, he, at St. Louis, entered the service of the Mountain Fur Company raised by our late fellow-citizen Gen. W. H. Ashley as a trapper and hunter; and in that capacity was he employed by Major Henry, in command of the Fort at the mouth of Yellow Stone river when the occurrence took place of which we write.

Mike, with many generous qualities, was always a reckless daredevil; but at this time, advancing in years and decayed in influence, above all become a victim of whisky, he was morose and desperate in the extreme. There was a government regulation which forbade the free use of alcohol at the trading posts on the Missouri river, and this was a continual source of quarrel between the men and the commandant, Major Henry,—on the part of Fink, particularly. One of his freaks was to march with his rifle into the fort and demand a supply of spirits. Argument was fruitless, force not to be thought of, and when, on being positively denied, Mike drew up his rifle and sent a ball through the cask, deliberately walked up and filled his can, while his particular "boys" followed his example, all that could be done was to look upon the matter as one of his "queer ways," and that was the end of it.

This state of things continued for some time; Mike's temper and exactions growing more unbearable every day, until, finally, a "split" took place, not only between himself and the commandant, but many others in the fort, and the unruly boatman swore he would not live among them. Followed only by a youth named Carpenter, whom he had brought up, and for whom he felt a rude but strong attachment, he prepared a sort of cave in the river's bank, furnished it with a supply of whisky, and with his companion turned in to pass the winter, which was then closing upon them. In this place he buried himself, sometimes unseen for weeks, his protege providing what else was necessary beyond the whisky. At length attempts were used, on the part of those in the fort, to withdraw Carpenter from Fink; foul insinuations were made as to the nature of their connection; the youth was twitted with being a mere slave, &c., all which (Fink heard of it in spite of his retirement) served to breed distrust between the two, and though they did not separate, much of their cordiality ceased.

The winter wore away in this sullen state of torpor; spring came with its reviving influences, and to celebrate the season, a supply of alcohol was procured, and a number of his acquaintances from the fort coming to "rouse out" Mike, a desperate "frolic," of course, ensued.

There were river yarns and boatmen songs and "nigger break-downs" interspersed with wrestling-matches, jumping, laugh, and yell, the can circulating freely, until Mike became some-what mollified.

"I tell you what it is, boys," he cried, "the fort's a skunk-hole, and I rather live with the bars than stay in it. Some on ye's bin trying to part me and my boy, that I love like my own cub—but no matter. Maybe he's pisoned against me; but, Carpenter (striking the youth heavily on the shoulder), I took you by the hand when it had forgotten the touch of a father's or a mother's —you know me to be a man, and you ain't a going to turn out a dog!"

Whether it was that the youth fancied something insulting in the manner of the appeal, or not, we can't say; but it was not responded to very warmly, and a reproach followed from Mike. However, they drank together, and the frolic went on until Mike, filling his can, walked off some forty yards, placed it upon his head, and called to Carpenter to take his rifle.

This wild feat of shooting cans off each other's head was a favourite one with Mike—himself and "boy" generally winding up a hard frolic with this savage but deeply-meaning proof of continued confidence;—as for risk, their eagle eyes and iron nerves defied the might of whisky. After their recent alienation, a doubly generous impulse, without doubt, had induced Fink to propose and subject himself to the test.

Carpenter had been drinking wildly, and with a boisterous laugh snatched up his rifle. All present had seen the parties "shoot," and this desperate aim, instead of alarming, was merely made a matter of wild jest.

"Your grog is spilt, for ever, Mike!"

"Kill the old varmint, young 'un!"

"What'll his skin bring in St. Louis?" &c., &c.

Amid a loud laugh, Carpenter raised his piece—even the jest-ers remarked that he was unsteady,—crack!—the can fell,—a loud shout,—but, instead of a smile of pleasure, a dark frown settled upon the face of Fink! He made no motion except to clutch his rifle as though he would have crushed it, and there he stood, gazing at the youth strangely! Various shades of passion crossed his features—surprise, rage, suspicion—but at length they composed themselves into a sad expression; the ball had grazed the top of his head, cutting the scalp, and the thought of treachery had set his heart on fire.

There was a loud call upon Mike to know what he was waiting for, in which Carpenter joined, pointing to the can upon his head and bidding him fire, if he knew how!

"Carpenter, my son," said the boatman, "I taught you to shoot differently from that *last* shot! You've *missed* once, but you won't again!"

He fired, and his ball, crashing through the forehead of the youth, laid him a corpse amid his as suddenly hushed companions!

Time wore on—many at the fort spoke darkly of the deed. Mike Fink had never been known to miss his aim—he had grown afraid of Carpenter—he had murdered him! While this feeling was gathering against him, the unhappy boatman lay in his cave, shunning both sympathy and sustenance. He spoke to none—when he did come forth, 'twas as a spectre, and only to haunt the grave of his "boy," or, if he did break silence, 'twas to burst into a paroxysm of rage against the enemies who had "turned his boy's heart from him!"

At the fort was a man by the name of Talbott, the gunsmith of the station: he was very loud and bitter in his denunciations of the "murderer," as he called Fink, which, finally, reaching the ears of the latter, filled him with the most violent passion, and he swore that he would take the life of his defamer. This threat was almost forgotten, when one day, Talbott, who was at work in his shop, saw Fink enter the fort, his first visit since the death of Carpenter. Fink approached; he was careworn, sick, and wasted; there was no anger in his bearing, but he carried his rifle, (had he ever gone without it?) and the gunsmith was not a coolly brave man; moreover, his life had been threatened.

"Fink," cried he, snatching up a pair of pistols from his bench, "don't approach me—if you do, you're a dead man!"

"Talbott," said the boatman, in a sad voice, "you needn't be afraid; you've done me wrong—I'm come to talk to you about—Carpenter—my boy!"

He continued to advance, and the gunsmith again called to him:

"Fink! I know you; if you come three steps nearer, I'll fire, by ———!"

Mike carried his rifle across his arm, and made no hostile demonstration, except in gradually getting nearer—*if* hostile his aim was.

"Talbott, you've accused me of murdering—my boy—Carpenter—that I raised from a child—that I loved like a son—that I can't live without! I'm not mad with you *now*, but you must let me show you that I *couldn't* do it—that I'd rather died than done it—that you've wronged me—"

By this time he was within a few steps of the door, and Talbott's agitation became extreme. Both pistols were pointed at Fink's breast, in expectation of a spring from the latter.

"By the Almighty above us, Fink, I'll fire—I don't want to speak to you now—don't put your foot on that step—don't."

Fink did put his foot on the step, and the same moment fell heavily within it, receiving the contents of both barrels in his breast! His last and only words were,

"I didn't mean to kill my boy!"

Poor Mike! we are satisfied with our senior's conviction that you did *not* mean to kill him. Suspicion of treachery, doubtless, entered his mind, but cowardice and murder never dwelt there.

A few weeks after this event, Talbott himself perished in an attempt to cross the Missouri river in a skiff.

The Last of the Girtys (1845)

CHARLES CIST

The graphic pen of Morgan Neville has given celebrity to Mike Fink, one of these river characters, to whose exploits as a marksman Mr. Neville has done justice; but to whose character otherwise he has done more than justice, in classing him with the boatmen to whose care merchandise in great value was committed with a confidence which the owners never had cause to repent.

This was true of those who had charge of the boat; but did not apply to Fink, who was nothing more than "a hand" on board, and whose private character was worthless and vile. Mike was in fact an illustration of a class of which I have spoken who did not dare to show their faces in their early neighborhoods or homes.

Mike's whole history in Missouri proves this, and especially is it made manifest in the closing scene of his existence. He takes the life of an unarmed youth whom he had raised from a child in a drunken fit of jealousy, probably without cause, and when reproved indignantly for his conduct by one of his comrades, draws his rifle to his shoulder to kill him also, provoking the quicker movement, which, in self defense, deprived himself of life.

Flatbootmen (1847)

FRIEDRICH GERSTÄCKER[3]

But this fighting and bragging [of the river boatmen] did not always end so peacefully, and the old bargeman Mike who for many years travelled on the Ohio and the Mississippi with his brother, provides a sad example. Mike was an excellent marksman, and when strangers came aboard he used to shoot a tin mug off his brother's head with a bullet, as Tell once shot down

3. Friedrich Gerstäcker (1816–72) was a German author who traveled in the United States before 1843 and who used materials collected in very popular travel books and in novels after the model of James Fenimore Cooper.

the apple with the crossbow. In Mike's days few steamboats as yet plied the big rivers, and for short distances and in pleasant weather travellers often preferred the calmer trip on such a barge. I am sure that many a man bet his last dollar to be able to watch with the others the terrible master shot; and Mike often bragged that, from the tiller up to the bow, a distance of about forty paces, he had shot down more than two hundred mugs from the head of his somewhat feeble-minded brother and in doing so had earned exactly that many dollars.

One evening, when he was travelling past the little town of Maysville which recently had been founded, two hunters came aboard to travel all the way down to Paducah, Kentucky, with him. When Mike saw their rifles, he started to brag and urged the hunters to make the usual bet. But they declined to encourage such an evil deed, and even vehemently protested against such atrocious behaviour as putting one's own brother in danger of being shot for the sake of a paltry dollar.

Finally, Mike was outraged. "Damn you!" he cried, "do you believe I can't do what I want on my own boat? Go, John, and get my rifle and three mugs and I'll be damned if I don't shoot down all three one after another."

John obeyed, stood up, and shortly thereafter the first mug fell, pierced through, on the aft-deck. With a spiteful glance towards the strangers, Mike reloaded, after first having carefully wiped the barrel. He aimed quickly, and the second one fell down with a rattle.

"Mike, that's enough!" said one of his people, coming up to him. "You have drunk a lot this afternoon and your hand is shaking—I saw how the front of the barrel was swaying back and forth."

"Go to the devil!" cried Mike angrily, "but don't get in front of my rifle. Remember what happened to Jim, when he tried to keep me from shooting."

"You killed him!" whispered the sailor slowly—"I know it very well even if you deny it, but damn you, you won't escape your punishment!"

"Go away! I say," cried Mike, angrily stamping his foot—"go away—the poor boy is standing there waiting—with the mug on his head. Here is the third one—and so much for your blabbering."

While he was still talking he raised the rifle, aimed, pulled the trigger. At the crack, the villain's unfortunate brother fell to the deck, dead, shot through the head. Frightened, Mike let his rifle fall and started to run forward, but that was his last movement. As soon as he saw the boy fall one of the hunters put his own weapon to his cheek, and Mike, shot through the heart, tumbled a few steps towards the side, then fell over the edge of the boat. He disappeared immediately in the water which lapped over him.

The crew, partly in agreement with the punishment of the man who had murdered his own brother, partly frightened by the bold act so typical of the pioneers, docked the boat and let the self-appointed judge and his friends walk up to the beach, a free man. They then buried poor John and continued their trip.

Report of an Examination of
New Mexico (1848)
J. W. ABERT

November 30 [1846, encamped near Valverde], . . . This afternoon we had a festive scene at the camp of a trader from Missouri, who still had some fine claret and some good old brandy. We had many tales of wild adventures of prairie life and hair-breadth escapes. We heard of Mike Fink, who, with two other desperadoes, for a time lived in the Rocky Mountains. There Mike would shoot a tin cup off the head of one of the trio for some trifling bet. One day, under the wager of a keg of whiskey, Mike fired away at the tin cup and his friend dropped. "There," said Mike, "I've lost the whiskey, I shot a little too low." True, the shot had entered between the eyes of the cup bearer. Shortly after this occurrence, Mike had an altercation with the second man, and, remarking that he had one of the best rifles that was ever shot, *the other* drew a pistol and killed Mike *dead*; and this man, on his way to St. Louis, to stand his trial, jumped overboard and was drowned in the waters of the Missouri. Thus, as the narrator stated, perished three of the most desperate men known in the west.

Mike Fink, a Legend of the Ohio (1848)
EMERSON BENNETT

For a number of years, Mike Fink continued upon the river, the same wild, humorous, and daring boatman we have described him. The introduction of steam upon the western waters completely destroyed his old occupation; and cursing it and all inventions connected with it, he retired in disgust. The latter part of his life is said to have been unhappy; and his end, as the fortune-teller predicted, was bloody. He continued the practice of shooting the tin cup from the head of another; and his last shot proving fatal to his friend—a spectator who fancied it intentional on the part of the old boatman at once shot him through the heart. So died Mike Fink.

Remembrances of the Mississippi (1855)
T. B. THORPE

If they [the boatmen] quarreled among themselves, and then made friends, their test that they bore no malice was to shoot some small object from each other's heads. Mike Fink, the best shot of all keel-boatmen, lost his life in one of these strange trials of friendship. He had a difficulty with one of his companions, made friends, and agreed to the usual ceremony to show that he bore no ill-will. The man put an apple upon his head, placed himself at the proper distance—Mike fired, and hit, not the inanimate object, but the man, who fell to the ground, apparently dead. Standing by was a brother of this victim either of treachery or hazard, and in an instant of anger he shot Mike through the heart. In a few moments the supposed dead man, without a wound, recovered his feet. Mike had, evidently from mere wantoness, displaced the apple by shooting between it and the skull, in the same way that he would have barked a squirrel from the limb of a tree. The joke, unfortunately, cost the renowned Mike Fink his life.

Lloyd's Steamboat Directory (1856)
JAMES T. LLOYD

The death of Mike Fink was melo-dramatic at least, if it wanted the dignified characteristics of tragedy. He had a friend, one of his barge companions, named Joe Stevens, on whom he had lavished his good offices, taught him the use of the rifle and many other accomplishments suited to his situation in life. Mike likewise had a sweetheart, the daughter of one of the early settlers, who dwelt in a cottage or shanty on the bank of the river, and performed the duties of laundress for the boatmen, among whom she had many admirers. Fink for some time appeared to be the most acceptable of this young lady's numerous lovers, but he was aroused at last from dreams of bliss, as delusive as they were delicious, by the fatal discovery that his friend Joe Stevens had fully *realized* all that felicity which he himself had enjoyed only in visionary perspective. Burning with rage and jealousy, Mike contrived to hide his resentment while he awaited a fair opportunity for vengeance. That opportunity came at last. On a certain fine autumnal afternoon, the crew of Fink's boat were recreating themselves on shore with the rifle exercise, shooting at a mark, which was a very common divertisement among gentlemen of their profession. Fink's reputation as an accurate marksman was so well established that his companions frequently allowed him to fire at a tin cup placed on the head of one of their number, and the man who supported this target, having a perfect reliance on Mike's skill, never considered the valuable contents of his knowledge-box endangered in the least by this experiment. On the occasion now referred to, a stranger was present, and Fink, apparently with a desire to show off his exquisite accomplishment, proposed to shoot at the tin cup in the manner just described. The person whom he selected to bear the target was his rival in love, and the object of his fierce but hitherto concealed resentment, Joe Stevens, who was wholly unsuspicious of the deadly malice which lurked in Mike's bosom. Joe cheerfully consented to be the cup-bearer, and having assumed the glittering but perilous diadem, he placed himself at the proper distance, and requested Mike to "blaze away." Mike *did* blaze away with a vengeance, but instead of aiming at the cup, as the spectators supposed he would, he directed the piece a few inches lower, perforated the skull of the unlucky Stevens, and laid him dead on the spot. A brother of Stevens was present, and he, suspecting that the bloody deed had been premeditated by Fink, levelled his gun at the latter, and shot him dead likewise. And thus the eventful life of this illustrious personage was brought to a sudden termination.

Edwards' Great West (1860)
RICHARD EDWARDS AND M. HOPEWELL, M.D.

One of the feats of Mike Fink was to shoot an apple with his rifle from the hand of a man by the name of Carpenter, which he had done over and over again for a gallon of whiskey, halving it on all occasions with Carpenter, who jeopardized his life so fearfully on these occasions.

The friendship which had so long subsisted between these brave and lawless men was interrupted by a quarrel, and before the rancor had entirely passed, some one offered Carpenter a gallon of whiskey if he would let some one shoot an apple from his hand. The temptation was irresistible to Carpenter, and he was unwilling that any one perform the feat but Mike Fink. Mike Fink was sent for, and, arrived at the spot, professed his willingness to do what he had so frequently done before successfully. Carpenter took his station at eighty yards, and as Mike Fink raised his rifle, his countenance changed to a demon's hue, black and fearful. In an instant his experienced eye ranged the lead with the sights, and then when every muscle was still and unmoved as a rock, the rifle was fired, and, to the horror of all, Carpenter fell dead upon the spot, the ball having perforated his forehead. Mike Fink pretended that the rifle hung fire, and the death was entirely accidental. However, in one of his drunken orgies he confessed to have done it designedly, and being threatened with arrest went far up the Missouri to escape from the meshes of the law. Pirate vengeance is more searching for life than public justice, and one of the boon companions of Carpenter followed the murderer to his wild haunts and stabbed him to the heart.

Early Days in St. Louis (ca. 1882)
JAMES HALEY WHITE[4]

Among the distinguished men of that day were two American boatmen, notorious for their crack shots with the Kentucky rifle, and their daring in shooting a common tin cup from off each other's heads at one hundred yards distance without a rest —off-hand as it was called. One of them was a large heavy, slow spoken, slow moving quiet man with a dark, sallow countenance, and having the appearance of being raised upon the diet of ague and fever, a very plentiful supply of which that country abounded in at that day. He was a popular man amongst his associates. He was called "Old Mike," or Mike Fink. His popularity was obtained from his qualities as a marksman. The other was a short, heavy, round built, square shouldered wide-headed man; also a remarkable marksman. He also was slow of motion and speech and also popular with his associates. They were cronies and almost always together, for they were from the same part of the country, near Pittsburgh, and belonged to the early class of boatmen who navigated the Ohio from Pittsburgh to New Orleans on flat boats. Many of the old citizens of the present, whose habitations bordered upon the Ohio River in those days, will recall their boat song which was sung to keep

4. James Haley White, born in Alexandria, Virginia, May 3, 1805, died in Suisun, California, October 17, 1882. He was the son of James and Nancy (Haley) White. In 1819 he moved with his father to St. Louis, where he remained for thirty years and gained considerable distinction as an architect. In 1849 he went to California. In 1882 White was writing his "Recollections," from which this was taken. It was first printed in 1939.

time with their oars, each stanza terminated with "All Way to Shawnee Town Long Time Ago." This other was named William Carpenter, or more popularly called Bill Carpenter. They had another companion in their journeyings and shootings. A native, also, of the vicinity of Pittsburgh, who went by the name of "Pittsburgh Blue," and was often made to bear the tin cup upon her head for each of them to shoot at. She was an abandoned woman, and like her shooting friends, fond of whiskey and always full of it. These characters have all passed away, and many of the early citizens of St. Louis who may be living at this day recollect well these characters and the scenes ascribed to them.

In the year 1821 there appeared another character as a boatman upon the stage of action by the name of Levi Talbot; he was a cooper by trade and was born and raised in Alexandria, Virginia. His tastes were different from those of Fink and Carpenter, except as to whiskey. He was a heavy set, well built and physically powerful man, and of loose bad habits and in principal he belonged to that class of boatmen who delighted in rough and tumble fighting. In one of his broils one night at the old Green Tree Tavern at St. Louis in an encounter, he had one of his fingers nearly bitten off. He applied to Mike Fink to cure it, for Mike sometimes acted in that capacity. Mike as a friend and without fee salved and poulticed him, and as soon as he was well he started for a trip to Council Bluffs. On leaving he stole Mike's blankets, which caused Mike to swear vengeance against him if they ever met. Time passed and they did meet for the last time. In 1822 Gen. William H. Ashley of St. Louis and others fitted out an expedition for the Rocky Mountains, embarking in the fur trade. They purchased several keel boats and had them fitted out with side wheels like our present steamboats, with shaft crank and fly-wheels and sliding frames erected upon the top deck of the boats, attached to the cranks to move back and forward. They had seats made across the boats under the frames, fore and aft of the shaft, to accommodate men sitting; with round cross pieces as handles for the men to move the frame and propel the boats.[5] He gathered a large company of men for the expedition, taking away from St. Louis many young men of good families, many who never returned. A part of his company went by land as well as by water for some of the distance.

Jim Beckwith, the old mountaineer accompanied the land portion of the expedition, and James Bridger of Fort Bridger notoriety, accompanied the boats. Mike Fink and Bill Carpenter accompanied this expedition, and far up the Missouri while the company were in camp, and Mike and Bill full of whiskey, they commenced their old game of shooting the tin cup. The result was that Mike shot his friend through the head and killed him. Talbot now made his appearance and accused Mike of murder. Mike now threatened to shoot Talbot for stealing his blankets. Talbot drew a pistol and shot Mike dead, and then attempted to cross the Missouri River to avoid arrest and was drowned. This is not a tale of fiction but a truthful narrative; the writer knew of these characters well and witnessed their tin-cup shootings, and their departure from St. Louis with the Ashley expedition; and also knew Beckwith and Bridger and their families.

5. The author's memory is probably in error here. Somewhat similar apparatus was used by General Atkinson on the Atkinson-O'Fallon Expedition up the Missouri in 1825.

Bibliography

Bibliography

I. ORIGINAL SOURCES AND REPRINTS, ARRANGED CHRONOLOGICALLY

(Under each original reference the reprints of that reference are listed under a, b, c, etc.)

Newspaper report of Fink's death, St. Louis Republican, July 16, 1823.

MORGAN NEVILLE, "The Last of the Boatmen," in The Western Souvenir, a Christmas and New Year's Gift for 1829, ed. JAMES HALL (Cincinnati, 1828).

a) SAMUEL CUMINGS, The Western Pilot, Containing Charts of the Ohio River and of the Mississippi . . . Accompanied with Directions for Navigating the Same (Cincinnati, 1829, 1832, 1834).

b) MARY RUSSELL MITFORD (ed.), Lights and Shadows of American Life (London, 1832), Vol. II.

c) The Athenaeum (London), June 2, 9, 1832, pp. 351–52, 365–66.

d) HIRAM KAINE, "Mike Fink," in the Cincinnati Miscellany or Antiquities of the West (October, 1845), pp. 31–32.

e) Description of Banvard's Panorama of the Mississippi, Painted on Three Miles of Canvas, Exhibiting a View of a Country 1200 Miles in Length, Extending from the Mouth of the Missouri River to New Orleans, Being by Far the Largest Picture Ever Executed by Man (Boston, 1847), pp. 33–34.

f) A. DE PUY VAN BUREN, Jottings of a Year's Sojourn in the South (Battle Creek, Michigan, 1859), pp. 305–12.

g) V. L. O. CHITTICK (ed.), Ring-tailed Roarers (Caldwell, Idaho, 1941), pp. 287–97.

h) B. A. BOTKIN (ed.), A Treasury of American Folklore (New York, 1944), pp. 30–34.

i) JOHN T. FLANAGAN (ed.), America Is West (Minneapolis, 1945), pp. 333–42.

j) WALTER BLAIR, THEODORE HORNBERGER, and RANDALL STEWART (eds.), The Literature of the United States (Chicago, 1946), I, 503–8; revised ed., 1953.

[281]

"Mike Fink: The Last of the Boatmen," *Western Monthly Review*, ed. TIMOTHY FLINT (Cincinnati, July, 1829), pp. 15–19.
a) *Missouri Republican*, July 21, 1829.
b) *Missouri Intelligencer*, September 4, 1829.
c) HENRY HOWE, *The Great West* (Cincinnati, 1847), pp. 245–46; this went through a number of editions.
d) BEN CASSEDY, *The History of Louisville, from Its Earliest Settlement to the Year 1852* (Louisville, 1852), pp. 72–74.
e) MORITZ BUSCH, *Wanderungen zwischen Hudson und Mississippi, 1851 und 1852* ... (Stuttgart und Tübingen, 1854), I, 372–77.
f) FRANK TRIPLETT, *Conquering the Wilderness* ... (New York and St. Louis, 1883).
g) H. M. CHITTENDEN, *History of the American Fur Trade in the Far West* (New York, 1902), IV, 707–12.
SMITH, JACKSON, and SUBLETTE, Record Book, Vol. XXXII, containing copies of letters from Indian agents and others to the Superintendent of Indian Affairs at St. Louis, from September 10, 1830, to April 1, 1832.
"Mike Fink, the Ohio Boatman," *Davy Crockett's Almanack, of Wild Sports in the West, Life in the Backwoods, Sketches of Texas, and Rows on the Mississippi, 1838* (Nashville, Tennessee, [1837]).
a) *The Crockett Almanacks*, "Nashville Series," ed. FRANKLIN J. MEINE (Chicago, 1955), pp. 149–50.
"Crockett Beat at a Shooting Match," *The Crockett Almanac, Containing Adventures, Exploits, Sprees, & Scrapes in the West, & Life and Manners in the Backwoods, 1840* (Nashville, [1839]).
a) WALTER BLAIR (ed.), *Native American Humor, 1800–1900* (New York, 1937), pp. 283–84.
b) B. A. BOTKIN (ed.), *A Treasury of American Folklore* (New York, 1944), pp. 7–8.
c) JACK CONROY (ed.), *Midland Humor* (New York, 1947), pp. 7–8.
WILLIAM T. PORTER, "To Correspondents," the *Spirit of the Times, a Chronicle of the Turf, Agriculture, Field Sports, Literature and the Stage* (New York), July 9, 1842, p. 217.
T. B. THORPE, "The Disgraced Scalp-Lock, or Incidents on Western Waters," the *Spirit of the Times* ... (New York), July 16, 1842, p. 229.
a) *Brother Jonathan* (1842), II, 342–44.
b) WILLIAM GILMORE SIMMS (ed.), *Transatlantic Tales, Sketches and Legends by Various American Authors* (London, 1842), pp. 60–65.
c) CINCINNATI MISCELLANY ... (1846), II, 332–34.

d) T. B. THORPE, *The Mysteries of the Backwoods; or Sketches of the Southwest Including Character, Scenery, and Rural Sports* (Philadelphia, 1846), pp. 118–36.

e) T. B. THORPE, "Mike Fink, the Keelboatman," *The Hive of the Bee-Hunter* (New York, 1854), pp. 163 ff.

f) JOSEPH DUNBAR SHIELDS, *Natchez, Its Early History* (Louisville, 1930), pp. 261–63.

g) JAMES DAUGHERTY (ed.), *Their Weight in Wildcats* (Boston, 1936), pp. 3–19.

h) ARTHUR PALMER HUDSON (ed.), *Humor of the Old Deep South* (New York, 1936), pp. 298–300.

i) V. L. O. CHITTICK (ed.), *Ring-tailed Roarers* (Caldwell, Idaho, 1941), pp. 274–86.

j) B. A. BOTKIN (ed.), *A Treasury of American Folklore* (New York, 1944), pp. 35–43.

JOSEPH M. FIELD, "The Death of Mike Fink," *St. Louis Reveille*, October 21, 1844.

a) "The Last of Mike Fink," *Louisville Journal*, December 25, 1844.

b) JOSEPH M. FIELD, *The Drama in Pokerville* (Philadephia, 1847), pp. 177–83.

c) *Paris Western Citizen* (Kentucky), Wisconsin Historical Society, Draper MSS 29CC45–46.

d) JAMES H. BRADLEY, *Sketch of the Fur Trade of the Upper Missouri River: Contributions to the Historical Society of Montana* (1923), pp. 320–24.

e) V. L. O. CHITTICK (ed.), *Ring-tailed Roarers* (Caldwell, Idaho, 1941), pp. 298–302.

f) B. A. BOTKIN (ed.), *A Treasury of American Folklore* (New York, 1944), pp. 47–50.

CHARLES CIST, "The Last of the Girtys," *Western Literary Journal and Monthly Review* (Cincinnati), February, 1845, p. 235.

a) *Cincinnati Miscellany* . . . February, 1845, pp. 125–26.

b) *The Western Boatman: A Periodical Devoted to Navigation* (Cincinnati), June, 1848, p. 129.

K, "Correspondence," *Cincinnati Miscellany* . . . February, 1845, pp. 156–57.

a) HENRY HOWE, *The Great West* (Cincinnati, 1847), p. 241; went through a number of editions.

b) B. A. BOTKIN (ed.), *A Treasury of Mississippi River Folklore* (New York, 1955), p. 129.

FRIEDRICH GERSTÄCKER, "Flatbootmen," *Mississippibilder: Licht- und Schattenseiten transatlantischen Lebens* (1847), *Gesammelte Schriften* (Jena, 1872), X, 582–83.

SOLITAIRE [JOHN S. ROBB], "Trimming a Darky's Heel," *St. Louis Reveille*, January 25, 1847.
  a) *Spirit of the Times* (New York), February 13, 1847, p. 605.
  b) B. A. BOTKIN (ed.), *A Treasury of American Folklore* (New York, 1944), pp. 43–46.
JOSEPH M. FIELD, "Mike Fink: The Last of the Boatmen," *St. Louis Reveille*, June 8, 9, 10, 11, 12, 13, 15, 18, 19, 20, 1847.
  a) *St. Louis Weekly Reveille*, June 14, 21, 1847.
EMERSON BENNETT, *Mike Fink, a Legend of the Ohio* (Cincinnati, 1848); revised ed. (Cincinnati, 1852).
"Lige Shattuck's Reminiscence of Mike Fink," *St. Louis Reveille*, February 28, 1848.
  a) *Spirit of the Times* (New York), April 15, 1848, p. 89.
  b) THOMAS W. KNOX, *The Underground World: A Mirror of Life below the Surface* . . . (Hartford and Chicago, 1873), pp. 683–84; reprinted in 1877.
  c) B. A. BOTKIN (ed.), *A Treasury of Mississippi River Folklore* (New York, 1955), p. 128.
"Report of Lieut. J. W. Abert on His Examination of New Mexico in the Years 1846–47," U.S. 30th Cong., 1st. Sess., Exec. Doc., No. 41 (Washington, 1848), IV, 503.
  a) U.S. Army Corps of Topographical Engineers . . . *Notes of a Military Reconnaissance* (Washington, 1848).
"Mike Fink Trying To Scare Mrs. Crockett," *Crockett's Almanac—Containing Life, Manners and Adventures in the Backwoods, and Rows, Sprees and Scrapes on the Western Waters, 1851* (Philadelphia, New York, Boston, [1850]).
"Rev. Peter Cartwright, Jocose Preacher," *Columbus Southern Sentinel* (Georgia), May 2, 1850.
  a) JAMES B. FINLEY, *Autobiography of Rev. James B. Finley; or Pioneer Life in the West*, ed. W. P. STRICKLAND (Cincinnati, 1854), pp. 309, 327–29.
  b) A. DE PUY VAN BUREN, *Jottings of a Year's Sojourn in the South* (Battle Creek, Michigan, 1859), pp. 312–14.
SCROGGINS, "Deacon Smith's Bull, or Mike Fink in a Tight Place," *Miltonian* (Milton, Pennsylvania), 1851 (exact date unknown).
  a) *Spirit of the Times* (New York), March 22, 1851, p. 22.
  b) *Missouri Courier* (Hannibal), May 5, 1851.
  c) *Holly Springs Mississippi Palladium*, June 6, 1851, p. 4.
  d) T. C. HALLIBURTON (ed.), *Traits of American Humour, by Native Authors* (London, 1852), III, 79–87.
  e) *Yankee Blade*, November 17, 1855.
  f) ARTHUR PALMER HUDSON (ed.), *Humor of the Old Deep South* (New York, 1936), pp. 301–4.
  g) CARL CARMER (ed.), *The Hurricane's Children* (New York, 1937), pp. 3–10.

h) V. L. O. Chittick (ed.), *Ring-tailed Roarers* (Caldwell, Idaho, 1941), pp. 269–73.

i) Ben C. Clough (ed.), *The American Imagination at Work* (New York, 1947), pp. 542–46.

"Mike Fink's Treat to the Indians"; "Mike Fink Hunting a Moose"; "Bravery of Mike Fink's Wife," *Crockett Almanac, Containing Life, Manners, and Adventures in the Back Woods, and Rows, Sprees, and Scrapes on the Western Waters, 1852* (New York, Boston, Baltimore, [1851]).

Ben Cassedy, *History of Louisville, from Its Earliest Settlement to the Year 1852* (Louisville, 1852), pp. 72–79.

a) *An Old Tale for the New Year, or Mike Fink* . . . (New York, 1928).

b) B. A. Botkin (ed.), *A Treasury of Southern Folklore* (New York, 1949), pp. 208–11.

"The Celebrated Mike Fink Attacked by a Wolf While Fishing in the Mississippi"; "Sal Fink's Victory over an Old Bear and Cubs"; "Mike Fink Killing a Wolf with His Fists," *Crockett Almanac, Containing Life, Manners, and Adventures in the Back Woods, and Rows, Sprees, and Scrapes on the Western Waters, 1853* (New York, Boston, Baltimore, [1852]).

"Mike Fink's First View of a Steamboat"; "Sal Fink, the Mississippi Screamer"; "How To Escape a Bear"; "Mike Fink's Idea of a Gymnastic School," *Crockett Almanac. Containing Life, Manners and Adventures in the Backwoods, and Rows, Sprees, and Scrapes on the Western Waters, 1854* (New York, [1853]).

a) "Sal Fink, the Mississippi Screamer," in Jack Conroy (ed.), *Midland Humor* (New York, 1947), pp. 9–10.

T. B. Thorpe, "Remembrances of the Mississippi," *Harper's Magazine*, December, 1855.

a) W. H. Milburn, *Ten Years of Preacher Life* (New York, 1859), pp. 216–22.

b) John C. Van Tramp, *Prairie and Rocky Mountain Adventures, or Life in the New West* (Columbus, Ohio, 1866), p. 95.

James T. Lloyd, *Lloyd's Steamboat Directory* (Cincinnati, 1856), pp. 35–38.

Peter Cartwright: The Backwoods Preacher: An Autobiography of Peter Cartwright, ed. W. P. Strickland (New York, 1857; other editions, London, 1858; Cincinnati, 1860).

Report of A. P. Redfield, September 1, 1858, to A. M. Robinson, 35th Cong., 2d Sess., Sen. Exec. Doc. I (Serial 974), p. 440.

Richard Edwards and Menra Hopewell, *Edwards' Great West and Her Metropolis, Embracing a General View of the West, and a Complete History of St. Louis* (St. Louis, 1860), p. 591.

MENRA HOPEWELL, Legends of the Missouri and Mississippi (London, [1874?]), pp. 372–78.

JAMES KEYES, Pioneers of Scioto County: Being a Short Biographical Sketch of Some of the First Settlers of Scioto County, Ohio (Portsmouth, Ohio, 1880), pp. 3–4.
  a) HENRY T. BANNON, Stories Old and Often Told: Being Chronicles of Scioto County, Ohio (Baltimore, 1928), pp. 116–18.

FRANK TRIPLETT, Conquering the Wilderness (New York and St. Louis, 1883; Chicago and New York, 1895).

HENRY HOWE, "A Talk with a Veteran Boatman," Historical Collections of Ohio (Ohio Centennial Edition; Columbus, 1888), I, 321–22.

WILLIAM EPLER, "Some Personal Recollections of Peter Cartwright," Illinois State Historical Society Journal, XIII (1920), 379.

WILLIAM E. CONNOLLEY, letter quoted in WALTER BLAIR and FRANKLIN J. MEINE, Mike Fink: King of Mississippi Keelboatmen (New York, 1933), p. 111.

JAMES HALEY WHITE, "Early Days in St. Louis" (ca. 1882), in Glimpses of the Past, VI (January–March, 1939), 5–10.

HENRY W. SHOEMAKER, "Mike Fink," The Capitol News (Harrisburg, Pennsylvania), December 1, 1950; November 10, 1952; March 31, 1953; January 9, 1956.

VANCE RANDOLPH, We Always Lie to Strangers (New York, 1951), p. 162.

ELLA CHAFANT (ed.), "Will of Mary Fink dated September 1, 1821," A Goodly Heritage: Earliest Wills on an American Frontier (Pittsburgh, 1955), pp. 146–47.

JULIAN LEE RAYFORD, "Two Stories about Mike Fink," letter to Walter Blair, dated January 1, 1956.

II. SECONDARY SOURCES: REWRITTEN STORIES AND REFERENCES TO MIKE FINK, ARRANGED CHRONOLOGICALLY

(This is not an exhaustive list; it is intended merely to indicate a typical group of references.)

JAMES HALL, Statistics of the West, at the Close of the Year 1836 (Cincinnati, 1837), p. 220.

J. W. MONETTE, History of the Valley of the Mississippi (New York, 1846), Vol. II, chap. i, sec. 2.

[JAMES H. PERKINS], "The Pioneers of Kentucky," North American Review, LXXII (January, 1846), 87.

DE GRACHIA, "The Old Bear of Tironga Bayou, Arkansas," Spirit of the Times, February 13, 1847.

JAMES HALL, The West: Its Commerce and Navigation (Cincinnati, 1848), p. 112.

CHARLES McKNIGHT, Our Western Border One Hundred Years Ago (Philadelphia, 1875).

J. THOMAS SHARF, History of St. Louis and County (Philadelphia, 1883), p. 1093.

W. H. PERRIN, J. H. BATTLE, and C. KNIFFIN, Kentucky, a History of the State (8th ed.; Louisville and Chicago, 1888), pp. 234–35.

EMERSON W. GOULD, Fifty Years on the Mississippi: Or Gould's History of River Navigation (St. Louis, 1889), pp. 4156–59, 4165.

FIRMAN A. ROZIER, Rozier's History of the Early Settlements of the Mississippi Valley (St. Louis, 1890), p. 64.

WILLIAM HENRY PERRIN, "Western River Navigation a Century Ago," Magazine of Western History, XII (August, 1890), 340–45.

W. H. VENABLE, Beginnings of Literary Culture in the Ohio Valley (Cincinnati, 1891), p. 228.

JOHN R. MUSICK, Stories of Missouri (New York, 1897), pp. 86–88.

ARCHER B. HULBERT, Waterways of Westward Expansion: The Ohio River and Its Tributaries (New York, 1903).

ARCHER B. HULBERT, The Ohio River (New York, 1906), pp. 211–16.

WALTER B. STEVENS, Missouri, the Center State, 1821–1915 (Chicago, 1915), pp. 707–8, 712–13.

T. J. DE LA HUNT, "A Holiday Gift Book from Out of the West in 1829," Evansville Courier (Indiana), December 1, 1918.

JOHN G. NEIHARDT, The Three Friends (New York, 1919).

JOHN G. NEIHARDT, The Splendid Wayfaring (New York, 1920).

ARCHER B. HULBERT, The Paths of Inland Commerce (New Haven, 1921), pp. 211–16.

EMERSON HOUGH, The Covered Wagon (New York, 1922), p. 281.

FRANK BIRD LINDERMAN, Lige Mounts: Free Trapper (New York, 1922).

OTTO A. ROTHERT, Outlaws of Cave-in-Rock (Cleveland, 1924), p. 327.

RALPH L. RUSK, Literature of the Middle Western Frontier (New York, 1925), I, 73, 275, 306.

CARL SANDBURG, Abraham Lincoln: The Prairie Years (New York, 1926), I, 78–79.

DOROTHY A. DONDORE, The Prairie and the Making of Middle America (Cedar Rapids, 1926), pp. 234, 401, 447.

HERBERT and EDWARD QUICK, Mississippi Steamboatin', a History of Steamboating on the Mississippi and Its Tributaries (New York, 1926).

Lucy L. Hazard, *The Frontier in American Literature* (Philadelphia, 1927), pp. 127–33.

V. L. Parrington, *The Romantic Revolution in America* (New York, 1927), pp. 138, 192.

Lyle Saxon, *Father Mississippi* (New York, 1927), pp. 137–38.

Lewis R. Freeman, *Waterways of Western Wandering* (New York, 1928), pp. 118–21, 168–73.

Popular Biography (New York, November, 1929), Vol. I, No. 1.

Edwin L. Sabin, *Wild Men of the Wild West* (New York, 1929), pp, 59–67.

Robert M. Coates, *The Outlaw Years* (New York, 1930), pp. 111–13.

Robert E. Riegel, *America Moves West* (New York, 1930), p. 165.

Frederick R. Bechdolt, *Giants of the Old West* (New York, 1930), pp. 32–34.

V. L. Parrington, *The Beginnings of Critical Realism in America* (New York, 1930), p. 92.

Charles Henry Ambler, *A History of Transportation in the Ohio Valley* (Glendale, California, 1931), pp. 53–58.

Helen Hardie Grant, *Peter Cartwright: Pioneer* (New York, 1931), pp. 115–16, 149–50.

Harris Dickson, "When New Orleans Was Young," *Collier's*, April 4, 1931, p. 25.

Constance Rourke, *American Humor: A Study of the National Character* (New York, 1931), pp. 53–55, 65, 152, 310.

Bernard DeVoto, *Mark Twain's America* (Boston, 1932), pp. 60, 92, 241.

V. F. Calverton, *The Liberation of American Literature* (New York, 1932), p. 314.

Walter Blair and Franklin J. Meine, *Mike Fink: King of Mississippi Keelboatmen* (New York, 1933).

C. B. Spotts, "Mike Fink in Missouri," *Missouri Historical Review*, XXVIII (October, 1933), 4–5.

Percy H. Boynton, *Literature and American Life* (Boston, 1936), pp. 612–13.

Herbert Asbury, *The French Quarter* (New York, 1936), pp. 81–82.

Carl Sandburg, *The People, Yes* (New York, 1936), p. 93.

Stanley Vestal, *Mountain Men* (Boston, 1937), pp. 6–7.

Walter Blair (ed.), *Native American Humor, 1800–1900* (New York and Cincinnati, 1937), pp. 81–82, 283–84.

Carl Carmer, *The Hurricane's Children* (New York, 1937), p. 103.

Leland D. Baldwin, *Pittsburgh: The Story of a City* (Pittsburgh, 1937), pp. 136, 143–44.

Thomas D. Clark, The Rampaging Frontier (Indianapolis, 1939), pp. 88–89.

Sydney Greenbie, Furs to Furrows (Caldwell, Idaho, 1939), pp. 173–75, 202–3, 327–29.

Leland D. Baldwin, The Keelboat Age on Western Waters (Pittsburgh, 1941), pp. 86, 109, 111–14, 216.

George D. Hendricks, Bad Men of the West (San Antonio, Texas, 1941), pp. 45, 97, 225, 275.

Richard M. Dorson, "America's Comic Demigods," American Scholar, X (autumn, 1941), 401.

Anne Malcolmson, Yankee Doodle's Cousins (Boston, 1941), pp. 129–37.

James D. Hart, The Oxford Companion to American Literature (New York, 1941), p. 243.

Eudora Welty, The Robber Bridegroom (New York, 1942).

Carl Carmer, America Sings (New York, 1942), pp. 86–89.

Bernard DeVoto, Mark Twain at Work (Cambridge, 1942), p. 65.

Pennsylvania Cavalcade, "American Guides Series" (Pennsylvania Writers Project, Works Project Administration [Philadelphia, 1942]), pp. 345–47.

Robert A. Hereford, Old Man River (Caldwell, Idaho, 1942), pp. 55–67.

Walter Blair, Tall Tale America: A Legendary History of Our Humorous Heroes (New York, 1944), pp. 34–65.

A. P. Hudson, "Folklore"; Harold W. Thompson and H. S. Canby, "Humor," in Literary History of the United States (New York, 1946), II, 720, 738; revised edition, 1953.

Walter Havighurst, Land of Promise: The Story of the Northwest Territory (New York, 1946), pp. 223–24.

Isabel McLennan McMeekin, Louisville, the Gateway City (New York, 1946), pp. 62–65.

Mody C. Boatright, Folk Laughter on the American Frontier (New York, 1949), p. 94.

Julian Lee Rayford, Child of the Snapping Turtle: Mike Fink (New York, 1951).

Louis O. Honig, The Pathfinder of the West: James Bridger (Kansas City, Mo., 1951), pp. 3, 13–14.

Dale L. Morgan, Jedidiah Smith and the Opening of the West (Indianapolis, 1953), pp. 7, 45–49, 79, 342, 379.

Nils Erik Enkvist, American Humour in England before Mark Twain (Abo Akademi, Finnland, 1953), pp. 27, 35.

Burl Ives, Tales of America (Cleveland and New York, 1954), pp. 157–69.

Ray Samuel, Leonard V. Huber, and Warren C. Ogden, Tales of the Mississippi (New York, 1955), pp. 11–12.

Walt Disney, Davy Crockett and Mike Fink (New York, 1956).